EXPLORING
DALLAS
with CHILDREN

EXPLORING DALLAS
WITH CHILDREN

A Guide for Family Activities

3RD EDITION

KAY McCASLAND THREADGILL

A Republic of Texas Press Book
Taylor Trade Publishing
Lanham • Dallas • New York • Boulder • Toronto • Oxford

A Republic of Texas Press Book

Published by Taylor Trade Publishing
An imprint of The Rowman & Littlefield Publishing Group, Inc.
4501 Forbes Boulevard, Suite 200
Lanham, Maryland 20706

Distributed by National Book Network

Library of Congress Cataloging-in-Publication Data

Threadgill, Kay McCasland.
  Exploring Dallas with children : a guide for family activities / Kay
McCasland Threadgill.— 3rd ed. ; 1st Taylor Trade Publishing ed.
    p. cm.
  "A Republic of Texas Press book."
  Includes index.
  ISBN: 978-1-58979-203-6
  1. Family recreation—Texas—Dallas—Guidebooks. 2. Family
recreation—Texas—Dallas Region—Guidebooks. 3. Dallas (Tex.)—
Guidebooks. 4. Dallas Region (Tex.)—Guidebooks. I. Title.
F394.D213T48 2005
917.64′28120464—dc22

                                                  2004023238

∞™ The paper used in this publication meets the minimum
requirements of American National Standard for Information
Sciences—Permanence of Paper for Printed Library Materials,
ANSI/NISO Z39.48-1992.

Manufactured in the United States of America.

To Whitney, Erin, and Abby, whose input is priceless, and to John for helping to make this happen.

CONTENTS

INTRODUCTION

Part of our Texas heritage is the spirit of adventure handed down from courageous, pioneer ancestors. The spirit of the West still urges both native Texans and those who have understandably adopted Texas as home to search out exciting and mind-expanding adventures around Dallas and the Lone Star State.

Usually, the major drawback is finding the time to plan ahead and to decide what a family, with a wide range of ages and interests, would find entertaining. That is where this guide will be invaluable, not only to those who live in and around Dallas but to visitors, youth organizations, and child-care institutions as well. The bulk of the legwork (literally) is done. Not only are vital statistics, like addresses and prices, listed, but special hints about things to try, notice, or bring are mentioned to make your visit as comfortable and worthwhile as possible.

I am thrilled to be able to publish this third edition. In five years, some favorite hangouts have closed their doors, but many new and exciting ones have opened to inform and amuse. Rewriting the guide has enabled me to rekindle friendships made while writing the first and to meet many new, enthusiastic people as well.

In the original 1993 edition, my family, with children ages five to thirteen, faithful friends, and Girl Scout Troop 956 were invaluable explorers in the quest to unearth and investigate a wide variety of places, some that entertain and excite, some that enlighten, and some that do an exceptional job of both. Having grown up with and in Dallas, I was astonished by what has been available for years that I had not known existed, such as a charming two-story Victorian farmhouse from the early 1900s and a large exhibit of mounted African animals housed in an oil company. Also, many landmark places offer opportunities of which many natives are unaware. Did you know that The Science Place hosts birthday parties or that a family may have a picnic at the Heard Museum and adopt a raptor? (What's a raptor?)

Dallas continues to grow and change. Because of changing needs and economy, attractions usually stipulate that all prices and hours are subject to change without notice. Some even go out of business without notice. Thus, it's always better to call before an outing to confirm information vital to your enjoyment of the trip. Also, many of the prices listed do not include tax.

Many of the museums and wildlife centers offer memberships, which not only keep members in close touch with programs but also supply financial support, which is vital to their existence. If your family is interested in science or nature or art or history, inquire about a family membership. Volunteer support is also essential to enable them to offer the range of educational programs and to schedule exhibits that make every visit fascinating.

We have had some wonderful times together compiling data for this guidebook. Few trips were disappointing. One unfailing, remarkable quality was the warm, Texas hospitality offered wherever we toured. Everyone wanted us to have a great time. And we did.

1. PLACES TO GO

Family entertainment at its Texas best is described in detail in this chapter. Turn off the television and the lights and head out for exciting adventures that may not be far from your own neighborhood but may offer literally acres of fun. Some attractions you seek may be listed in Chapter Two because they are smaller or attract a more specialized interest group.

AFRICAN AMERICAN MUSEUM

Fair Park: 3536 Grand, P.O. Box 15053, Dallas, Texas 75315-0153 (214) 565-9026 Website: www.aamdallas.org

In 1993, the 38,000-square-foot African American Museum opened its new building in Fair Park. The museum is dedicated to research and the acquisition of visual art forms and historical documents that relate to the life and culture of the African American community, as well as to an outreach program to enable all to understand the African American experience through exhibits, classes, day camps, and workshops. The building houses both permanent and traveling exhibits.

Architect Arthur Rogers designed a building with a rotunda capped by a sixty-foot dome. Four galleries, which represent Africa's quadrants, radiate outward from the central rotunda. The floor tiles are terra-cotta, the ceilings are exposed yellow pine, and the effect is light and airy.

On the first floor is a cafe and bookstore, and a balcony is on the second floor. Classrooms, a library, and an amphitheater are in the basement. The museum is designated by the state of Texas as the official repository for African American culture, so it houses important historical documents and collections.

- Call for information about group tours: (214) 219-2049.
- Restrooms and water fountains are available.
- The museum is handicapped accessible.

Hours: Closed Monday; Tuesday to Friday, 12 PM to 5 PM; Saturday, 10 AM to 5 PM; Sunday, 1 PM to 5 PM.
Admission: Free.
Directions: Take the Grand Ave. entrance from Robert B. Cullum Blvd. in Fair Park. Parking is free except during the state fair and special events.

AGE OF STEAM RAILROAD MUSEUM

Fair Park: 1105 Washington St., Dallas, Texas 75210 (214) 428-0101 (Mailing address: P.O. Box 153259, Dallas, Texas 75315-3259) Website: dallasrailwaymuseum.com

One of Dallas's oldest train depots, built around 1905, rests at the Age of Steam Railroad Museum alongside an outdoor exhibit of passenger cars, freight trains, and engines, which operated from 1896 to 1969. The world's largest steam locomotive, named Big Boy, cabooses, and a 1920s passenger train, including sleeping cars, are part of this tribute to the glory days of the railroad. Children may observe that these trains have definitely seen better days, but they will come to understand how the engines and cars evolved and catch some of their old spirit.

The depot was renovated to house the gift shop, as well as other memorabilia from the days when it was a vital part of railroad life. The depot is also the entrance to the museum, except during the state fair when visitors enter at the east end. An extensive booklet is available for sale, as is a souvenir guide. The tour begins at the east end and goes the length of the trains and then back up again. Visitors climb steps to peek in some of the trains, and some of the passenger cars may be boarded.

Look for *Doodlebug*, the 1931 Santa Fe Railroad self-propelled railcar that made the rounds between Carlsbad and Clovis, New Mexico. The GG1 electric locomotive #4903 that pulled the 1968 funeral train of Senator Robert Kennedy rests in the museum. In all, twenty-eight vintage trains are on display.

- Browse in the gift shop for railroad-related items, including toys.
- There is a soft drink machine outside the depot. Have lunch Tuesday to Saturday at the Old Mill Inn located near the Music Hall on the Fair Park grounds, or bring a picnic lunch.
- Guided tours for groups may be arranged with reservations. Tours for children are $2.50 per child. Adults are $2.50, and one adult is free with a group of fifteen people. To schedule a tour, call the museum or ArtReach at (214) 219-2006.
- The museum is somewhat handicapped accessible. The path between the trains is sometimes rocky, and stairs lead up to all the doors. Go on a dry day, and wear comfortable shoes.
- Restrooms are available in the nearby Hall of State. A water fountain is in the depot.
- Parking is free except during the state fair. A parking lot is at the east end of the train yard.

Hours: Wednesday to Sunday, 10 AM to 5 PM. Call before going in bad weather. Closed major holidays. Hours change during the fair.

Admission: Adults, $3; ages 12 and under, $1.50.

Directions: See directions to Fair Park. The train museum is on the north side of Fair Park on Washington east of Parry Ave.

AMERICAN MUSEUM OF MINIATURE ARTS

**Hall of State at Fair Park, 3939 Grand Ave., Dallas, Texas 75226
(214) 969-5502, (214) 421-4500 Website: www.minimuseum.org**

Housed in the Sharp Gallery of the Hall of State at Fair Park, the American Museum of the Miniature Arts features a thirty-piece collection of miniature houses and room boxes portraying lifestyles and work habits of Americans over 200 years. Various architectural styles are clearly seen on all the houses, which are completely lighted and furnished with accessories consistent with the time period. Other outstanding exhibits are a 16th-century armorer's shop, an Indian trading post, and a miniature Tudor home made in England.

Kids enjoy the scavenger hunt in which they search for particular items in the houses.

The exhibit may relocate to Children's Medical Center.
• Group tours are available. A guided tour is $3 per person.
• The museum is handicapped accessible.
• Water fountains and restrooms are available.
• Parking is located across the street from the Hall of State and is free, except during the State Fair of Texas.

Hours: Tuesday to Saturday, 9 AM to 5 PM; Sunday, 1 PM to 4 PM. Closed major holidays.

Admission: Free.

Directions: From north on US 75 (Central Expwy.), take US 75 South, exit I-30 East, and take the Second Ave. exit. Turn left onto Parry, turn right at Washington. After passing the Railroad Museum at Fair Park, turn right into the large parking lot.

BACHMAN LAKE

**3500 W. Northwest Hwy., Dallas, Texas 75220
(214) 670-6374, (214) 670-4100**

A popular oasis amid the noises of Love Field Airport and business traffic, the 205-acre Bachman Lake offers a wide variety of entertainment, most of which is good for the body and spirit.

On a 3.08 bike/hiking trail along the lake, joggers, skaters, and bicyclists pursue fitness and fun. Occasionally, you see the rowing club out on the lake and paddleboats during warm months. Motorboats and swimming are not allowed.

On days when the park is not too crowded, it's a great place to picnic and feed the birds. At Northwest Hwy. and Lakefield is a covered pavilion that can hold about eight picnic tables. It and three other sites are available for rent. One grill for cooking is on the north side, and another is on the south side of the lake.

During the Christmas season, the Park Department sometimes organizes a beautiful display of lights at Bachman.

For ten years, the **Bachman Lake Recreation Center**, located at 2750 Bachman Dr., has offered special programs for those with special mental and physical needs. Serving ages six to elderly, it is therapeutically color coordinated and has rails along the walls. Call (214) 670-6266 for a brochure.

- Paddleboat and skate concession is by contract, so check with the Park Department to see if it is being offered. Try (214) 670-8860.
- Lake traffic is one way, and the driving gate is closed on Saturday and Sunday.
- Always lock your car, and do not leave valuables in it.
- Restaurants are nearby on Northwest Hwy.
- The trail is handicapped accessible.
- The two permanent restrooms are at the Northwest Hwy. entrance and the Shorecrest entrance, but they are closed December through March to prevent freezing. Portables are available then. Water fountains are by those restrooms, and two are along the trail. Accompany your children to the restroom.
- Parking is free. On weekends, you may want to park at the concession and recreation center parking area.

Hours: Open 5 AM to midnight, but staying after dark is not advisable.
Admission: Free.
Directions: Take the W. Northwest Hwy. (Loop 12) exit off Central (US 75) or off N. Dallas Tollway and go west. The lake is on the south side. Or from I-35E, exit Northwest Hwy. and go east.

THE BALLPARK IN ARLINGTON/AMERIQUEST FIELD

1000 Ballpark Way, Arlington, Texas 76011

Tickets: (817) 273-5100

Executive offices: (817) 273-5222

Website: www.texasrangers.com

"Take me out to the ballgame . . ." became an even more frequent request in April 1994 when Ameriquest Field opened as the new home of the Texas Rangers. Costing $189.4 million to build, the stadium complex consists of a sunset-red granite and redbrick exterior, eight towers, five seating levels, three concourses, and a Home Run Porch. The asymmetrical playing field is natural grass. Entrances are provided at each of the four corners.

The two sections of the main concourse provide many food and beverage concessions, as well as the following seating options: field boxes, terrace boxes, left-field reserved, and bleacher seating. The upper-concourse/upper-deck seating offers upper boxes, upper reserved, and grandstand reserved. The other levels are suites and club seating. **Rawlings Grille** at (817) 469-8900 is located on the upper suite level behind the Home Run Porch.

As you walk around the exterior of the stadium, notice the thirty-five cast-stone steer heads and twenty-one Lone Stars, as well as ten murals of Texas scenes located between the upper and lower arches that surround the stadium.

Fans may only bring in paper and plastic containers (no cans or glass bottles) and coolers measuring 16 × 16 or smaller that will fit underneath the seats. No alcoholic beverages may be brought in. No flash photography is allowed, but cameras and handheld video cameras are acceptable. Tailgate parties are allowed as long as they do not take over more parking spaces. Fans may also picnic in **Vandergriff Plaza**, a park area behind the center-field fence.

In addition to Ranger games, the complex provides the **Dr Pepper Youth Park** baseball facility for ages-12-and-under organized youth groups, birthday parties, tournaments, summer camps and clinics, rental, and other occasions. Call (817) 273-5238.

The **Legends of the Game Baseball Museum** features baseball memorabilia and exhibits from the National Baseball Hall of Fame in Cooperstown, New Jersey. In the third floor **Learning Center**, interactive exhibits for school-age fans include the Science of Baseball, Baseball History Tunnel, Baseball Geography and Math, and Baseball Communications. Special programs, such as summer day camps, sleepovers, story time, and special day activities, are scheduled throughout the year. Call (817) 273-5600 or (817) 273-5087 for information, hours, and admission fees.

If you need help, the Fan Assistance Center is located behind home plate on the main concourse.

- **Tours** of the ballpark may be arranged by calling (817) 273-5222. Combination tickets for the tour and the museum may be purchased.
- A Wiffle Ball park, two tee-ball cages, Speed Pitch, Ring-a-Coke, and picnic tables are some of the attractions at the **Coca-Cola Sports Park** in Center Field's Vandergriff Plaza. Games cost one or

two tokens. The park opens two hours before game time. Call for information about pregame birthday parties: (817) 273-5143, ext. 2.

- The lower-level picnic area is behind Sections 39 and 40. Upper-level picnic areas are across the upper concourse.
- Fans age 13 and under are invited to join the **Dr Pepper Jr. Rangers**. Call (817) 273-5143.
- Arrange a birthday party by calling (817) 273-5099.
- To be included in the Birthday and Anniversary Parade on the video board, call (817) 273-5137. Advanced purchase is required.
- Areas of the stadium are handicapped accessible. Call (817) 273-5222 for more information.
- Water fountains and restrooms are provided. Diaper changing areas are in both men's and women's restrooms.
- ATMs are located on all three levels.
- Section 335 is designated as a nonalcohol section. Smoking is prohibited in restrooms and all seating areas.
- **The Texas Rangers Grand Slam Shop** is on ground level behind center field. Call (817) 273-5222.
- Parking is $8 per car and $20 per bus. Season parking pass holders park in a designated area. Everyone else parks in general parking. The lots open three hours before the game.
- Almost everything can be purchased in advance online.

Hours: For evening games, the gates open three hours early, and for afternoon games, two hours early. This is subject to change. On nongame days, ticket office hours are Monday to Friday, 9 AM to 6 PM, and Saturday, 10 AM to 4 PM. Night-game hours are Monday to Saturday, 9 AM to 9 PM, and Sunday, 12 PM to 9 PM.

Admission: Tickets may be purchased at the ticket office, online, or by phone at (817) 273-5100 and may be charged on Visa, MasterCard, or American Express. Tickets may also be purchased at Dillards. Ticket prices depend on selection of seating. There are some discounts for ages 13 and under.

Directions: From Dallas, take I-30 West and exit at Six Flags Dr. Take Six Flags Dr. to Randol Mill Rd. and turn right. Continue to the parking lots. Another route is to take I-30 to the Ballpark Way exit. Go right on Ballpark Way and continue to the parking lots.

CEDAR RIDGE PRESERVE

7171 Mountain Creek Pkwy., Dallas, Texas 75249
Website: www.audubondallas.org

Just thirty minutes south of downtown Dallas, the Cedar Ridge Preserve encompasses 630 acres of environmentally rich land on the White

Rock Escarpment. In April 2003, **Audubon Dallas** took over management of the preserve, formerly the Dallas Nature Center. The organization is very busy with habitat restoration and the development of educational programs. Please check the website for new events and information.

Families enjoy hiking on ten miles of trails through prairie and woodlands where native animals and birds live in a protected environment. Visitors may spot native plants, such as yucca, sunflowers, and orchids.

In spring, the butterfly garden comes alive with brilliant flowers to attract the butterflies, and the orchards are in bloom.

- A picnic area is available.
- The trails are not handicapped accessible at this time.
- Parking is free.

Hours: Grounds open Tuesday to Sunday from 7 AM to dusk.
Admission: Free. Donations are appreciated.
Directions: Go south on I-35 to Hwy. 67 South (sign says Cleburne). Take I-20 West (sign says Ft. Worth); exit at Mountain Creek Pkwy. and go south (under the highway). Drive two miles to the center's gate on the right.

CELEBRATION STATION

4040 Towne Crossing Blvd., Mesquite, Texas 75150
(972) 279-7888 Website: www.celebration.com

Daniel and the Dixie Diggers, animated hounds with musical talent, steal the show at Mesquite's family entertainment park. Indoors in the 16,000-square-foot facility is a restaurant downstairs offering great pizza, hot dogs, and more. On the first level are games, which give tickets that may be redeemed for prizes, and on the second level are more challenging video games.

Go-carts, bumper boats, batting cages, a few kiddie carnival rides, laser tag, paintball, and two miniature golf courses are offered for more fun outdoors in the six-acre park. Height and age requirements are enforced for some activities.

- Group rates (for fifteen or more) are available. Birthday parties (minimum of six) are welcome. Call for reservations. Lock-ins and special holiday events are popular.
- Miniature golf courses are handicapped accessible.
- Restrooms and water fountains are available.
- Parking is free.

Hours: Open daily, weather permitting. Hours change seasonally.

Admission: No entrance admission fee. Purchase tokens for games. Various packages are available, depending on what you want to do. All-day, unlimited-play passes are offered.

Directions: Going east on I-30 toward Mesquite, take the Gus Thomasson Rd. exit. Pass Gus Thomasson, stay on the service road to Towne Crossing, and turn right. From I-635, exit at Town East Blvd. and go west. Turn right on Towne Crossing.

DALLAS AQUARIUM AT FAIR PARK

1462 First Ave. and Martin L. King Blvd. at Fair Park, Dallas, Texas 75226 (214) 670-8443 (Mailing address: P.O. Box 150113, Dallas, Texas 75315-0113) Website: www.dallaszoo.com

The Dallas Aquarium building, which dates from the 1936 Texas Centennial at Fair Park, houses thousands of species of both freshwater and saltwater fish. In addition, there are amphibians, reptiles, various invertebrates, and cases of beautiful shells and other nonliving material.

Exhibits include other fish from the Gulf, Red Sea, Caribbean reef, and Australian Great Barrier Reef. The little Australian scavengers, cleaner wrasses, actually clean the parasites off of other fish. A 10,500-gallon Amazon Flooded Forest Exhibit has been added, as has a fish breeding lab for endangered species, such as the Texas blind salamander, Barton Springs salamander, and endangered desert fish.

The walking batfish, a fish that actually walks on legs (modified fins), will catch the attention of children, as will the five-foot electric eel, piranhas, seahorses, and 135-pound alligator snapping turtle.

- The Education Center at the Dallas Zoo coordinates summer classes at the aquarium. Call (214) 670-6832 for more information.
- In the Adopt-a-Fish program, for $15 to $100 your family, Scout troop, or business can select from a list of aquatic friends one to adopt. Call (214) 943-2771, ext. 311, for further details.
- There are no concessions, but the Old Mill Inn is within walking distance in Fair Park. It is open Tuesday to Sunday, 11 am to 2:30 pm. The aquarium does have candy and soft drink machines. On a nice day, you may wish to bring a blanket and have a picnic. Picnic tables are usually between the aquarium and the Planetarium Building.
- The building is handicapped accessible.
- Restrooms and water fountains are available.
- Parking is free except during the state fair.

Hours: Open daily 9 AM to 4:30 PM. Closed Thanksgiving Day and Christmas Day. Hours extended during the state fair.

Admission: Ages 2 and under, free; ages 3–11, $1.50; ages 12 and over, $3. Educational group rates are available. Call (214) 670-6832.

Directions: From the Robert B. Cullum Blvd. side of Fair Park, enter at the Martin L. King Blvd. gate and park. The aquarium is just past the Texas Discovery Gardens to the left, very close to the Texas Star Ferris Wheel. See directions to Fair Park.

DALLAS ARBORETUM AND BOTANICAL GARDENS

8617 Garland Rd., Dallas, Texas 75218 (214) 515-6500
Website: www.dallasarboretum.org

Even before arriving at the entrance, you can see some of the gorgeous, lush gardens of the sixty-six-acre Dallas Arboretum from the road, but that is only a glimpse of the acres of beauty to come. Located on the eastern shore of White Rock Lake, the arboretum provides education in horticulture, a haven for wildlife, vibrant flower displays, and numerous special events for families. Children love not only the trees and flowers but also the winding paths and fountains. Here, they really have room to stretch and enjoy the outdoors. In 1996, the $1.4 million **Women's Council Garden**, which is behind the DeGolyer House, was opened to the public. The 1.8-acre garden incorporates water as a symbol of strength and unity. Don't miss the frog sculpture, an interactive fountain in which four bronze frogs shoot twenty-foot streams of water.

Favorite times to visit include Dallas Blooms Spring in March and April and Dallas Blooms Autumn in October. The Jonsson **Color Garden** features more than 2,000 varieties of azaleas, while more than 30 varieties of ferns grow in the Palmer **Fern Dell**. More than 200,000 flowers bloom during this festival, and children's activities are scheduled on weekends.

The $20 million Trammel Crow **Visitor Education Center** built with native limestone opened in 2003. It provides indoor classrooms, an exhibit hall, gift shop, gazebo, orientation theater, and an outdoor dining terrace, which provides year-round dining.

- Tours of the **DeGolyer's Spanish Colonial Revival Mansion**, now a museum, include the Oilman's Study and other rooms filled with interesting art and furniture. Tours leave every thirty minutes.
- Garden hunt sheets are available daily and change seasonally.
- Picnics are encouraged, and food service is offered year-round in the dining terrace and increased during special events.
- Christmas at the Arboretum in December includes a holiday market and many festive decorations and activities.
- Children's Nature Club events are usually held in May and June for ages 4–12. Classes last two to three hours. Classes are offered for pre-K through sixth grade all year long.

- In June through August are family focus summer events with special activities for kids during each event.
- An annual tour for special needs children and adults, called Gardens for Everyone, is held in the spring. Call for specific dates. Most of the paths are handicapped accessible. Trams are available.
- Restrooms and water fountains are provided.
- Parking is $4. The fee may be higher during special events.

Hours: Open daily, year-round, from 10 AM to 5 PM. Evening hours are often extended for summer musical programs on Thursday.

Admission: Adults, $7; seniors (65+), $6; ages 3–12, $4; members and children under 2, free. Memberships are available.

Directions: Located on the north side of Garland Rd. at Whittier, just west of the intersection of Garland Rd. and Buckner Blvd. Signs direct visitors to the parking area.

DALLAS CHILDREN'S MUSEUM

308 Valley View Center, Dallas, Texas 75240 (214) 386-6555
Website: www.dallaschildrens.org

Pushing grocery carts, getting checkups from their doctors, taking an eye exam, playing musical instruments—all are part of daily life but munchkin size at Dallas Children's Museum.

Here, at this 6,500-square-foot museum, activities, events, and programs are devoted to play and educational growth.

The Cultural Bridges exhibits change regularly as they focus on stimulating an understanding and celebration of different cultures. Special events are often coordinated with the particular culture presented.

Permanent exhibits include ScEYEnce Laboratory, Your Own Backyard, PresbyHealth Care Systems Hospital, Kroger Grocery Store, Dairy Farm, Arts District, Computer and Technology, and Toddler Discovery Area.

- The museum offers programs, classes, special events, and camps related to stories, the arts, yoga, Spanish, and other interesting topics about our world.
- Birthday parties include a 1.5 hour playtime and a private room for refreshments.
- Groups should preregister.
- No food or drink. A food court is on the lower level of the mall. Chuck E. Cheese is nearby on the west side of the mall at 13364 Montfort.
- The museum is handicapped accessible. Elevators are in the mall.

- Parking is free. Park by JC Penny to enter close to the museum.
- Memberships are available.

Hours: Monday to Friday, 9 AM to 6 PM; Saturday, 11 AM to 6 PM; Sunday, 12 PM to 6 PM. Closed Thanksgiving Day, Christmas Day, and Easter Sunday.

Admission: Adults, $3; seniors, $2; ages 2–12, $4. Under 24 months, free.

Directions: From Central Expwy. (US 75), exit going west on LBJ Fwy. (635). From LBJ, exit going north on Preston Rd. Valley View Mall is on the northwest corner of LBJ and Preston.

THE DALLAS FIREFIGHTER'S MUSEUM: OLD TIGE

3801 Parry Ave., Dallas, Texas 75226 (214) 821-1500

Located in the 1907 Old No. 5 Hook and Ladder Co. Station, the Dallas Firefighter's Museum houses a collection of wonderful, retired fire trucks. *Old Tige*, named after then mayor W. L. Cabell, is the 1884 horse-drawn steam pumper.

Recapture the early days of firefighting in the alarm office complete with clanging bell and in the old firehouse setting with its wood-burning stove. Visitors see the progress of the last 100 years in firefighting equipment through the collection of photos, fire tools, helmets, suits, and extinguishers. Sometimes you can hear today's Dallas Fire Department radio as dispatchers conduct business. A favorite of most children is the fire engine, which they can climb on, as well as the collection of toy fire trucks. Pieces of wooden water main unearthed from the Farmers Market area, which date to around the 1880s, are on display.

The museum is dedicated to firemen who have fallen in action, a tribute to their courage and devotion to duty.

- Tours are available with reservations.
- There is no food or drink in the museum, but the Old Mill Inn just across Parry in Fair Park is open for lunch Tuesday to Sunday.
- Only the lower floor is handicapped accessible.
- Restrooms and water fountains are provided.
- Parking is available in front or on the side street. During the state fair, park at the Fair Grounds and walk across Parry.

Hours: Tuesday to Saturday, 9 AM to 4 PM. Open daily during the state fair. Closed major holidays.

Admission: Adults, $2; children, $1; over 65, under 3, and members, free.

Directions: Located on the northwest corner of Parry at Commerce. If on I-30 going west, take Fair Park First Avenue exit, and circle under the bridge to Exposition. Take it to Parry and turn left. If on I-30 going east, take the Fair Park Second Avenue exit to Parry. Turn left and go three blocks.

DALLAS HOLOCAUST MEMORIAL CENTER

7900 Northaven Rd., Dallas, Texas 75230 (214) 750-4654
Website: www.dallasholocaustmemorialcenter.org

Dedicated as a tribute to the memory of the six million who died during the Holocaust and in the hope that such an atrocity will never occur again, the Dallas Museum for Holocaust Studies was conceived by a group called Holocaust Survivors, who wished to tell their stories and help others understand the impact of the Holocaust on themselves and world history.

Poems, paintings, and a tapestry are exhibited in the entry stairwell, with a boxcar at the bottom of the stairs that actually transported Jewish victims to the death camps. After the boxcar are the museum and exhibition rooms. Here, visitors see a pictorial history, items from the camps, and a video screen. An extensive library of 2,500 books, periodicals, and European government record books is available for use by the public on site. An audiovisual materials catalog on Holocaust topics is available. The Memorial Room includes a symbolic sculpture and plaques that list the names of victims, survivors, and courageous people who risked their lives to save others. Some of these people have videotaped their memories, and visitors may ask to view the tapes. Expansion is planned.

- Museum personnel recommend that only children fifth grade and higher should tour. Some knowledge of the Holocaust prior to the tour is advisable.
- Group tours are available by appointment; self-guided tours are available daily.
- Books and postcards are for sale.
- There is no food or drink.
- Handicapped access is through an elevator in the Jewish Community Center.
- Restrooms and water fountains are in the Jewish Community Center.
- Parking is free.

Hours: Monday to Friday, 9:30 AM to 4:30 PM; Sunday, 12 PM to 4 PM from September through June. Closed on Jewish and most national holidays.

Admission: Suggested donation for adults, $3; students, $2. Memberships are available.

Directions: From US 75 (Central), exit Royal Ln. and go west. Turn right on Freda Stern and right again into the parking lot. The museum is located on the lower level.

DALLAS MUSEUM OF ART

1717 N. Harwood, Dallas, Texas 75201 (214) 922-1200
Website: www.dm-art.org

The Dallas Museum of Art is known internationally for both special exhibitions and permanent collections. One fascinating collection on long-term loan from Boston is Eternal Egypt: Objects of the Afterlife, which includes both funerary objects and pieces from the daily life of ancient Nubia. Other major collections include post–World War II, contemporary, and African, Asian, and Oceanic art objects; American and European paintings, sculptures, and decorative arts; and the Wendy and Emery Reves Collection in which they recreated six rooms of their Mediterranean villa, featuring prized impressionist paintings.

The 140,000-square-foot Hamon Building includes larger exhibition areas, the Museum of the Americas, the Atrium Café, and performance space for jazz and classical music.

One of the finest ways for families to develop and share a love of art is at the Dallas Museum of Art's **Gateway Gallery**, a 3,200-square-foot, informal exhibition area, which has magnetic appeal for everyone with its interactive permanent and temporary exhibits.

The gallery offers both free and fee-based art activities, classes, and tours. Call (214) 922-1822 for information about programs, such as Drop-In Art on Saturday and Sunday and family art activities.

Another favorite area for children, especially those who need to stretch, is the outdoor sculpture garden with its cascading wall fountains and sculptures in a mazelike layout. Children cannot climb on the sculptures, but they can take their lunch out there to enjoy the garden. The nearby Trammel Crow building has more sculptures encircling it, and the Nasher Sculpture Center is across the street.

- Thursday activities include Art Talk by docents and staff at 7 PM, Meet the Artist on the first Thursday of the month at 7 PM, and special-interest tours at 12:15 PM for thirty minutes. On Wednesday at 12:15 PM is a thirty-minute gallery talk.
- An information desk, which has maps and information about current exhibits, is at the entrance.
- The museum shop invites youngsters to select art-related books, puzzles, calendars, games, and toys.
- Free public tours meet at the information desk. School tours are free but require three weeks notice. Call (214) 922-1331. For $3 for

nonmembers, a tour of the Reves Collection is given at 1 PM on Tuesday to Friday.

- The museum has the noncirculating Mayer Library and Teacher Resource Room. Call for details about use.
- The Go van Gogh program offers free, one-hour art programs for school classrooms. Call (214) 922-1230.
- The second-floor Seventeen Seventeen Restaurant prepares lunch Tuesday to Friday from 11 AM to 2 PM. Call (214) 880-9018. The Atrium Café is open Tuesday, Wednesday, and Friday, 11 AM to 2:30 PM, and Saturday and Sunday from 11 AM to 2 PM. Call (214) 922-1835.
- The museum is handicapped accessible.
- There are restrooms and water fountains.
- Underground parking is available from Harwood or St. Paul. A fee is charged for parking. The trolley route brings you to St. Paul and Ross, right by the museum.

Hours: Tuesday and Wednesday, Friday to Sunday, 11 AM to 5 PM; Thursday, 11 AM to 9 PM. Closed Mondays, New Year's Day, Thanksgiving, and Christmas Day.

Admission: Adults, $6; seniors and ages 12 and older, $4; under 12 and students with current ID, free, except for special exhibitions. Also free, Thursday 5 pm to 9 pm and the first Tuesday of each month. Memberships are available.

Directions: Located downtown in the Arts District on Harwood between Woodall Rodgers Frwy. and Ross Ave. From US 75, exit at Woodall Rodgers. Take the St. Paul exit if traveling from Central toward I-35. Coming from the west, exit at Field-Griffin in the right-hand lane.

DALLAS MUSEUM OF NATURAL HISTORY

3535 Grand Ave. at First in Fair Park, Dallas, Texas 75210 (214) 421-DINO (Mailing address: P.O. Box 150349, Dallas, Texas 75315) Website: www.dallasdino.org

Parents may have problems getting their children into the Dallas Museum of Natural History because they have discovered the giant mammoth sculpture and want to stay out on the lawn and play on it. They will notice the exterior walls of shell stone in which fossils of early Texas ocean life are embedded. This Art Deco building was built by the Works Progress Administration for the Texas Centennial in 1936 and has intrigued its visitors ever since with its collections of Texas fossils, mounted native birds and animals in more than fifty lifelike dioramas, land and freshwater mollusks, and Texas pollinating insects.

More than 400,000 visitors every year stand in awe of the remains of a thirty-one-foot Heath Mosasaur found at Lake Ray Hubbard and the 20,000-year-old, thirteen-foot tall skeleton of a mammoth. Look for the giant prehistoric sea turtle and live insect zoo. A hands-on, interactive discovery center called City Safari for ages four to ten is now on permanent exhibit.

An annual event is Dino Day, which focuses on those creatures of long ago.

- The Dallas Museum of Natural History offers classes and workshops for children ages four to twelve. Day trips take young naturalists to explore fossil sites and grassland prairies. Summer family programs include taking nature walks and discovering critters in the creek. Once each month, usually on Saturday, is Family Festival Day from 11 AM to 4 PM. Check the website for the calendar of events.
- Tours for classes are available with reservations. Call (214) 421-3466 for group reservations. Themed sleepovers may also be arranged.
- The museum sponsors a naturalists' lecture series, which includes famous speakers such as Jean-Michel Cousteau.
- Nature Presents, the gift shop, stocks books, tapes, toys, and more of interest to young naturalists. It is open during the same hours as the museum.
- An amphitheater is available for rental for community cultural performances.
- No food is available in the museum, but the Old Mill Inn is a short walk from Fair Park. Open Tuesday to Sunday for lunch, 11 AM to 2:30 PM. You can also bring a blanket and picnic by the lagoon.
- Handicapped access is available.
- Water fountains and restrooms are provided.
- Parking is free, except during the state fair.

Hours: Monday to Saturday, 10 AM to 5 PM; Sunday, 12 PM to 5 PM. Closed Thanksgiving, Christmas, and New Year's. Hours subject to change.

Admission: Adults, $6.50; seniors (55+), $5.50; students (13–18), $5; children (3–12), $4; children under 3, free. There is an additional fee for some special exhibits. Memberships are available, and members receive free admission.

Directions: Enter Fair Park through the Grand Ave. gate from Robert B. Cullum Blvd. The museum is to the right of Grand.

THE DALLAS WORLD AQUARIUM AND
ORINOCO RAINFOREST

1801 N. Griffin, Dallas, Texas 75202 (214) 720-2224
Website: www.dwazoo.com

Something fishy is going on at Daryl's By Design catering company, located at Hord and N. Griffin in the West End Historic District. Owner Daryl Richardson is combining business and his hobby of observing marine life by bringing in a 20,000-gallon tank with a tunnel visitors can walk through and thirteen 2,000-gallon tanks in which he beautifully displays aquatic life from all over the world. Each tank represents a different area, such as the Red Sea exhibit, and the corals and other plants are also from that region. It doesn't take long for visitors to discover the lively black-footed penguins, which were used in a Batman movie.

Self-guided tours are available with a brochure that explains each tank and provides a list of feeding times. Group tours with a guide may be requested. **Orinoco**: Secrets of the River is modeled after a Venezuelan rain forest. Visitors usually enter at the treetop level and see various exotic birds, monkeys, crocodiles, and piranhas as the bamboo-planked path spirals down through the fauna and habitats. A waterfall inspired by the Venezuelan Orinoco river basin, adds to the tropical atmosphere. An elevator also goes to each level.

The newest addition is the **Mundo Maya** exhibit, which features a shark tank, Jabiru storks, sea turtles, flamingos, rattlesnakes, beaded lizards, and other Mayan creatures.

- A restaurant, eighteen-O-one, is open for lunch, 11:30 AM to 2:30 PM, and the Jungle Café is open from 11 AM to 4 PM.
- The gift shop offers nature-related gifts.
- The aquarium offers education programs to study marine life for students in the third grade and above. Classes have interesting names, such as Romancing the Reef and Fish Colors: Not Just for Looks. Call (214) 720-2224 on Monday to Friday to schedule. Classes are held Monday to Friday from 9:30 AM to 12:30 PM and last about thirty minutes, but schedule additional time to see the aquarium and rainforest. Sack lunches are available at an additional cost.
- During the summer, the education department offers keeper talks every half hour between 10 AM and 2:30 PM. Feeding times are also posted.
- The West End Marketplace and restaurants are within easy walking distance.

- Visitors may park on a surface lot across the street for a fee. The West End Parking Garage is nearby.

Hours: Open daily, 10 AM to 5 PM. Closed Thanksgiving and Christmas.
Admission: Adults, $15.95; children (3–12), $8.95; seniors (60+), $12.95. Additional tax.
Directions: From Central (US 75), exit onto Woodall Rodgers. Take the Field exit and turn left. Stay in the right-hand lane, which will curve to Griffin. The first right is Hord. You can see the fish sculptures on top of the building. The DART rail line stops at the West End, about two to three blocks from the aquarium.

DALLAS ZOO

650 South R. L. Thornton (I-35E), Dallas, Texas 75203 (214) 670-5656 Website: www.dallas-zoo.org

Since 1888, the Dallas Zoo has been fascinating families with its collection of exotic and endangered species. In 1997, a 67.5-foot giraffe sculpture, the largest sculpture in Texas, was installed at the Marsalis entrance to welcome visitors. The zoo covers ninety-five acres and was the first zoo to open in Texas. A family favorite at the zoo is **The Wilds of Africa** exhibit in which zoo visitors travel through six habitats on a one-mile monorail ride with a narrator. More than eighty-six species of mammals and birds roam freely in this twenty-five-acre exhibit. It's open from September 15 to December 1 and March 1 to June 15. One adult is required for every seven children. This safari continues as visitors then walk along a wooded quarter-mile nature trail. Of further interest is the two-acre Jake L. Hamon **Gorilla Conservation Research Center** where gorillas may be viewed without their realizing that they are being observed. A rain forest is simulated, and everything in it is edible. The Dallas Zoo is a breeding facility for both Sumatran and Indochinese tigers. The ExxonMobil **Endangered Tiger Habitat** allows guests to come face-to-face with tigers through glass viewing areas and to find out how to help save these big cats from extinction.

The **Lacerte Family Children's Zoo** offers educational, interactive exhibits for toddlers to preteens and features The Farm, with touchable animals, pony rides, and activities; The Underzone, with naked mole rats, mongooses, and other underground creatures; and The Nature Exchange, where children can trade objects from nature at a hands-on store.

- The zoo sponsors special events, such as Safari Days, Summer Fun Weekend, and Boo at the Zoo. Check the website or call for the dates of special events.

- Summer classes are offered for children. Call (214) 670-6832. A popular volunteer program for ages eleven and twelve is **Junior Zookeeper**, and applications need to be requested in November for summer jobs. Youths ages thirteen and older may apply in early March for positions as **Conservation Guides**, and **Junior Camp Counselors** apply in February.
- The zoo has an Adopt-an-Animal program.
- The Jungle Shop located in the entry plaza offers a variety of souvenirs, books, and toys related to birds, reptiles, and mammals.
- The Ndebele Cafe offers hamburgers and the like, and Subway has sandwiches. Picnic tables are provided.
- The paved pathways are accessible to wheelchairs, but the area is hilly. Parts of the zoo are hard to negotiate.
- Restrooms, benches, and water fountains are available.
- Parking is $5.

Hours: Daily, 9 AM to 5 PM; 9 AM to 4 PM in winter. Closed Christmas Day. Monorail rides begin at 10 AM.

Admission: Ages 12–64, $8; ages 3–11, $5; seniors, $4; ages 2 and under, free. Monorail rate: Ages 3 and over, $2. Endangered Species Carousel rides: $2 for ages 3 and up. Pony rides: $2. Group rates and memberships are available.

Directions: Three miles south of downtown off I-35 South. Take the Marsalis exit, go north on the service road, and turn right at the base of the giant giraffe statue into the zoo parking lot. A separate entrance for DART riders is available on Clarendon Dr., just across the street from the **DART light rail Dallas Zoo station.**

FAIR PARK

1300 Robert B. Cullum Blvd., Dallas, Texas 75226 (Mailing address: P.O. Box 15009, Dallas, Texas 75315) (214) 565-9931

State fair: (214) 670-8400

Website: www.bigtex.com

Fair Park, location of the outstanding **State Fair of Texas**, has been close to the hearts of native Dallasites and those who visit from around the state since R. L. Thornton Sr. persisted in the selection of Dallas as the site of the Texas Centennial in 1936. The largest historical landmark in Texas, this 277-acre park is well known for its major museums, **Music Hall**, **Cotton Bowl Stadium**, **Smirnoff Music Centre**, and the **Coliseum**, which are active year-round.

Fair Park should be visited at its finest during the state fair, which lasts for three weeks beginning at the end of September. During that time young children pet furry animals in the Barnyard, giggle at puppets in the Midway Puppet Show, and try Midway rides designed especially for them. The 212-foot Texas Star Ferris Wheel and seventy-eight-year-old carousel are yearly favorites. Museums prepare fascinating exhibits for the fair, and the Texas–Oklahoma football classic is a thrill for all fans. Families look over prime livestock brought from area farms and ranches and attend rodeos in the Coliseum, watch amazing free-flight bird shows in the Band Shell, select the car of their dreams in the Automobile Building, puzzle over exotic displays of wares in the International Bazaar, and admire prize-winning crafts in the Creative Arts Building.

Those who love the night lights of the fair stay for the Starlight Parade and the TXU Energy Extravaganza, where lasers, fireworks, and familiar tunes create dazzling special effects nightly on the Esplanade.

Many families will confess that although the shows and exhibits alone are worth the trip and putting up with the crowds, the real draw is the tantalizing aroma and anticipation of foods, such as corny dogs and greasy fries, followed by giant cinnamon rolls, cotton candy, and ice cream. Indoors at the Tower Building and outside at Cotton Bowl Plaza and other locations are foods for every palate. The blend of these aromas, the tumultuous sounds of the Midway, and the welcoming voice of a fifty-two-foot-tall cowboy named Big Tex invite everyone to relax and have a wonderful time.

Families are advised to arrive early enough to park in well-lighted areas inside the fair grounds and to walk in groups. Do not wear expensive jewelry. Police are highly visible on raised stands, on horses, and in small vehicles. Their headquarters are southeast of the Cotton Bowl. At the entrances, there are usually identification tags that children can wear as necklaces. Their names should not be written where a stranger could easily read it and call to them. Families should agree on a meeting place in case they are separated.

- The *Dallas Morning News* reports special events daily during the fair, and at the gates, the fair provides a map and guide to activities.
- Talented family members might enjoy entering one of the arts-and-crafts or food contests in September. Winning entries are displayed during the fair.
- Children especially love climbing on the orange serpentine sculpture between the Museum of Natural History and The Science Place. Picnics in this area are fun. There may be some ducks to feed.
- Museums at Fair Park are listed individually. They include The Science Place with its Omni-Max Theater and Planetarium Building,

Museum of Natural History, Dallas Aquarium, Texas Discovery Gardens, Age of Steam Railroad Museum, Hall of State, D.A.R. Building, African American Museum, and Women's Museum. Most museums are closed on Monday.

- The Fair Park Passport offers a 40 percent discount on admission to eight museums. Call (214) 428-5555 or check online.
- Most of Fair Park is handicapped accessible. Midway rides during the fair will vary.
- Restrooms are not plentiful, but there are some in the major exhibition buildings, outside the Cotton Bowl steps, near the Magnolia Lounge, and in the livestock area. All major museums have restrooms, and most have water fountains. Outdoor water fountains are turned off during the winter.
- The **Old Mill Inn** is a restaurant located near the Magnolia Lounge and the Music Hall. It is open for lunch Tuesday to Saturday from 11 AM to 2:30 PM and is generally open during the state fair from 10:30 AM to 8 PM. A kids' menu is available. Call (214) 426-4600.
- Flea markets are scheduled, as are special events, such as football games, ethnic celebrations, and craft fairs.
- Smirnoff Music Centre and Dallas Summer Musicals provide wonderful summer and fall entertainment. Special concerts featuring popular artists are held during the fair at the Chevrolet Main Stage. The Dallas Opera also performs in the Music Hall.
- Another museum kids love is the Firefighter's Museum located across Parry from Fair Park.
- Parking for about 10,000 vehicles is available on the grounds. A fee of around $7 is charged during the fair. Call DART at (214) 979-1111 for information about State Fair Flyers bus service and ticket combinations.

Hours: The grounds are open daily. The museums are listed under individual headings in this text. Their days and hours of operation vary.

Admission: Some of the museums are free, and some charge a fee. State fair admission is approximately $11 for adults; ages 3 and over, $7. Discount coupons are usually available at Tom Thumb. Tickets and coupons may be purchased online at www.bigtex.com.

Directions: Fair Park is two miles east of downtown. From Central Expwy. (US 75), exit Fitzhugh or Haskell. From I-30W, exit Barry or Carroll and head southwest. From I-45 North, exit Martin L. King Blvd. and proceed northeast. Scyene Rd. going west becomes Robert B. Cullum Blvd. and leads to Fair Park. Or take Abrams Rd. south, which changes name to Columbia, turn left on Carroll, and then right on Parry, which goes around the park.

FRONTIERS OF FLIGHT MUSEUM

Frontiers of Flight Museum at Love Field Terminal, LB-38, Dallas, Texas 75235 (214) 350-3600 Website: www.flightmuseum.com

The Frontiers of Flight Museum moved into a spacious new two-story museum in 2004. The new facility provides a 20,000-square-foot education-experience center with interactive display exhibits for three age groups. A collection of rare aviation artifacts will guide you from Early Concepts of Flight through The Jet Era to Aviation Opportunities.

Eras in aviation history are illustrated through mounted newspaper and magazine articles; personal items such as uniforms of famous aviators and the fur parka belonging to Rear Adm. Richard Byrd; and items used during flights of various airships, such as remnants of the Hindenburg.

Visitors look at models of the *Kitty Hawk Flyer*, the Red Baron's favorite triplane, and large replicas of modern passenger planes and space shuttles. In the Love Field Gallery, they can hear the Love Field Control Tower as planes depart and land. Aviation enthusiasts can look over more that twenty-five full-size aircraft and twenty major aviation history galleries.

- The Friends of the Museum and museum personnel present special Focus Nights programs, such as bringing aircraft used in the Persian Gulf and the Confederate Air Force to Dallas, as well as authors and specialists in fascinating aspects of the aviation field.
- Group tours are available with reservations.
- Children who can read and have some knowledge of major figures in aviation would benefit most from the tour.
- A brochure is available.
- A small food court setting offers fountain drinks, vending machines, and simple foods like hot dogs and popcorn.
- A gift shop carries books, videos, and toys related to aviation, as well as freeze-dried food for astronauts.
- The museum is handicapped accessible.
- Restrooms and water fountains are available.

Hours: Monday to Saturday, 10 AM to 5 PM; Sunday, 1 PM to 5 PM. Closed some holidays.

Admission: Adults, $8; seniors, $6; children (3–17), $5; children under 3, free. Memberships are available. Children under 12 must be accompanied by an adult.

Directions: The museum is located at Love Field Airport on Lemmon at University.

HALL OF STATE

Fair Park: 3939 Grand Ave., Dallas, Texas 75226 (214) 421-4500
(Mailing address: P.O. Box 150038, Dallas, Texas 75315)
Website: www.hallofstate.com

Operated by the Dallas Historical Society, the Art Deco–style Hall of State residing at the end of the Esplanade in Fair Park is the home of both permanent and temporary exhibits that reflect the history of Dallas and Texas. As part of the 1936 centennial, the Hall of State was built of Texas limestone in a T-shape for $1.2 million. A statue of a Tejas warrior occupies the niche above the entrance, and the blue background represents the state flower, the bluebonnet. The symbols in the bronze grills on the entry doors, cotton bolls, spurs, and oil wells, are representative of Texas agriculture and industry. The statue out front is of R. L. Thornton, who was largely responsible for bringing the centennial to Fair Park, for his forty-one years of service to Dallas.

Just inside is the Hall of Heroes, where bronze statues of heroes of the Republic of Texas reside. The four-story Great Hall to the back has an Aztec motif in its hand-stenciled ceiling. A gold-leafed medallion with a five-pointed star and the six figures around it represents the rulers over Texas. The large murals on each side tell the story of Texas history and industry. The shafts of light indicate changes in time. Notice native wildlife in mosaics on the floor.

The other four exhibit rooms, two on each side of the Hall of Heroes, represent East, West, North, and South Texas through murals, figurines, frescos, photographs, and mosaics. In the north and south rooms is a permanent history exhibit on Texas.

- The "Hall of State: Tour Guide" brochure is a helpful guide available at the museum.
- Guided tours for groups are available with reservations. A small fee may be charged.
- Currently, the American Museum of Miniature Arts has its dollhouse exhibit in the Sharp Gallery.
- The G. B. Dealey Library is housed in the West Texas Room.
- In a display case are some books about Dallas and Texas for sale.
- There is no food or drink in the museum.
- Handicapped access is available.
- Restrooms and water fountains are on the lower floor. A water fountain is on the upper level.
- Parking is free on Washington Ave., except during the state fair. The Hall of State is near the Age of Steam Railroad Museum.

Hours: Tuesday to Saturday, 9 AM to 5 PM; Sunday, 1 PM to 5 PM. Closed Christmas Day and New Year's Day.

Admission: Free. Memberships are available.

Directions: From Parry Ave., go east on Washington in Fair Park past the railroad museum. It's the large building across from the parking lot at Grand and Nimitz inside Fair Park.

HAWAIIAN FALLS ADVENTURE PARK

4550 N. Garland Ave., Garland, Texas 75040 (972) 546-3046

Second location: 4400 Paige, The Colony, Texas 75056

Website: www.hawaiianfalls.com

Aloha, Hawaiian Falls Adventure Park invites swimmers to challenge the sixty-two-foot-high Waikiki Wipeout and shoot the loop on the Hawaiian Halfpipe. When you need a break, relax on the Kona Kooler lazy river, floating along, carefree in your tube. Music in the background keeps things lively.

Smaller children never seem to tire of the Keiki Cove, where they can climb, splash, and explore. This jungle-themed kiddie park has interactive water guns and sprinklers.

Grab some lunch and relax on this island of family fun in W. Cecil Winters Regional Park.

- Concessions for food and drinks are available. You cannot bring in coolers, food, alcohol, or beverages. Exceptions include things necessary for infants and special needs.
- A public picnic area is located outside the main gate. Visitors can leave and reenter with a hand stamp.
- Group ticket prices and birthday parties are available.
- Restrooms and water fountains are in the park.
- The park is handicapped accessible for many activities.

Hours: Open seasonally. Monday to Saturday, 10:30 AM to 6:30 PM; Sunday, 11 AM to 6:30 PM.

Admission: Adults, $12.99; children under forty-eight inches in height and seniors (60+), $7.99; ages 3 and younger, free.

Directions: From LBJ Fwy. (I-635), exit Garland Ave. going east.

HEARD NATURAL SCIENCE MUSEUM AND WILDLIFE SANCTUARY

One Nature Place, McKinney, Texas 75069 (972) 562-5566

Website: www.heardmuseum.org

The 289-acre wooded wildlife sanctuary, the legacy of Miss Bessie Heard, is dedicated to preserving and encouraging native wildlife and vegetation, as well as educating the community to appreciate and conserve nature. Around 100,000 visitors wander each year along the nature trails, spotting rabbits, raccoons, and hawks, as well as favorite wildflowers and native trees. Self-guided trails and guided trails are available. Groups, such as Scouts or bird watchers, may take special guided tours. The Hoot Owl Trail, the basic three-quarter-mile trail, takes about an hour to cover. Outings in canoes and night hikes are sometimes offered.

In addition to the looping, beautiful trails, there is the 16,250-square-foot museum, which has added another 8,000 square feet for classrooms. On the upper floor are exhibit halls, and live-animal displays are on the lower floor. Visitors marvel at the collections in the Natural Science Hall, Seashell Room, and the Rock and Mineral Hall. Artwork is displayed in the Print Gallery and Activity Hall. In the live-animal exhibit, families may see the grandeur of an eagle or sharp eyes of a hawk close up.

More than 6,000 students, grades two through junior high, each year take part in the education program, which includes subjects such as animal families and astronomy, with related arts and crafts. A nature photography contest is also held each year for community entries.

Around 100,000 injured or orphaned birds of prey are treated and released in the **Heard Raptor Center**. If an injured raptor is found, call the museum for assistance at (972) 652-5560. Support for this program and the live-animal exhibit partially comes from the Wild Child Adoption Program through which supporters may adopt a creature, such as a golden eagle for $250, a tiger salamander for $25, or a three-toed box turtle for $25.

- Consider bringing binoculars or a camera.
- Ask about special events, such as the Outdoor Nature Festival (on a weekend in September), Wild Bird Seed Days, and Native Plant Sale in April.
- The Heard Museum offers birthday parties. Overnight programs are planned for Scouts.
- Volunteer opportunities are available for ages 14 and up.
- The Nature Store offers a variety of nature-oriented gifts.
- A small picnic area is available. A soft drink machine is on the outside balcony. School groups sometimes picnic at Finch Park on Kentucky St. or Town Lake Park in McKinney.
- A paved trail and the museum building are handicapped accessible.
- Restrooms and water fountains are in the museum.
- Parking is free.

Hours: Open Monday to Saturday, 9 AM to 4:45 PM with last departure for self-guided trails at 4 PM; Sunday, 1 PM to 4:45 PM with last departure for self-guided trails at 4 PM; guided trails on Saturday and Sunday at 2 PM from September through mid-July. Groups contact the Education Department. Closed some holidays.

Admission: To the grounds: Adults, $5; ages 3–12 and seniors, $3. To both grounds and exhibits: Adults, $8; ages 3–12 and seniors, $5. Memberships are available.

Directions: From US 75 (Central), take Exit 38 (Hwy. 5) north and stay in right lane. Proceed one mile, turn south on Hwy. 5, and go another 3/4 mile. Turn left on FM 1378. Drive east on FM 1378 one mile to the museum, which is located on the north side. It's located southeast of McKinney about twenty-five miles from downtown Dallas.

HERITAGE FARMSTEAD

1900 W. 15th St., Plano, Texas 75075 (972) 881-0140 Website: www.heritagefarmstead.org

Behind a bank of trees, which shields it from the noises of progress, lies a two-story Victorian blackland prairie farm home and twelve outbuildings. One step onto its wrap-around porch, and visitors step back in time to 1891, when it was located on a 360-acre working farm owned by Dudley and Ammie Wilson.

A short film in the Orientation Center explains what farm life was like at the turn of the century through the advent of the tractor and what farm families did to survive. As the tour goes into the main house, the rooms, such as the two parlors, music room, Ammie's sewing room, Dudley's farm office, and the kitchen with a wood-burning stove, come alive. Check under the beds for chamber pots and in the children's bedrooms for period toys. On the first floor, look for the framed hair wreath.

Some items in the rooms are changed periodically to reflect the way they would have looked during a particular season or holiday. Adult visitors will likely find items they remember from their grandparents' houses, a way of life that would be lost to the younger generation if not for the efforts of preservationists.

Other favorite buildings are the curing shed, corn crib, brood house for chickens, and livestock area with its mule, sheep, and pigs. Look under a shelter for a horse-drawn carriage, Model T truck, and Fordson tractor. Throughout the growing season, cotton, sorghum, and various vegetables and herbs are planted. The pole barn has picnic tables and a small stage, which may be rented for outdoor meetings, such as wedding receptions. Children also find interesting the cistern, windmill, and storm cellar. A reproduction one-room school allows visitors to sit at the connected desks, write on slates, and imagine sharing the small building with eight grades and one teacher. There is also a small auxiliary farmhouse on site, dating to the 1880s, which is used for educational programs. This structure, too, may be rented.

Opened as a museum in 1978, the four-acre museum is listed on the National Register of Historic Places, and tour guides dressed in period costumes explain life as it once was on a Collin County farm.

- Special events include the Lantern Light Tour. Usually only the house's lower floor is toured on event days. Call for more special events or check the website.
- Self-guided tours of the grounds are available Tuesday to Friday from 9 AM to 3 PM and on weekends from 1 PM to 5 PM. Going on a dry day is recommended. Self-guided tours with children can be enhanced by borrowing seek-and-find scavenger hunt clues at the museum entrance. See the guided-tour schedule below.
- There is handicapped access to the lower floor. Pictures of the upstairs are by the first-floor telephone. Pathways and most outbuildings are accessible.
- Group tours of ten or more are asked to preregister at least six weeks ahead. Spanish-speaking docents may be available.
- There is no concession.
- The Country Store has farm-related children's books, stuffed toy animals, dolls, and other toys, as well as gifts with historical emphasis and items made on the farm by crafters.
- Restrooms are located in the altered hen houses, and a water fountain is nearby.
- Parking is free.

Hours: Guided tours: November 1 to July 31, Tuesday and Wednesday 10 AM; Thursday and Friday 10 AM and 12 PM. August 1 to October 31, 10 AM and 12 PM. Year-round, Saturday and Sunday, 1 PM and 2:45 PM. Closed Monday and major holidays.

Admission: Under 3, free; ages 3–12 and senior citizens, $2.50; ages 13 and over, $3.50. Fee includes guided tour. Memberships are available.

Directions: Take the 15th St. (544) exit off Central (US 75) and go west. Turn south on Pitman, which is between Alma and Custer. Look for signs and the two-story house on the left.

LAS COLINAS

204 Mandalay Canal, Irving, Texas 75039
(972) 869-1232, (972) 556-0625

Las Colinas is a carefully planned, 12,000-acre development of attractive office buildings, homes, recreational businesses, and retail stores.

Boy Scouts of America, Kimberly-Clark, Exxon, and others have their world headquarters there.

If you enter the Las Colinas Urban Center on O'Connor Rd. from the south, be sure everyone looks to the right for the beautiful **flower clock** with the words "Las Colinas" spelled out in shrubs just before driving under Hwy. 114 (Carpenter Fwy.).

On the west side of O'Connor just past Las Colinas Blvd. is a parking garage and then the west tower of Williams Square. Between the west and east towers is a plaza larger than two football fields on which nine larger-than-life Spanish horses called the **Mustangs of Las Colinas** appear to be galloping across a stream. Fountains under the horses' hooves give the look of splashing water. Families can climb steps along the water and cross it on granite stepping stones. In the lobby of the west tower is the **Mustang Sculpture Exhibit**, which explains the process used to sculpt and install the horses through photographs, models, and a slide presentation. Other African wildlife sculptures by mustang sculptor Robert Glen are also on display. The exhibit is open Wednesday to Saturday. Call (972) 869-9047.

Near the Urban Center on the east side of Hwy. 114 at Rochelle Rd. is the **Marble Cow Sculpture**, which includes five large marble cows atop Bluebonnet Hill. A sidewalk goes up the hill, and kids love running from cow to cow. Benches are under the trees. The sculpture is across the street from the Texas Commerce Tower.

North of Las Colinas Urban Center on O'Connor Rd. are the **Las Colinas Equestrian Center** and **The Movie Studios at Las Colinas**.

A bike trail runs through Las Colinas.

Williams Square is handicapped accessible. The canal is accessible through an elevator in the Tower East parking garage elevator on Las Colinas Blvd.

Admission: Free.

Directions: Located in Irving, the Urban Center is at O'Connor Rd. and Hwy. 114.

MESQUITE CHAMPIONSHIP RODEO

1818 Rodeo Dr., Mesquite, Texas 75149 (972) 285-8777
Website: www.mesquiterodeo.com

Don your Levis and Ropers and recapture the thrilling days of the Wild West with its daring cowboys and powerful livestock at the Mesquite Championship Rodeo. Families can experience the true flavor of Texas, beginning with hickory-smoked barbecue at the 300-seat Bull's-eye Pavilion. Pony rides and the Kiddie Korral barnyard entertain young buckaroos awaiting the exciting prelude to rodeo events, the majestic Grand Entry.

Eyes widen and pulses race as the crowds watch calf ropers, steer wrestlers, and bronc-and-bull riders brush with danger and conquer it with courage and skill. Lovely barrel racers, crazy clowns, and country music add to the entertainment. Even the young 'uns have their turn in the arena with the Kids' Calf Scramble for ages eight and under.

The $8 million, air-conditioned Mesquite Arena has grandstand and reserved box seating, as well as seventy luxury Champion Suites, some of which can be leased nightly for $1,250. Call for the date of the Mesquite Rodeo Parade, which kicks off the rodeo season, usually in April.

- A gift shop and emporium are on the rodeo grounds.
- Concessions sell food and beverages.
- The arena is handicapped accessible.
- Restrooms and water fountains are available.
- Parking is $3. Arrive around 7 pm to miss heavy traffic. There is sometimes a long line exiting from I-635.

Hours: April through September, Friday and Saturday nights, 8 PM to 10 PM. The gates open at 6:30 PM.

Admission: Tickets range from $5 to $30. Group rates are available for twenty-five people or more. Bull's-eye Barbecue costs $6.50 to $9.50.

Directions: Exit Military Pkwy. off I-635 (LBJ Fwy.) in Mesquite. The Arena is visible from the freeway on the west side.

THE MOVIE STUDIOS AT LAS COLINAS

6301 N. O'Connor Rd., Irving, Texas 75039 (972) 869-3456, (972) 869-FILM Website: www.studiosatlascolinas.com

Housed in the 112-acre Dallas Communications Complex at Las Colinas, the studios tour takes visitors behind the scenes to a working motion picture and TV sound stage. You'll see sets and memorabilia from movies and TV shows, such as *Star Trek, Forrest Gump, Hunt for Red October, Wayne's World, Gerbert,* and *Robocop.* A tour of the studios lasts about 1.5 hours.

Fascinating displays illustrate special effects, makeup, and costumes. Audiences like the sound- and visual-effects show. Kids ages eight to eighteen can enroll in movie-making workshops and camps. Call (972) 869-3300.

- The Hollywood Company Store is open for movie and TV fans. Call 869-7723.
- The studios is handicapped accessible for most of the tour.
- Water fountains and restrooms are available.
- Group tours may be arranged.
- Parking is free.

Hours: June through August: Monday to Saturday, 10 AM to 8 PM; Sunday, 12 PM to 8 PM. September through May: Monday to Saturday, 10 AM to 4 PM; Sunday, 12 PM to 4 PM. Tours are at 10:30 AM, 12:30 PM, 2:30 PM, and 4 PM. Possibly closed on Mondays in January and February. Call to confirm times.

Admission for studio tour: Adults, $12.95; seniors (65+), $10.95; ages 5–12, $8.95; 4 and under, free.

Directions: The studios are located at Royal Ln. and O'Connor Rd., between O'Connor and Valley View and north of Northwest Hwy. in Irving.

NASHER SCULPTURE CENTER

2001 Flora, Dallas, Texas 75201 (214) 242-5100
Website: www.nashersculpturecenter.org

An "oasis in the city," the $70 million Nasher Sculpture Center is the only spot in the world completely dedicated to the display and advancement of sculpture. The $400 million masterworks collection of Ray Nasher and his late wife, Patsy, covers 2.4 acres. Its focus is on the history of modern sculpture, and the pieces are by artists ranging from Rodin to Richard Serra. A 55,000-square-foot building, designed by Italian architect Renzo Piano, houses sculpture galleries, a café, and a store. Larger pieces are installed in the outdoor garden, where 175 trees shade the sculptures, fountains, terraced theater, and three granite walkways. At the far end of this "roofless" museum is the Turrell skyspace *Tending*, a twenty-six-foot, black-granite cube that seats twenty-five people who can look at the sky through a 10 × 10–foot opening. The play of light is most spectacular at dawn and twilight. Nasher plans to rotate the works in his collection.

- Across the street is the Dallas Museum of Art, which also has an outdoor sculpture garden. The two will collaborate on some special exhibits.
- The center is in the process of developing an art-education curriculum. School and other group tours may be arranged by calling (214) 242-5170.
- Inside the museum building are restrooms, water fountains, and a café.
- No flash photography, tripods, or video cameras are allowed.
- The museum is handicapped accessible.
- Parking: Ace and Star lots are between Flora and Woodall Rodgers. A fee is charged. The Dallas Museum of Art garage has entrances on St. Paul and Harwood.

Hours: Tuesday, Wednesday, and Friday through Sunday, 11 AM to 6 PM; Thursday, 11 AM to 9 PM. Closed Mondays and major holidays.

Admission: Adults, $10; seniors, $7; students, $5; children under 12, free. The price includes the audio tour.

Directions: From N. Central Expwy. (US-75 S), merge onto Woodall Rodgers (TX 366W) via exit 1A toward I-35E S/Waco (0.70 mi.). Take the St. Paul exit. Turn left onto the Woodall Rodgers service road and turn right onto N. Harwood.

OLD CITY PARK

1717 Gano, Dallas, Texas 75215 (214) 421-5141
Website: www.oldcitypark.org

One of Dallas's historical and architectural treasures is Old City Park, thirteen acres on which rest thirty-six restored 19th-century homes, buildings, and preserved arts.

The tour may begin with a short film at the 1887 MKT Railroad Depot and continue to the Drummer's Hotel, Flower Garden, General Store, and Miller Log House. Children will love the Miller's Log Playhouse. The barn often serves as a potter's workshop. Notice that the Gano cabin dogtrot house has an open breezeway with rooms on each side to allow for circulation. A windmill stands nearby. The Renner School, Victorian George House, Pilot Grove Church, and Brent Place (a house that could be ordered in a kit) will also be of interest.

With younger children, the best days to visit are the special event days. Other highlights are the July 4 celebration, Treat St. at Halloween, and the Candlelight Christmas Tour.

Three tour options are available: a self-guided tour with a map; the Home Life Tour at 1:30 PM on Tuesday to Saturday and at 2:30 PM on Sunday; and the historical audio tour, $3.

McCall's Store, a Victorian gift shop, carries some interesting toys, especially at Christmas. The corral may be open with Heritage Livestock farm animals.

On the grounds, Brent Place restaurant may be open for lunch; call (214) 421-3057. Outside McCall's is a soft drink machine. A McDonald's is at Harwood and Gano. To the west on Griffith is a Ramada Inn with a dining room on the top floor. Visitors may bring a picnic lunch.

- There is handicapped accessibility to the grounds but not to all of the buildings.
- Restrooms with wheelchair access are located in the Fisher Road House. There are water fountains.
- Parking is free.

Hours: Grounds are open Tuesday to Saturday, 10 AM to 4 PM; Sunday, 12 PM to 4 PM. Tours are self-paced and self-guided. Audio tours add to your enjoyment.

Admission: Adults, $7; seniors, $5; ages 3–12, $4.

Directions: From the west on I-30, exit at 46B Ervay. Turn left at St. Paul and left again at Gano. From the east, take exit 46A Downtown Central. At Harwood, turn right. The first right is Gano.

OWENS SPRING CREEK FARM

1401 E. Lookout Dr., Richardson, Texas 75082 (972) 235-0192
Website: www.owensinc.com/owens_scfarm.htm

Rolling green hills and white buildings complete the home of Owens Country Sausage at Spring Creek Farm. The Owens Museum, located near the entrance, takes visitors 100 years back in time in the Butcher Shop, Country Store, Country Kitchen, and Farmer's Workshop.

Outside the museum are farm animals and the Antique Wagon Showroom. What children remember most about the farm are the stables, which house the Owens Gentle Giant, one blonde, magnificent Belgian draft horse, which weighs about 2,300 pounds. The stable also has an eight-horse pony hitch with matched miniature horses that pull a variety of miniature wagons. The ponies are favorites in area parades.

Just inside the gates is a two-story farmhouse dating to 1887 and called **Miss Belle's Place** after the spinster schoolteacher who held classes in her home. Tours of the home may be arranged through the Junior League of Richardson. Call (972) 644-5979.

- Free guided tours are available with reservations. Call (972) 235-0192.
- There is no food or drink at Owens, but at the intersection of Plano Rd. and Campbell are Purdy's and The Feed Bag for burgers.
- Handicapped access is available.
- Restrooms and water fountains are provided.
- Parking is free.

Hours: Open daily, 9 AM to 4 PM. Closed 12 PM to 1 PM for lunch. Tours on the hour from 9 AM to 3 PM with reservations. Closed major holidays.

Admission: Free.

Directions: Exit Campbell Rd. east from US 75 and go north on Plano Rd., or take Plano Rd. north from I-635. The farm is on the right.

THE PALACE OF WAX AND
RIPLEY'S BELIEVE IT OR NOT!

601 E. Safari Pkwy., Grand Prairie, Texas 75050 (972) 263-2391

Two very unique attractions located together just five minutes east of Six Flags are The Palace of Wax and Ripley's Believe It or Not! Lifelike figures of the famous and infamous have eyes that seem to follow visitors as they go from one vignette to the next. Those remembered in wax vary from Jesus Christ to Hollywood's stars and starlets to Sleeping Beauty and her prince. Walk through Behind the Scenes to a working wax studio and costume shop to see how these amazing wax figures are created.

Bring a camera to capture the collection of incredible oddities in Ripley's Believe It or Not! museum. Eight major theme galleries invite visitors to experience tornadoes and earthquakes and walk across coals of fire. On display is an enormous collection of curiosities that Robert Ripley collected on his tour of 198 countries. Visitors marvel at his strange treasures, such as a leaning Tower of Pisa made of matchsticks, The Lord's Prayer handwritten on one-fourth of a postage stamp, and a mask formed from human skin. Many hands-on exhibits challenge guests to Believe It or Not!

- The Haunted House at The Palace of Wax is a favorite Halloween event. Families might call for more information before taking young children.
- Facilities include a gift shop, snack bar, and game area.
- The museums are handicapped accessible.
- Restrooms and water fountains are available.
- Parking is free.

Hours: Open daily year-round, except Thanksgiving, Christmas, and New Year's Day. Memorial Day to Labor Day: 10 AM to 9 PM. Remainder of year: Monday to Friday, 10 AM to 5 PM; Saturday to Sunday, 10 AM to 6 PM. The ticket office closes one hour before the listed closing time.

Admission: To see only one of the two museums: Ages 13 and up, $14.95; ages 4–12, $8.95; 3 and under, free. To see both museums: Ages 13 up, $17.95; seniors, $15.95; ages 4–12, $12.95; 3 and under, free. Discount rates are available for groups of twelve or more.

Directions: From I-30, exit north at Belt Line Rd. The museums can be seen from the highway. They're seven minutes east of Six Flags.

SANDY LAKE AMUSEMENT PARK

I-35E North at Sandy Lake Rd. (Exit 444), Carrollton, Texas 75006 (972) 242-7449 (Mailing address: P.O. Box 810536, Dallas, Texas 75381) Website: www.sandylake.com

A favorite swimming hole of Dallasites for more than thirty years, Sandy Lake continues to delight families with its large pool designed for all ages. Lifeguards watch the pool area closely.

A hilly miniature golf course, paddleboats, and nineteen amusement rides add to the fun. Screened in along the lake area in the Bird Barnyard are peacocks, ducks, geese, guineas, and turkeys to watch.

During April and May, local school bands, orchestras, and choirs compete there.

- Tickets are bought for the attractions, and discount books are available.
- Birthday party packages, which may include a meal, are offered.
- Paddleboat riders must meet height requirements or ride with an adult. Small children wear life jackets.
- Four concessions with hamburgers, hot dogs, and snacks are convenient. Families may bring only home-prepared food with no glass bottles for picnics. Picnic tables are provided, but groups of fifteen or more need a reservation, and there is a fee.
- Most areas are handicapped accessible, but the miniature golf course is too hilly.
- Restrooms and water fountains are available.
- Parking is free.

Hours: Open April through September. Hours and days vary from month to month.

Admission: General admission at the gate: Ages 4 and up, $2; 3 and under, free. Swimming, $4; paddleboats and miniature golf, $2; amusement rides, $1 to $2.

Directions: Take I-35E north and exit at Sandy Lake Rd. (Exit 444) in Carrollton. Go west a short distance to the park on the right.

THE SCIENCE PLACE

1318 Second Ave., Dallas, Texas 75210 (214) 428-5555
(**Mailing address**: P.O. Box 151469, Dallas, Texas 75315)
Website: www.scienceplace.org

Housed in two buildings in Fair Park, The Science Place has been fascinating children with scientific marvels for over thirty-four years. Exciting traveling exhibits, such as Whales: Giants of the Deep, which has five active, full-sized robotic whales, regularly team up with permanent exhibits to challenge the minds of onlookers. Hands-on activities and demonstrations allow families to become active participants in the world of scientific discovery. The TI Founders **IMAX Theater**, which has a seventy-nine-foot domed screen, presents larger-than-life films daily.

Permanent exhibits include **Kid's Place**, which delights children up to age seven with the Number Forest, Building Things, Senses, and Waterworks. The basics of math and physics and environmental concerns may be explored in a variety of exhibits.

Demonstrations such as **Electric Theater** feature electricity. Call for times and news about other current demonstrations.

The Science Place **Planetarium** in the SP Planetarium Building presents programs that often coincide with current exhibits. Look for the annual program about the Christmas Star. Call (214) 428-5555 for programs and times. There are special showtimes during the state fair.

Lectures given by experts in fields of science, such as Jane Goodall, are regularly on the events calendar.

The **SP Preschool Program** offers an exciting curriculum for children during the week and special weekend workshops for preschoolers through eighth graders year-round. Summer classes and family work-shops are also scheduled. Call for a brochure.

ImagiNature Gallery by Kid's Place has critters, bees, birds, and fish.

- Birthday parties may be celebrated on weekends with a staff person to assist. Call for information and reservations.
- The Science Plays Store offers books, toys, games, costumes, and other science-related items.
- The Science Place Cafe offers light fare from soups to sandwiches and a variety of snacks. Open daily, 9:30 AM to 3:30 PM. Picnic ta-bles are usually located behind the museum by the lagoon.
- Handicapped access is available.
- Restrooms and water fountains are provided.
- Parking is free, except during the state fair.

Hours: Tuesday to Friday, 9:30 AM to 4:30 PM; Saturday, 9:30 AM to 5:30 PM; Sunday, 11:30 AM to 5:30 PM. Closed Christmas Day.

Exhibit admission: Adults, $7.50; ages 3–12, $4; seniors (60+), $6.50; members and ages under 3, free. Planetarium, $3 for the show only. Memberships are available. IMAX only: Adults, $7; ages 3–12 and sen-iors, $6. Various combo prices are offered. Advance tickets are available online.

Directions: Enter Fair Park through the Grand Ave. gate off of Robert B. Cullum Blvd. Parking is available in front of the museum.

SIX FLAGS HURRICANE HARBOR

1800 E. Lamar, Arlington, Texas 76006 (817) 265-3356
Website: www.sixflags.com/parks/hurricaneharbordallas

Aptly named, the forty-seven-acre Hurricane Harbor water park offers an exhilarating way to cool off during the hot Texas summertime.

Whether taking a leisurely inner tube cruise around Arlington's Lazy River ride or dropping into a free fall from seventy-six nautical feet of Der Stuka, family members will find nonstop entertainment during their day at Hurricane Harbor. Young and old are drawn to Captain Hook's Lagoon, which has five stories of fun on net ladders and slides. Next, they may want to try Suntan Lagoon, an activity pool with geysers, fountains, and waterfalls surrounded by a deck.

The more adventuresome might try the Bubba Tub, in which four ride a rubber tub from a six-story height. The white water rafting of Colorado is replicated in the inner tube ride on the Ragin' Rapids of a man-made river with slides and waterfalls to add to the experience. Rides like Banzai Banzai and the Black Hole live up to their names in thrilling speed and splashing finales.

- Lifeguards are professionally trained and are very visible. Some rides have height requirements or caution those with heart problems or women who are pregnant.
- Soft rafts and tubes for the wave pool are available for rent or sale, but you will probably want to bring your own.
- Adults must accompany young children, who use approved flotation devices. Watch children very carefully in the pools, especially on crowded days.
- Picnic tables are available. Visitors may bring their own food and nonalcoholic drinks. No glass containers are allowed. Concessions provide drinks and fast food.
- Across the highway is Six Flags Over Texas amusement park.
- There are coin-operated lockers for valuables, shower facilities, an arcade, a gift shop, sand volleyball courts, and lounge chairs.
- There is handicapped access to the pool areas.
- Restrooms and water fountains are provided.
- Parking is $7.

Hours: Open from mid-May through mid-September. Hours vary. Call for specific days and times. Summer hours are usually Fridays and Saturdays from 10:30 AM to 9 PM, Sundays through Thursdays from 10:30 AM to 8 PM.

Admission: A one-day pass to the Arlington park: Adults, $28.99; seniors (55+) and kids under forty-eight inches tall, $18.99; ages 2 and under, free. Discount rate is sometimes given for evening admission. Season passes are available.

Directions: The Arlington park is just off I-30, directly across from Six Flags Over Texas. Exit onto the Hwy. 360 service road. The park is on the north side.

SIX FLAGS OVER TEXAS

2201 Road to Six Flags, Arlington, Texas 76010,
Metro (817) 640-8900 Website: www.sixflags.com/texas

As children see the bright, waving flags and dancing fountains of Six Flags Over Texas, excitement and anticipation of the thrills to come overflow. For over thirty years, this 205-acre family theme park has entertained all ages with a variety of rides, shows, and special events.

Young children are drawn to the antique Silver Star Carousel, Looney Tunes Land, and the Good Time Theater where Bugs Bunny and pals entertain. Older children brave the roller coasters, which range from the tamer Mini-mine Train to the fourteen-story wooden roller coaster called The Texas Giant. Towering 325 feet into the air, the Superman Tower of Power fits riders into a launch vehicle, sends them up "faster than a speeding bullet," pauses, and then sends them hurtling down. For those who need a cooldown, a liberal drenching is promised by the Roaring Rapids and the Log Ride.

Everyone loves the shootouts between Six Flags cowboys, the shows at the Crazy Horse Saloon and Southern Palace, and the special concerts at the 10,000-seat Music Mill Amphitheater. The lush landscaping, cheerful employees, and cleanliness are always appreciated. Emporiums with T-shirts and other souvenirs are plentiful.

- Some rides have height and age requirements.
- Discount coupons and information about special events are often available in Friday newspapers or other promotions. Special prices are sometimes offered for purchasing evening tickets or bringing designated soft drink cans.
- Special events include September's Heritage Craft Fair, Halloween Fright Nights, and Holiday in the Park in December and January.
- There are diaper stations and Lost Parents headquarters in Looney Toon Land. Stroller rental at the main gate is about $7.
- Admission to the park includes all rides and shows, except some special concerts in the amphitheater. Some rides have a height requirement. Food, arcade games, and souvenirs are not included in the fee but may be needed in the budget.
- Indoor restaurants serve fried chicken, Mexican dishes, burgers, and pizza, as well as other fast foods, at food stands with picnic-type outdoor seating. A shaded family picnic area with tables is located in the parking lot between rows 25 and 30. Get your hand stamped at the gate for reentry.
- There is handicapped access to the park. Accessibility to rides varies. A guide to ride accessibility is available at the gate.

- Restrooms and water fountains are available throughout the park and are noted on the park map. Lockers are provided near the entrance.
- Parking is about $9. Trams transport visitors from the remote parking to the entrance and back. A park map is distributed at the entrance to the parking lot.

Hours: Open weekends in spring and fall; daily in summer; special schedule for Holiday in the Park. For specific hours and information, call Metro (817) 640-8900, ext. 517. In summer, hours are usually daily, 10 AM to 10 PM.

Admission: One-day pass: Adults, $39.99; children under forty-eight inches and seniors (55+), $24.99; ages 2 and under, free. Two-day passes and individual and family season passes are available. Discount rates are available for groups of twenty-five or more.

Directions: Located between Dallas and Ft. Worth off I-30 on the south side. Exit at Hwy. 360 in Arlington. The orange observation tower can be seen for miles.

THE SIXTH FLOOR MUSEUM

411 Elm St., Dallas, Texas 75202 (214) 653-6660, (888) 485-4854
Website: www.jfk.org

The Sixth Floor Exhibit: John F. Kennedy and the Memory of a Nation is a permanent collection of historical information regarding the assassination of President John F. Kennedy on November 22, 1963. Located on the sixth floor of the former Texas School Book Depository, photographs, forty minutes of documentary film, and significant artifacts are presented to help visitors understand the events leading to and following this tragic event. Museum personnel believe all materials are appropriate for viewing by families.

An audio tour is available, and about seventy-five minutes should be allowed to cover the exhibit adequately. The museum brochure recommends a walking tour around Dealey Plaza following a map that notes points related to the motorcade and theories about the gunman. As visitors leave the sixth floor, they are invited to write their own memories of the assassination in books that will always be part of the historic record.

No photography is allowed.

- The Visitor Center has a small bookstore. You may write or call for a free brochure.
- Oliver Stone's movie *JFK* was filmed here.
- On Market between Commerce and Main is the John F. Kennedy Memorial Plaza.

- Restaurants are located in the nearby West End Historic District.
- The handicapped-accessible entrances are on the north side of the building at Pacific and on the west side.
- There are restrooms and water fountains.
- Paid parking is available to the north of the Visitor Center. Ample parking is next to the Visitor Center on the west side of the building. Visitors can ride the DART train, get off at the West End station, and walk about a block west.

Hours: Open daily, 9 AM to 6 PM; last ticket sold one hour prior to closing. Closed Christmas Day.

Admission: Exhibition only: Adults, $10; seniors, students, and children 6–18, $9; children under 6, free. There is an audio tour for ages 6–12 as well as adult audio tours in seven languages. Group rates are available.

Directions: The Visitor Center faces Dealey Plaza on Houston St. between Elm and Pacific in the old Texas School Book Depository Building, which is now called the Dallas County Administration Building.

SURF 'N SWIM

440 Oates Rd., Garland, Texas 75043 (972) 205-3993, (972) 205-2757 Website: www.ci.garland.tx.us

Nestled in a shady greenbelt area, this large wave pool is operated by the City of Garland in Audubon Park. Excited whoops go up as the surf is turned on, producing rolling waves that lift and lower inner tube riders.

Lifeguards carefully monitor the area and can push a button to stop the waves if necessary. Only soft flotation devices are allowed.

Plenty of shaded and unshaded grassy areas are provided for spreading out beach towels. Picnic tables are provided, and food may be brought in, but glass bottles and alcoholic beverages are not allowed. Ice chests are checked at the entrance.

- Inner tubes may be purchased, or a swimmer's own tube can be aired up for 50 cents. A tube makes the waves more enjoyable.
- Very young children should be watched carefully, especially on crowded days, to see that they do not get caught underneath the tubes. The waves will lift them off their feet, and their heads go under water.
- Audubon Park has a wonderful shaded playground area east of the pool. Passes are honored all day, so swimmers may leave and return on that day.
- Call ahead if the weather has been stormy. The pool is closed if the water is clouded. Even in summer, it can be cool there on a cloudy, windy day.

- Rental after closing time is offered for groups. Three birthday packages are available.
- The concession sells fast food and snow cones.
- Handicapped accessible into pool area is available.
- Restrooms, an open shower, water fountains, and a pay telephone are available.
- Parking is free.

Hours: Open from Splash Day about mid-May on weekends to daily while school is out until Labor Day, 11 AM to 7 PM. Open Friday until 9 PM. Crowds thinnest in the early morning and late afternoon.

Admission: Sixty inches and taller, $5.50; under sixty inches, $4.50; 2 and under, free. Group rates are available for twenty-five or more.

Directions: Take the Oates Exit off LBJ Fwy. (I-635) and go east. The pool is past the baseball fields on the right at Audubon Park.

TELEPHONE PIONEER MUSEUM OF TEXAS

One Bell Plaza, 208 S. Akard, Dallas, Texas (Mailing address: P.O. Box 655521, Dallas, Texas 75265-5521) (214) 464-4359

The many unique and entertaining venues for explaining the history and operation of the telephone at the Telephone Pioneer Museum of Texas attract all ages. In the theater, an audiovisual presentation explains how far communication has come and where it is going. Alexander Graham Bell, as a lifelike figure, is diligently pursuing his new invention, the telephone, while a huge, bright-red telephone with a face in its receiver explains telephone etiquette to all who will listen.

A Norman Rockwell print reminds visitors of the diligence of the cable repairman perched at the top of a pole. A number of telephones and similar inventions are displayed. In one exhibit, visitors may dial and watch the call being completed. At the Party Line display, children may listen in on lively dialogue between characters, such as Ma Bell, Big Tex, Superman, and Thomas A. Edison. Don't leave without listening to the talking bear, who explains the services of the Telephone Pioneers. The Pioneers and the telephone company worked together in assembling this museum, which is open only with reservations, so call ahead for your group.

- Browse in the gift shop for T-shirts, toys, and telephone-related items.
- The museum does not allow food or drink.
- The museum is handicapped accessible.
- There are restrooms and water fountains.
- Call about parking before coming to the museum. DART buses stop within walking distance. Call (214) 979-1111 for the bus schedule.

Hours: Open Tuesday to Friday; tours at 10 AM and 12 PM by reservation only. Call at least two weeks in advance. Closed holidays and weekends.

Admission: Free.

Directions: Located in downtown Dallas at One Bell Plaza, second floor, between Commerce and Jackson with Browder on the east.

TEXAS DISCOVERY GARDENS IN FAIR PARK

3601 Martin Luther King Blvd., Dallas, Texas 75210 (214) 428-7476 (Mailing address: P.O. Box 152537, Dallas, Texas 75315)
Website: www.texasdiscoverygardens.org

Celebrating its sixtieth birthday in 2001, the Texas Discovery Gardens in Fair Park continues to share "butterflies, bugs, and botany" with children and adults. This Art Deco building is a National Historic Landmark, built for the 1936 Texas Centennial Exposition. An urban oasis, it maintains a 15,000-square-foot visitor center and 7.5 acres of outdoor gardens. Children delight in wandering around the paths and identifying green plants and blooming flowers. The gardens provide a natural habitat for butterflies and other native wildlife.

Featuring more than 266 species of African flora, the William Douglas Blachly Conservatory, a 6,800-square-foot glass house, demonstrates how plants adapt to different environments and relate to other plants, animals, and humans. Roses and over forty different perennials are featured in the Rose Garden. In addition to the wonderful smell of roses, families will enjoy the Herb and Scent Garden and the Xeriscape Garden, which demonstrates low water use and teaches families how to save the environment one yard at a time. The fountains and pools enhance the beauty.

The Texas Discovery Gardens offer educational classes and tours for school children. Topics include Life in a Compost Bin, Terrarium Worlds, and Butterflies, Bugs and Botany. Other special events are scheduled throughout the year. The live-butterfly exhibit is a favorite during the state fair, when more than 1,000 butterflies are released per week.

- Areas of the center may be reserved for parties and meetings.
- There is no food service, except during the state fair. The Old Mill Inn, across from the Music Hall, is within walking distance (Tuesday to Sunday, 11 AM to 2:30 PM).
- Handicapped access is available.
- There are restrooms and water fountains.
- Parking is free except during the state fair and Fair Park special events.

Hours: Open Tuesday to Saturday, 10 AM to 5 PM; Sunday, 1 PM to 5 PM. Open Memorial Day and Labor Day, 10 pm to 5 pm; closed other Mondays, Thanksgiving, Christmas, and New Year's Day.

Admission: Wednesday to Sunday: Members and children under 3 admitted free; adults, $3; seniors (60+), $2; children (ages 3–11), $1.50. Tuesday, free admission for everyone. These rates and hours vary during the state fair.

Directions: Enter Fair Park through the Martin L. King entrance off Robert B. Cullum Blvd. Parking is to the right. See directions to Fair Park.

WEST END MARKETPLACE

West End Historic District, 603 Munger Ave. at Market St., Dallas, Texas 75202 (214) 748-4801

Always festive at any time of year, the West End MarketPlace entertains families on four floors of the former cracker factory. My father worked at the factory as a young man before World War II. Located in the fifty-five-acre West End Historic District, the MarketPlace houses more than forty specialty retail shops and pushcarts, including Cats Canines and Critters, Dallas Cowboys Pro Shops, and Wild Bill's Western Wear.

Children are happy to spend the day on the Fountain Level at Tilt in Dallas Alley, with more than 200 electronic video games and a motion simulation theater. Also, they can watch the singing fudge makers on the first floor at the Fudgery. When hunger strikes, take the escalator to the fourth floor for a variety of casual eateries.

While on this floor, duffers may want to compete in miniature golf at CityGolf, an eighteen-hole, indoor miniature golf course. It's a favorite place for year-round birthday parties.

The West End hosts several festivals and special events, such as Hoop It Up, Taste of Dallas, the circus exhibit, the elephant walk, Disney on Ice, and the Police Motorcycle Competition. Call for a calendar of events or watch for newspaper announcements on Friday. More than twenty restaurants, such as Spaghetti Warehouse, Sonny Bryan's, and Friday's, serving a variety of foods, are located just outside the MarketPlace.

- The West End is near the Dallas Arts District, Dealey Plaza, Dallas World Aquarium, and the Sixth Floor Museum.
- The Dallas Surrey Service and Max-a-Million provide horse-drawn carriage rides around the West End and downtown, weather permitting. Call (214) 946-9911 or (214) 914-8600 for information.
- The MarketPlace is handicapped accessible.
- Restrooms and water fountains are available.

- Various parking lots with fees are available; there is also some metered street parking and the six-story West End Parking Garage at Munger and Lamar, one block east of the MarketPlace. It's better not to travel alone or wear flashy, expensive jewelry after dark.

Hours: Monday to Wednesday, 11 AM to 9 PM; Thursday, 11 AM to 10 PM; Friday and Saturday, 11 AM to 12 AM; Sunday, 12 PM to 6 PM. Closed Thanksgiving, Easter, Christmas Day, and New Year's Day.

Admission: Free to enter and look around. A fee may be charged to participate in special events.

Directions: From I-35 (Stemmons Fwy.), exit Continental, which changes name to Lamar (at Munger). Turn right for the MarketPlace or turn left for the garage. From US 75 (N. Central Expwy.), take Woodall Rogers (I-35E) to Field St. Veer left under the highway to Lamar, and turn left on Lamar. At Munger, turn right for the MarketPlace or turn left for the parking garage. The DART rail line stops at the West End.

WHITE ROCK LAKE

(214) 670-8281 Website: dallascityhall.org/dallas/eng/html/park_ and_recreation.html

Park directory website: www.whiterocklake.org/directory/ directory.html

Built for water supply in 1910, White Rock Lake is now operated as a public park that consists of over 1,000 acres of lake and 1,000 acres of parkland. Main avenues surrounding White Rock include E. Northwest Hwy., Buckner Blvd., Mockingbird Ln., Garland Rd., and Lawther Dr. On sunny days, the shaded park is highly populated with sailors, fishermen, joggers, bicyclists, skaters, and picnickers.

On a 9.33-mile trail around the lake, those jogging, skating, and bicycling get their exercise protected from city traffic. An eight-to-ten station par course is between Emerald Isle and Poppy Dr. on the lake's east side. The 7.3-mile White Rock Creek Trail continues north through the greenbelt area to Valley View Park. A pretty ride is from Greenville Ave. and Royal Ln. to Lawther Dr. A new **playground** has been built at Tee Pee Hill, as have six pieces of par course equipment. Close by are bathrooms, a drinking fountain, and cool spray. Enter the park at Williamson and W. Lawther.

Boats with motors of ten horsepower or less, as well as sailboats, kayaks, canoes, and paddleboats, are welcome on the lake. Sailing clubs sometimes hold regattas, which are beautiful to watch. Fishermen line the creek banks and piers, hoping for white crappie, largemouth bass, and catfish. They should have a fishing license and follow length and limit regulations. White Rock provides twelve fishing piers and five boat ramps, two on the east side and three on the west.

At one time, visitors could take Lawther all around the lake, but the crowds were unpopular with residents of the area. Now it is divided into four sections with entrances at Emerald Isle, from Poppy to the Dreyfus Club building off Buckner, by the spillway on Garland, and at Lawther off Mockingbird. Visitors can drive the entire length of the west side.

Shaded picnic areas with nearby playgrounds are plentiful. Covered pavilions and buildings may be rented for large groups. The old **Pump House** at the south end is now a historical site and management office for the Water Department. A sculpture is in front of the building. At Sunset Bay is a life-size bronze statue called **CCC Worker**, honoring Civilian Conservation Corps Company 2986, which helped develop White Rock Lake Park from 1935 to 1942. From Buckner Blvd., go west into the park on Poppy. Turn left on E. Lawther, and go 3/10 mile to Sunset Bay, near the Park Office and the ducks.

- At Mockingbird Point, 8000 Mockingbird, just west of Buckner Blvd., is a **dog park**. Call (214) 670-8895 or visit www.dallasdogparks.org. Closed Monday.
- Perched on the hill on the southeast corner of Mockingbird and Buckner is a small, pretty playground and covered picnic table that overlooks the lake. Another picnic/play park is just a little further north beside the baseball diamonds on Buckner.
- **Flag Pole Hill**, with its playground, covered pavilion for picnics, and wonderful hill to climb, is also a great place to fly a kite, throw a Frisbee, or listen to special outdoor summer programs by the Dallas Symphony.
- Since swimming has not been allowed for many years, the old 1930s bath house is now the **Bath House Cultural Center**, which is used as a gallery, center for performing arts, and educational center for various workshops.
- The **White Rock Lake Museum** is open at the Bath House. Its mission is to present the natural and human history of the lake with an emphasis on the ecology of water. From Buckner Blvd., go west on Northcliff to E. Lawther. Call (214) 670-8751 for a calendar of events.
- Bikes, including tandem, may be rented from Jack Johnston's Bikes; call (214) 328-5238. Canoes may be rented from High Trails Canoe in Garland; call (214) 2-PADDLE. Both businesses are near the lake on Garland Rd.
- Call the Park Department about building and pavilion rental at (214) 670-8748.

- For tennis court reservations, call (214) 670-8745. For information about bike trails and maps, call (214) 670-4272.
- **For the Love of the Lake** is an organization of enthusiastic volunteers who are dedicated to the preservation and enhancement of White Rock. They organize second-Saturday lake spruce ups and other events. PMB 281, 381 Casa Linda Plaza. For information, call the Lakeline at (972) 622-SAVE or e-mail info@whiterocklake.org.
- The **Dallas Arboretum** is near the spillway on Garland Rd. The casual White Rock Yacht Club restaurant is just a little farther down Garland where it splits to the left on E. Grand.
- Portable restrooms in winter are not handicapped accessible. After April 1, five permanent restrooms are opened that are accessible. Water fountains are located nearby. Eight water fountains are along the trail.
- Free parking. Lock your car. Do not leave valuables in sight.

Hours: Daily, 6 AM to 12 AM. It is not advisable to be there after dark.
Admission: Free.
Directions: Access to the park is on Garland Rd., E. Northwest Hwy., Lawther Dr., and N. Buckner Blvd. Signs direct visitors.

THE WOMEN'S MUSEUM

3800 Parry Ave. at S. Washington in Fair Park, Dallas, Texas 75226
(214) 915-0860 Website: www.thewomensmuseum.org

Once a 1910 coliseum in Fair Park that served as both a cattle-auction barn by day and a symphony hall by night, the $25 million Women's Museum: An Institute for the Future has blossomed.

Designed by New York architect Wendy Evans Joseph, the three-level museum celebrates the history and contributions of women in America. The Art Deco look was added in 1936 for the Texas Centennial Exposition. A statue of Venus rising from a cactus greets visitors at the front door.

Inside, exhibits focus on a variety of topics, such as inspirational quotes, unforgettable women, health and sports, "mothers of invention," art, computers, and the future. A thirty-foot-tall electronic quilt publishes thirty-five still and moving messages concerning the lives of women.

- Ongoing classes, events, and camps get girls involved in areas, such as Web design, TV production, creativity, sports, and fitness.
- Tours are available for groups of ten or more.
- Soft drink, juice, and snack machines are located in the museum.
- The museum is handicapped accessible. There are some wheelchairs on site.

- Restrooms and water fountains are available.
- Parking is free, except during the state fair.

Hours: Tuesday, 10 AM to 9 PM; Wednesday to Saturday, 10 AM to 5 PM; Sunday, 12 AM to 5 PM. Winter hours may be from 12 AM to 5 PM daily.

Admission: Adults, $5; students and seniors, $4; ages 5–11, $3; under 5, free.

Directions: The museum is located at the Washington Ave. entrance to the Fair Park across from the Music Hall. From downtown Dallas, take I-30E and exit at Second Ave. Turn left onto Parry in front of the Music Hall and follow the signs to the Women's Museum parking lot.

2. TIDBITS: MORE GOOD THINGS TO DO

The first chapter just scratches the surface of the many things to see and do in and around Big D. The listings in this chapter may be a little smaller or appeal to a certain age or interest group, but they still offer entertaining and educational activities to explore and enjoy. As Dallas grows, sometimes getting off the beaten path is the most rewarding.

MORE AMUSEMENTS

There is always something to do around town, no matter how old one is or what the ever-changing Texas weather is doing. In addition to these listed, many shopping malls also have an arcade, such as Cyber Zone or Tilt, to entertain family members who would rather play than shop. Look under **Individual and Family Sports** for activities, such as ice hockey, skateboarding, go-carting, rock climbing, ice-skating, paintball, hiking, and miniature golf.

ADVENTURE LANDING

17717 Coit Rd. between Frankford and Campbell, Dallas, Texas 75252 (972) 248-4966 Website: www.adventurelanding.com

Three eighteen-hole miniature golf courses allow players to test their swings, after which they may want to visit the large arcade, take a few laps on the speedway in go-carts, hit a few balls at the batting cages, or relax in the cafe with some pizza. A special Adventure Pass for three hours of unlimited fun is $19.99 plus tax.

AIR COMBAT SCHOOL

921 Six Flags Dr., #117, Arlington, Texas 76011, Metro (817) 640-1886 Website: www.aircombatschool.com

To get the feeling of being a real top gun, attend Air Combat School. For this experience, the aviator must be at least four feet, eight inches tall and may want to bring other family members or friends because they can communicate with each other on radios while they fight in this intense, simulated flying experience.

From ground school, the pilot goes to the equipment room for the flight suit, helmet, and other necessities. An F-106 Delta Dart egress trainer will test the trainee's survival skills and strap him or her into a motion base flight simulator. From this jet fighter cockpit, the trainee will be pitted against all kinds of threats. Other experiences are in an A-4 Skyhawk, F-8 Crusader, F-111 Aardvark, and F-16 Fighting Falcon and an ejection seat simulator. This is not recommended for anyone who is claustrophobic or has heart or breathing problems. Someone who has a severe problem with motion sickness might consider taking some doctor-approved preventative medicine. The price for each person is $40 plus tax for a 1.5 hour program, and birthday parties are welcomed. Gift certificates are available. Call for operating hours or to schedule a flight. To reach the Air Combat School, exit Hwy. 360 from I-30.

FUNFEST

3805 Belt Line Rd., Addison, Texas 75244 (972) 620-7700

The daily fun at FunFest includes bowling, billiards, laser tag, and virtual reality. Children must be accompanied by an adult in the evening. Open Sunday to Thursday, 11 AM to 12 AM; Friday and Saturday, 11 AM to 2 AM.

PLANET PIZZA

3000 Custer Rd. at W. Parker, Unit 310, Plano, Texas 75075 (972) 985-7711

Ferrari bumper cars, a swinging pirate ship, and a large soft-play area with tunnels, balls, tubes, and slides are only part of the fun at Planet Pizza, an indoor play park. Arcade games with a ticket-redemption center and a fast food menu add to the entertainment for children ages two to ten. Individual tickets or unlimited rides and soft-play hand stamps may be purchased. The unlimited play is about $7 to $9. Birthday party packages are available for a minimum of six children. Special deals are offered on Wednesday.

MAIN EVENT

3941 N. Central Expwy., Plano, Texas (972) 422-3350

2070 I-35N, Lewisville, Texas (972) 459-7770

407 W. Hwy. 114, Grapevine, Texas (817) 416-1111

Website: www.mainevent.com

Fun at Main Event takes the form of bowling, billiards, laser tag, arcade games, and a cafe. On Monday, Wednesday, and Friday, Main Event has **Laser Jam**: Blacklight bowling, fog, lasers, and music. Hours are Sunday to Thursday, 11 AM to 12 AM; Friday, 11 AM to 2 AM; Saturday, 10 AM to 2 AM. Only ages eighteen and older may remain Sunday to Thursday after 10 PM and Friday to Saturday after midnight.

NICKEL MANIA

2661 Midway Rd., Carrollton, Texas 75006 (972) 713-9500
Website: www.nickelmania.com

Nickel Mania is a nickel arcade where the games are played with real nickels. The arcade hosts birthday parties and serves Simple Simon Pizza.

RONALD'S PLAYPLACE

14770 Preston Rd., Dallas, Texas (972) 233-8788

105 Montfort at LBJ Fwy., Dallas, Texas (972) 233-5952

Both of these McDonald's have entertaining indoor play parks with tunnels and slides and toddler areas. The unique McDonald's on Montfort was built to look like a Happy Meal box.

SPEEDZONE

1130 Malibu Dr. (I-35E at Walnut Hill), Dallas, Texas 75229 (972) 247-RACE Website: www.speedzone.com

The focus is on race cars of various types at the twelve-acre Speedzone. In addition to the race cars, which are primarily for adults, Speedzone also has two miniature golf courses, a restaurant, and the Electric Alley game room, which has 100 simulator and skill-redemption games.

Hours are Friday and Saturday, 11 AM to 1 AM; Sunday to Thursday, 11 AM to 11 AM (18 and older only after 9 PM).

WHIRLYBALL

3541 W. Northwest Hwy. at Webb Chapel, Dallas, Texas 75220 (214) 350-0117 or (214) 350-0129
Website: www.whirlyball.homestead.com/entrance.html

Whirlyball is a unique team game that combines jai alai, basketball, and hockey. Team members ride in bumper cars while they try to score points. There is a video arcade, two courts, and two party rooms. Teams must have a minimum of ten players, and the courts rent for $157 per hour daily and $17 per person with six-person minimum. Players must be nine or older.

WHIRLYBALL LASERWHIRLD

3115 W. Parker, Plano, Texas 75075 (972) 398-7900
Website: www.whirlyball.homestead.com/entrance.html

This location has both **Whirlyball**, as listed above, and **Laserwhirld**, a two-story laser-tag arena where up to twenty-five people engage in active play for twelve minutes each game. Participants can play solo or in team competition. Birthday parties are welcome. For laser play, players must be at least forty-eight inches tall.

NATURE, ECOLOGY, SCIENCE

As the Metroplex grows in population and the natural areas are developed to accommodate new and expanding families and businesses, preservation of those natural areas and their wildlife in preserves and parks has become a priority of both state and local park departments and organizations, such as the Texas Committee on Natural Resources and the Sierra Club, as well as of families who wish to escape city life to undisturbed settings. Even though "The stars at night are big and bright deep in the heart of Texas," sometimes city lights obscure all but the brightest stars. If you can't get out of town, local planetariums offer celestial programs day and night. Of further interest to naturalists is the progress in recycling and other conservation efforts in the Dallas area. Some local businesses are specializing in products to encourage and equip families who are interested in science and outdoor activities. Try the **Natural History of North Central Texas** website to explore flora, fauna, fossils, frogs, and so forth at www.nhnct.org. It's a collection of links, data, and original content to promote appreciation of the natural world in North Central Texas. "Nature Study" allows you to click on the county you're interested in to reach nature preserves, hiking trails, and wildlife in that particular area. Some links include Texas Parks and Wildlife, Butterflies of Texas, Dallas/Ft. Worth Herpetological Society (reptiles), and Texas Freshwater Fisheries Center in Athens.

About a two-hour drive southwest of Dallas is **Comanche Peak Nuclear Plant**. Area colleges and businesses are offering courses, such as computer science, to help youngsters understand this field. Although some of the Dallas area's science museums and nature centers are listed in **Places to Go**, the following should be of special interest.

NATURE

CONNEMARA CONSERVANCY

Website: www.connemaraconservancy.org

Located along Rowlett Creek north of Plano, Connemara Conservancy is a seventy-two-acre nature preserve featuring **outdoor sculpture** and presenting performances of music and dance at various times beginning in

March. Cars must be left outside the preserve. It is very popular for hiking and informal picnicking on the rolling, grassy terrain. From US 75 North, take exit 34 (McDermott Dr.) and proceed west for 1.6 miles. Turn south and go one mile to a stile with a fence at left on the east side of the road. Call (214) 351-0990 for details.

DALLAS COUNTY AUDUBON SOCIETY, INC.

P.O. Box 12713, Dallas, Texas 75225

Metro rare bird alert: (817) 329-1270

Website: www.audubondallas.org

Woods, Wings, and Water is a publication of the active **Audubon Dallas**, and the title is very descriptive of their activities. Their monthly meeting is held at Clark Auditorium in the Scottish Rite Hospital on the second Monday of each month from September through April at 7:30 PM. The guided birding field trips to places like Hagerman Wildlife Preserve and Woodland Basin are wonderful outdoor experiences, and beginners are welcome. The society is involved in wildlife preservation and helps injured birds. Annual dues are $15 for local chapter membership only. Bring along binoculars and a field guide on the field trips.

Wild Birds Unlimited, 4300 Lover's Ln., sells a wide variety of bird-related products. Call 891-9793.

DALLAS COUNTY PARK AND OPEN SPACE PROGRAM

411 Elm, Ste. 250, Dallas, Texas 75202 (214) 653-6653

Beginning in 1977, Dallas County and various private interests have been working together to acquire natural areas to preserve as public, open-space parkland. More than 3,000 acres are in the system. The terrains vary from grassland to wetlands to woods, and visitors are welcome free of charge to all of them. Most are suitable for hiking and informal picnicking. Insect repellent would be handy to have along. Remember to bring water and something to store trash in to leave the area undisturbed. These areas are maintained by the cities in which they are located. For more information, call the city's park department or Dallas County Park and Open Space Administrator at 653-6653. You might ask for a **brochure** that outlines all of the preserves.

Cottonwood Creek Preserve is known for its beautiful display of wildflowers in the spring. It includes 220 acres of natural land. Points of interest are noted along the creek trail. It's recommended for hiking on a two-mile natural-surface trail that loops around, nature study, and picnicking. To reach this preserve in Wilmer, take I-45 South and turn east on Belt Line. Turn north on Goode and then east to the end of Cottonwood Valley Rd. Call (972) 441-3222.

Elm Fork Preserve is forty-four acres of heavily wooded land in northwest Dallas County used for hiking and nature study. Take Sandy Lake Rd. west from I-35 to R. J. McInnish Park, and go south through the park entrance to the preserve at the southeast corner of the park. Park at the back by the softball complex in McInnish Park. There are restrooms and a picnic/playground area. A trail has been paved along the river. Call the Carrollton Parks and Recreation Department at (972) 466-3084.

Cedar Ridge Preserve covers 604 acres of wilderness in Cedar Hill next to City of Dallas Escarpment Park. It's suitable for study of plants and animal habitats and hiking. Go south on I-35 to Hwy. 67 South (sign says Cleburne) and take I-20 West (sign says Ft. Worth). Exit onto Mountain Creek Pkwy. and go south (under the freeway). Drive two miles to the preserve, formerly the Dallas Nature Center. Restrooms and picnic areas are in the Audubon Dallas buildings. Call (214) 321-2182.

Grapevine Springs Park Preserve in Coppell is the latest acquisition in the Open Space program. Originally established as a park in 1936, it was abandoned after a few years and became very overgrown. Now, it is again part of the park system and the subject of interest to both archaeologists and historians. In 1843, it was the temporary capital of Texas for about three weeks while Sam Houston tried to sign a treaty with a delegation of Cherokee Indians. The treaty was to be executed at the full moon, but it was a blue moon month, with one full moon at the beginning and one at the end of the month. Sam Houston was at the site for one moon and the Indians at the other. They met at another place later.

The fifteen acres of this park are said to look like a sunken water garden when it rains, for the Works Progress Administration built channels in a drainage pattern along the creek. The park has one mile of bark-covered pathway and a natural-surface nature trail, as well as picnic tables. To reach the park, go north on Denton Tapp Rd. to Bethel Rd. and turn west. Go about one mile to Park St. and turn south. Park St. dead ends into the preserve. Call Coppell Parks at (972) 462-8495.

Lemmon Lake Preserve includes a 142-acre lake along the Trinity River, which is surrounded by 133 acres of prairie woodland. A footpath is suitable for hiking and nature study. Picnicking near the park entrance and bank fishing are popular. Take Old Central Expwy.–Texas 310 South from Loop 12 (Ledbetter Dr.) to River Oaks and go east to the preserve. Call the Dallas Parks Department at (214) 670-4100 or (214) 670-0967.

McCommas Bluff Preserve covers 111 wooded acres on the Trinity River's east bank. It's the site of a historical marker called the Navigation of the Upper Trinity concerning the barge commerce and the locks on the Trinity from 1900 to 1910, as well as the river way for the *Sally Haynes* steamboat. But the area is just as famous because it contained the spring where notorious characters like the Daltons, Jesse James, and Belle Starr watered their horses. It is being surveyed by archaeologists because it was also the site of the abandoned Trinity City, which was inhabited from 1871 to 1911. Now it has a nature trail and is used for hiking, fishing, nature study, and informal picnicking. From Loop 12 in Dallas, go south on Longbranch (which becomes Riverwood at the dead end) and then west to the preserve. Or from Longbranch, go west at Fairport to the dead end. Call (214) 670-4100.

Post Oak Preserve features an ADA trail that is 1.7 miles round-trip from the parking area to the lake and back. An additional 1.75 miles of interlocking natural-surface trails are cleared as well. Here is the last large stand of Post Oak savannah that once stretched through this part of the county. It's located in southeast Dallas County on Bowers Rd. just south of the DISD Environmental Education Center in Seagoville. There's no formal parking lot. Call DISD at (972) 749-6900.

Trinity River–Mountain Creek Preserve offers an all-weather parking lot, pavilions, tables, grills, playground, canoe launch, equestrian parking lot, and a two-mile ADA trail that loops through the preserve. This fifty-five-acre preserve is located at 1000 Hunter-Ferrell Rd., south of Bolden St. in western Dallas County. Call Irving Parks at (972) 721-2501.

DUCK CREEK GREENBELT

For those who prefer some development in their nature areas, Duck Creek Greenbelt offers three miles of concrete trails that loop along Duck Creek in Garland. In February 1992, a Garland girl found a bison bone that was more than 500 years old beside Duck Creek and donated it to the Museum of Natural History. Visitors often enter the area at Audubon Park at 342 Oates Rd., east of I-635, where there is paved parking, a picnic table area, and a playground, as well as a Surf 'N Swim wave pool. Call (972) 205-2750.

EARTH DAY

Every year on April 22, many families in Dallas and the surrounding areas celebrate the Earth and dedicate themselves to bettering its condition through efforts such as preservation of natural environments and wildlife, elimination of hazardous products, and recycling. Activities range from planting begonias in the front yard to cleaning a local park to attending a city festival. Watch local newspapers, *Dallas Family*, or *dallas child* for announcements of activities or call the U.S. Environmental Protection Agency at (214) 665-6444.

The Sierra Club or the Texas Committee on Natural Resources may also know of other family-oriented Earth Day events. The Heard Museum and the Museum of Natural History plan special events in honor of the Earth. The state parks also participate with special activities. Call to find out what they have planned at the ones near Dallas.

HOME AND GARDEN SHOW

Begin watching newspapers the last week of February for announcements about the Dallas Home and Garden Show, a favorite event for many years. It's usually held during the first weekend in March at Market Hall. The entrance gardens have colorful spring flowers, and beautiful designer gardens are located inside. Usually, The Science Place has exhibits to educate and inspire young gardeners, and children will also enjoy the exhibits about hobbies and ecology. Kids under twelve enter free, and discount coupons may be available. Parking is free. You may want to bring your camera.

L. B. HOUSTON NATURE AREA

More than 300 acres on the Elm Fork of the Trinity River make up the L. B. Houston Nature Area. It is near the area where gold seekers crossed the Trinity River in the 1800s to reach California. Trails with names like River Trail, Beaver Trail, and Wilderness Way Trail vary from a half-hour walk to a 2.5-hour walk. Restrooms and picnic facilities are at California Crossing Park north of the preserve. Birding and spotting animal tracks are popular activities here. Wait at least two days after a rain. Enter from Tom Braniff Pkwy. north of Hwy. 114 near Irving. Call (214) 670-6374 for details.

PLANETARIUMS AND OBSERVATORIES

Richland College Planetarium has special programs such as laser concerts and holiday programs that are open to the public. On the first Friday night of each month is a program and telescope observation. A planetarium program is presented on the second and third Saturday at 2 PM and at 3 PM. Contact the planetarium director at (972) 238-6013 for dates and times or look them up at www.rlc.dcccd.edu/ce/planet.htm. The campus is located at 12800 Abrams at Walnut.

St. Mark's School of Texas Observatory is open to the public occasionally for special programs. A program about the Star of Bethlehem is a Christmas favorite. Call (214) 346-8000 for specific dates. The address is 10600 Preston Rd.. Occasionally, the Texas Astronomical Society hosts novice observer meetings. Call (972) 758-3849.

The Science Place Planetarium is located in the Planetarium Building at Fair Park. Programs are changed periodically and often coincide with Science Place exhibits. It's a public planetarium for Dallas residents and visitors, and times are extended during the state fair. The building has a snack bar and permanent and changing exhibits. Also, planetarium birthday parties may be arranged. Buy tickets at The Science Place just west of the Planetarium Building. The planetarium show is $3. Enter Fair Park through the Grand Ave. gate off Robert B. Cullum Blvd. Parking is available in front of the museum. Website: www.scienceplace.org.

University of North Texas Sky Theater often performs family planetarium shows at 2 PM and 8 PM on Saturday. It's located in the Environmental Education, Science and Technology Building. Park in Lot 10 across Avenue C in Denton. Admission: $2 to $4. Call (940) 369-7655 or visit www.skytheater.unt.edu.

ROWLETT NATURE TRAIL

Rowlett Nature Trail is a 1.3-mile path following the shore of Lake Ray Hubbard in Rowlett. As visitors enter the greenbelt, there is a parking area, picnic tables under ancient pecan trees, and a fishing pond. It's also great for bird watching as well as hiking and other nature studies. Take I-635 to I-30 East. Exit at Belt Line and go left under the overpass. Turn right on Rowlett Rd. and travel about five miles. Turn left on Miller and go about one mile to the trail located on the right side of the street. For further details, call (972) 475-2772.

SIERRA CLUB

The Sierra Club is a national organization that was founded about 100 years ago by naturalist John Muir. The club is dedicated to preserving, studying, and enjoying the environment and plans activities for all ages to achieve these goals. It publishes a catalog and newsletter. The newsletter, *The Compass*, includes notice of environmental issues and activities by nature centers, such as the Heard, as well as a calendar of hiking and canoeing outings. Meetings are held on the second Wednesday of each month from 7 PM to 8:30 PM at E. D. Walker school auditorium located at Montfort and Wozencraft. For information about the local chapter, call (214) 369-5543 or consult their website at www.texas.sierraclub.org/dallas.

TEXAS COMMITTEE ON NATURAL RESOURCES

Austin, Texas (512) 441-1122 Website: www.tconr.org

This nonprofit membership organization works with state and local government agencies to acquire and preserve natural areas. Their task forces present programs to school children and other groups on a variety of subjects such as recycling, water and air quality, wildlife, pesticides, forests, and wetlands. Each March, the committee hosts the **Texas Buckeye Trail**, a walk in the **Great Trinity Forest**, to see Buckeyes in bloom, as well as numerous species of shrubs and flowers. A favorite outing is the annual **Texas Wilderness Pow Wow**, which is usually held on an April weekend and includes activities for all ages.

TEXAS TREES FOUNDATION
(FORMERLY DALLAS TREES AND PARKS FOUNDATION)

2121 San Jacinto, Ste. 1111, Dallas, Texas 75201 (214) 953-3028
Website: www.dallastpf.org

The Texas Trees Foundation is dedicated to preserving, beautifying, and expanding parks and other public, natural, green spaces in a six-county area around Dallas. Through educational programs, this organization hopes to inspire others to build and protect our "urban forest." Two of their education programs are Growing Together, a hands-on tree-planting experience for elementary-age students, and Shadekeepers, which is a tree-planting education resource group. Texas Trees recommends a trip downtown to **Pioneer Plaza** for a combination history and green field trip. The foundation dedicated the park, which once was a 4.2-acre parking lot, in 1995. In addition to the bronze sculptures of forty longhorn steers being driven to market by a black cutter, vaquero, and trail boss, look for a trail map and granite replicas of brands from historic cattle ranches, as well as native plants and trees and a stream.

Through the Trees for Dallas program, qualifying local nonprofit organizations and schools may request a ten-to-twenty gallon tree for about $25 to $50. Call (214) 953-1184 or e-mail dtpf@swbell.net. Since the organization's name has changed, the e-mail may change later.

TURTLE CREEK GREENBELT

Turtle Creek Greenbelt is also for those who like their trails a little less woolly. Both paved and unpaved paths in Dallas and Park cities begin at Reverchon Park, 3535 Maple Ave., with two miles of paved trail to Stonebridge. The path breaks as it changes from Dallas to Highland Park. It continues along the creek beside Lakeside and St. John's in a beautiful area in Highland Park. In Dallas, call (214) 670-8895; in Highland Park, call (214) 521-4161.

WHOLE EARTH PROVISION CO.

5400 E. Mockingbird Ln., Dallas, Texas 75206 (214) 824-7444

Exploring the Whole Earth Provision Co. is the next best thing to being outdoors. Provisions include clothing and shoes designed for outdoor activities, as well as travel tools, such as an excellent selection of guidebooks for outdoor activities in Texas and elsewhere. Technical gear includes sleeping bags, tents, compasses, mess kits, and telescopes. Children love the stuffed wild animals, animal masks, backpacks, bug kits, puzzles and books, and many other nature games and toys.

WILDFLOWERS AND SPRING TRAILS

Spring in Texas is gorgeous as the state flower, the bluebonnet, begins to bloom alongside other hardy favorites. Certain areas along highways are seeded and designated nonmowing areas. Towns, such as Ennis (25 miles south of Dallas), often create festivals around the bluebonnet in April and feature trails that are great for photography. Contact the Ennis Chamber of Commerce at (888) 366-4748 or visit www.visitennis.org. Bardwell Lake is near the festival.

The Texas Department of Transportation provides recorded information updated weekly in the spring about where to find wildflowers, and it has published a pamphlet called *Wildflowers of Texas;* call (800) 452-9292. Richardson also hosts an annual wildflower festival, and Palestine has the annual **Dogwood Trails**, which is a popular time to ride the Texas State Railroad. Tyler has the annual **Azaleas and Spring Flower Trail**.

WOODLAND BASIN NATURE AREA

Located in a marshy area on Rowlett Creek at Lake Ray Hubbard in Garland, Woodland Basin Nature Area has a 1,000-foot boardwalk lined by cattails and sedges that extends out into the lake. This is a popular area for fishing and bird watching, and it is wheelchair accessible. There is paved parking. From I-635, go east on Centerville, and turn east on Miller. Follow Miller about half a mile to the park at 2323 E. Miller Rd. Call the Garland Park and Recreation Department at (972) 205-2750.

ECOLOGY

RECYCLING AND CONSERVATION

Families and businesses are becoming very involved in recycling efforts in their communities, from sorting materials at home and using natural alternatives to hazardous house and garden products to buying recycled paper products for home and office uses. The **Dry Gulch Recycling Center** located at 9500 Harry Hines is a nonprofit recycling collection center initiated by the Texas Committee on Natural Resources and many others with the City of Dallas. Call (214) 353-9986 for hours and to hear what materials they accept or to arrange a tour. You may also want to visit the **Rock Tenn** mill for paper recycling in Oak Cliff; call (214) 358-1533. **DFW Can Recycling** benefits Habitat for Humanity; call (972) 293-9226 for a convenient site. Call SBC Southwestern Bell at (800) 953-4400 for locations to recycle your old phone books. Curbside recycling has been initiated in several communities. After Christmas, ask the Parks Department for places to drop off your Christmas tree so it may be recycled as mulch for park gardens and trails. For more information about recycling in Dallas, call (214) 670-4475.

Each March for many years, the Dallas Water Utilities has sponsored the **Water Conservation Poster Contest** for students in first through eighth grade. The posters are displayed at City Hall during Drinking Water Week. The water education program of Dallas Water Utilities includes a speaker's bureau. Call (214) 670-3155 for more information.

SCIENCE

COMANCHE PEAK NUCLEAR POWER PLANT

Visitors Information Center, Texas Utilities Generating Company, P.O. Box 1002, Glen Rose, Texas 76043 (254) 897-5554

Located about a two-hour drive southwest of Dallas, the Comanche Peak Nuclear Power Plant generates electricity through the nuclear fission process. The plant has two Westinghouse-built reactors. At the visitors information center, families may watch a video presentation and look over exhibits and displays that explain the operation of the first nuclear power plant in Texas. See **Day Trips** for other places of interest around Glen Rose. Call or write for visitor center hours or group tour information and reservations.

COMPUTER SCIENCE

Since Dallas-area elementary schools and some preschools have incorporated computer literacy into their curricula, today's children are growing up with computers and see them as useful tools and toys in their daily lives. Dallas libraries and museums allow children to use them to gather information and create artwork. For further instruction in computer science, contact local universities' and community colleges' continuing education departments for courses and summer day camps. St. Mark's School of Texas, Greenhill School, and Hockaday offer summer day camps centering on science and computer science.

NATIONAL SCIENCE BALLOON CENTER

From the end of April to the end of August is the best time to see this NASA contractor near Palestine launching high-altitude balloons for scientific experiments. The forty-five-minute tour may be arranged by calling (903) 723-8002 seven to ten days in advance.

SCIENCE FAIR AND DESTINATION IMAGINATION

Dallas-area school children participate each February and March in the Science Fair and Destination Imagination, formerly the Invention

Convention. Winners are selected at each school to go to the regional competition. An excellent way to foster curiosity, problem-solving skills, and an interest in science is to be a participant and, win or lose, to visit the fair and the convention at the regional competition level. Check with your local school for dates and locations in March or April.

Some college bookstores carry science supplies. In addition to **The Science Plays** store at The Science Place in Fair Park, area businesses that aid in science-related projects are the following:

- **Science Projects** 13440 TI Blvd. # 6, near Texas Instruments on LBJ Fwy., Dallas, Texas (972) 470-0395
- **Heath Scientific** 320 Texas St., Cedar Hill, Texas (972) 291-4223

HIGH TECH KIDS OF THE SCIENCE PLACE

Northpark Center at Northwest Hwy. and Central Expwy. (214) 696-5437 Website: www.scienceplace.org

High Tech Kids is a Science Place satellite located on the upper level of Northpark Center near Neiman Marcus. Here kids and parents conduct kitchen-science experiments, listen to stories at the Dr. Seuss Story Theater, take computer classes, learn Spanish, go to camp, and much more. Services include drop-off classes offered hourly for about $15 per hour and birthday parties. Reservations are recommended.

FARMERS MARKETS AND PICK YOUR OWN

FARMERS MARKETS AND NURSERIES

Stopping by the farmers market can be a wonderful experience each week for your family. First, the markets are outdoors, and you can meet the farmers themselves. You are supporting your local economy and encouraging your family to select fruits and vegetables that are so good for their health. Children learn to compare prices among the vendors, to look for ripeness and quality in the produce, and to discover in which seasons certain fruits and vegetables are harvested. Often, the markets make holidays even more special with truckloads of pumpkins or Christmas trees grown in East Texas. Some markets include beautiful plants, crafts, country music, and sometimes barnyard animals. The *Dallas Morning News*'s Wednesday food section lists local markets and what seasonal produce is in good supply. Call the markets for hours. Some are only open spring through fall.

BIG TOWN FARMERS MARKET
U.S. 80 at Big Town Blvd., Mesquite, Texas

CITY OF DALLAS FARMERS MARKET
1010 S. Pearl, Dallas, Texas 75201 (214) 939-2808
Website: www.dallasfarmersmarket.org

Serving Dallas for more than fifty years, the City of Dallas Farmers Market has row after row of beautiful fruits, vegetables, and house and garden plants. It also publishes an informative yearly calendar. The Fall Harvest Festival at the end of October is a favorite event. The downtown market is located between Harwood and Central, north of I-30 West and is open daily.

FAIRVIEW FARMS MARKETPLACE
3314 N. Central Expwy. (Exit 30), Plano, Texas (972) 422-2500
Website: www.fairview-farms.com

The marketplace has produce, plants, and flowers in spring and summer. Call for days and times. Sometimes the management offers wagon rides and other entertainment.

FARMERS BRANCH FARMERS MARKET
Denton Dr. at Valley View, Farmers Branch, Texas

NURSERIES
A relatively free (unless, like most, you can't resist buying some plants or seeds) nature excursion is one to a local nursery. Children can learn a great deal about the identification and care of flowers, trees, and vegetables from this visit. Nurseries usually carry supplies for birds, as well as books on gardening, such as Neil Sperry's *Texas Gardener*. Popular nurseries include Nicholson-Hardie, Calloway's, Northhaven Gardens, and Plants N Planters. Southwest Landscape Nursery Company at 2220 Sandy Lake Rd. in Carrollton has 40,000 square feet of greenhouse growing space on ten acres.

PICK YOUR OWN FOOD AND CHRISTMAS TREES AND COMMUNITY-SUPPORTED AGRICULTURE

One of the most rewarding family experiences is to leave early, before the Texas sun heats up the air, and drive out to a **Pick Your Own (PYO)** farm to handpick fruits and vegetables that could not be any fresher. Not only can children see on what kind of tree, vine, or bush the produce grows, but they have the experience of doing something for themselves and will be more likely to enjoy it served later at a meal. Blueberries, peaches, and a variety of vegetables are most often offered at the farms. Usually, the farm provides a basket, but asking about containers, restrooms, and picnic areas, as well as hours is a good idea. Do not wear perfume or hair spray because they attract insects. Bringing a hat or visor, tennis shoes, insect repellent, and sunscreen would be wise. Yearly, the Texas Department of Agriculture compiles a list of **PYO farms** and roadside sales, as well as a list of certified farmers markets, and posts them at gotexan.org. At www.picktexas.com is "Kid's Corner," which has fun activities and veggie characters. The **Texas Fresh Produce Guide**, which lists the top twenty fruits and vegetables and when they are available, may be ordered from the Texas Department of Agriculture at 1720 Regal Row, Ste. 118, Dallas, Texas 75235, or call (214) 631-0265 or visit www.gotexan.org/produce/index.html.

FRUITS AND VEGETABLES

DENTON COUNTY

Smith's Pumpkin Patch at Katie's Country Market. Pick a pumpkin from the field in October. Stock up on homemade jam and crafts. 736 Rock Hill Rd., Aubrey, Texas (940) 365-2201 Website: www.the-pumpkinpatch.com.

FANNIN COUNTY

Walker's Blueberry Farm (northwest of Bonham), 2933 FM 274/Mulberry Rd., Ravenna, Texas 75476 (903) 583-4739.

Jenkins Fruit Farm, 269 CR 1600, Bonham, Texas 75418 (903) 583-2220.

GRAYSON COUNTY

Bailey's Berry Patch, 905 Crawford Rd. (north of Sadler, Texas, off FM 901) (903) 564-6228 Website: www.txberry.com. Blackberries and muscadine grapes.

HENDERSON COUNTY

Blueberry Basket, 12462 FM 2588, LaRue, Texas 75770 (903) 677-3448 (near Athens). Blueberries and blackberries.

SMITH COUNTY

Barron's Blueberries, 16478 Co. Rd. 431, Lindale, Texas 75771 (903) 882-6711 (near Tyler).

Rozell's Peach Orchard, 14278 SH 64 W, Tyler, Texas 75704 (903) 592-2074.

The Berry Farm, 9628 CR 429, Tyler, Texas 75704 (888) 584-8054. Blackberries, blueberries, raspberries, and preserves; picnic tables, wheelchair accessible, brochure available.

VAN ZANDT COUNTY

Blueberry Hill Farms Inc., south of Edom on FM 314 (903) 852-6175 Website: www.bbhf.net.

COMMUNITY-SUPPORTED AGRICULTURE

At **Good Earth Organic Farm**, the family offers organically grown items at an affordable price. Members of the Texas Organic Growers Association, Good Earth produces free-range eggs; pasture-raised lamb, chicken, and turkey; squash and greens; fruit and shade trees, and more. Farm hours are most Thursdays and Saturdays from 9 AM to 5 PM. The farm is located about fifteen minutes north of Greenville. Children are welcome but must be supervised by parents. Dogs are not permitted. Call or write Good Earth Farms, 8571 FM 272, Celeste, Texas 75423 (903) 496-2070 Website: www.goodearthorganicfarm.com.

CHRISTMAS TREE FARMS

Not many holiday activities are as festive as loading up the family and heading out to a Christmas tree farm to find the perfect tree for your house. Many of the farms offer extras, such as wagon rides, picnic areas, nature trails, hot apple cider and coffee, crafts, jars of homemade goodies, Santa, small petting zoos, coloring books, and mazes. Children can learn how the trees grow and how the farmer replants as the trees are cut. The farms usually open for business right after Thanksgiving Day. Some offer tours for schools and other organizations. For more Texas locations and details, visit www.texaschristmastrees.com.

GRAYSON COUNTY

Elves Christmas Tree Farm, 601 Harvey Ln., Denison, Texas (903) 463-7260 Website: www.elveschristmastreefarm.com. Virginia pines, school tours.

HUNT COUNTY

KADEE Farm, Hwy. 69 South, Greenville, Texas 75402 (903) 883-3279 Website: www.p-and-g-a.com/K-DEE. Seven miles south of Greenville, school tours.

KAUFMAN COUNTY

Wells Family Farm, 11051 CR 2312, Terrell, Texas (972) 524-9000 Website: www.wallsfamilyfarm.com. Virginia pines, Leyland cypress.

VAN ZANDT COUNTY

Canton Christmas Tree Farm, one mile east of Canton, I-20, Exit 528 at FM 17 (214) 808-6467 Website: www.cantonchristmastreefarm.com. Fraser fir, **school tours**.

WOOD COUNTY

McNew Star M Plantation, 2914 Hwy. 276 W, Quinlan, Texas (903) 356-2195 Website: www.christmastreemcnew.net. Virginia pines, **school tours**.

PETS AND WILDLIFE

PETS

Bonding between children and their pets is a very important part of childhood, providing them with a loyal friend and teaching them about kindness and responsibility. A trip to a pet store can be very educational and entertaining whether or not you plan to adopt. A highly recommended place to find a family friend is a local animal adoption center or shelter. Check your city's offices or look up humane societies in the *Yellow Pages* for their numbers and call for hours. Then go by for a visit. Most will arrange tours for groups and also mention opportunities for volunteers. These organizations can give you information about low-cost spaying/neutering surgery for pets you already own. The Texas Kennel Club presents an All-Breed Dog Show and Obedience Trials and the North Texas Cat Club schedules cat shows.

CITY OF DALLAS PET ADOPTION CENTERS

The City of Dallas operates two centers where citizens may bring homeless animals or adopt a pet. A homeless animal without a collar or tags is kept for seventy-two hours and then checked for adoptability. If not adoptable, it is euthanized. Adopting a pet may cost about $12 to $57. The **Dallas Coalition of Animal Owners** rescues purebred dogs that are not adopted and tries to find them a home. Call (214) 349-4897 if interested in these pets.

The two shelters are open to adopt or to search for lost pets Monday to Saturday, 8 AM to 4:30 PM, and closed holidays. Located behind the Dallas Zoo, the **Oak Cliff** location is 525 Shelter Place, (214) 670-6800, and the **Pleasant Grove** location is 8414 Forney Rd., (214) 670-8226. The **Lost Pet Hotlines** are (214) 670-1965 and (214) 670-8389. Locate the pet shelters online at www.dallascityhall.org. To register your pet, Dallas requires about $7 for neutered/spayed pets and $20 for other pets. Send the registration information to **City of Dallas Animal Registration**, 5215 N. O'Connor Blvd., Ste. 760, Irving, Texas 75039, or call (214) 821-3400.

THE SOCIETY FOR THE PREVENTION OF CRUELTY TO ANIMALS OF TEXAS

362 S. Industrial Blvd., Dallas, Texas 75207
(214) 651-9611, (888) ANIMALS
McKinney, Texas, shelter (972) 562-7297
Website: www.spca.org

The SPCA was established in 1938, and volunteers have been active ever since in finding homes for homeless animals, offering low-cost spaying/neutering surgery, investigating complaints of cruelty, locating lost pets, gathering stray animals for their safety and the safety of citizens, and scheduling youth programs on pet care and responsibility.

The dogs are divided into rooms according to whether they are large or small, male or female, or puppy or full grown. Cats usually occupy a separate room. The SPCA does almost everything a family vet would do, including spaying/neutering, and offers the pets for about $80 to $134. They ask families questions about the animal's new home and the length of time he or she will be left alone. Also, they answer your questions about health care, behavior, and feeding.

The SPCA holds owner and pet fun runs, parades, and walk-a-thons. This is a fun way to show children the multiple breeds of pets. Volunteers are needed at these events. **Repeats** is the name of their resale store at 14350 Marsh Ln. in Spring Valley, where the SPCA accepts donations of clothes, furniture, and household items that are still in good condition; call (972) 241-8066. If you lose a pet or find a lost one, call the SPCA's computerized lost-and-found service at (214) 651-WAGS.

If your family would like to adopt a pet, the SPCA is also at Northpark Center before Christmas, and the PetSmart stores periodically offer adoptable cats and dogs from the SPCA. Groups may call to schedule a free tour.

OPERATION KINDNESS

3201 Earhart Dr., Carrollton, Texas (972) 418-PAWS
Website: www.operationkindness.org

Operation Kindness is a no-kill adoption agency for pets. Each year they sponsor a family and pet festival called Dog Day Afternoon.

ANIMAL ADOPTION CENTER

117 N. Garland Ave., Garland, Texas 75040 (972) 494-KIND

This no-kill animal welfare organization receives homeless animals and cares for them until they are adopted. They operate on donations of money and volunteer time. Visitors may come by Monday to Tuesday, 11 AM to 4:30 PM; Wednesday to Saturday, 11 AM to 5:30 PM; and Sunday, 1 PM to 4:30 PM. They offer flea dips from April through October at low cost.

DOG AND KITTY CITY

2719 Manor Way, Dallas, Texas 75235 (214) 350-7387
Website: www.dognkittycity.com

Located near Love Field Airport, Dog and Kitty City is a no-kill shelter operated by the Humane Society of Dallas County. They rescue and care for dogs and cats, which are spayed/neutered before adoption.

THE NORTH TEXAS RABBIT SANCTUARY

1013 Lesa Ln., Garland, Texas 75042 (972) 494-1994
Website: www.ntrs.org

This animal sanctuary rescues and cares for rabbits. The rabbits are neutered, litter-box trained, and placed up for adoption as "house rabbits." The sanctuary is certified by the Association of Sanctuaries.

PETMOBILE PET HOSPITAL

608 W. I-30 at Belt Line, Garland, Texas (972) 423-PETS

The Petmobile Pet Hospital offers city pet registration, low-cost vaccinations, dips, nail clipping, and other services at Dallas city parks and various locations year-round. Before leaving, ask for a phone number that will be answered by a person in case the pet has a reaction to the vaccination.

EMERGENCY ANIMAL CLINIC

12101 Greenville Ave., Dallas, Texas 75243 (972) 994-9110

The Emergency Animal Clinic is a veterinary clinic offered as a service by more than fifty veterinarians for after-hours pet care. Hours are Monday to Thursday, 6 PM to 8 AM, and Friday from 6 PM through Monday at 8 AM.

FRITZ PARK PETTING FARM

312 E. Vilbig, Irving, Texas 75060 (972) 721-2501,
(972) 721-2640

Offered by the Irving Parks and Recreation Department only in June and July, the Fritz Park Petting Farm opens with a neighborhood parade and special events at the park. Cows, horses, goats, sheep, chickens, and more graze and nap among admiring children. The Little Red School House is home to smaller critters. The farm also has an incubator where children can watch chicks hatch right out of the eggs. A birthday room may be reserved for parties. Tours are available and volunteers are appreciated at the farm, which is open Tuesday to Saturday, 10 AM to 6 PM, and Sunday, 2 PM to 8 PM if the weather permits. Free admission.

PET PARKS FOR DOGS

Dallas has two parks designed for dogs, and more are in the planning stages. **Bark Park Central** is located at the corner of Good Latimer Expwy. and Commerce St. downtown. **White Rock Lake Dog Park** is at Mockingbird Point, 8000 Mockingbird, near Buckner Blvd. Look on the website at www.dallasdogparks.org for new parks and further details.

WILDLIFE

Texas has abundant wildlife in spite of development, and environmentalists are working diligently to protect it as well as exotic wildlife imported from other lands. In addition to **Dallas Zoo**, the **Dallas World Aquarium**, the **Museum of Natural History**, **Dallas Aquarium**, and the raptor center at the **Heard Natural Science Museum and Wildlife Sanctuary**, which were discussed in **Places to Go**, wildlife may be studied at some other museums, zoos, and wildlife refuges and parks near Dallas. See **Day Trips** for wildlife areas in Ft. Worth, Tyler, Gainesville, Denison, Waco, and Glen Rose. One of the best places to see local wildlife is in the open space preserves listed earlier in this chapter. The purchase of a **Texas Parks and Wildlife Conservation Pass** allows you access to many places that are closed to the general public and offers a variety of field trips.

CANYON OF THE EAGLES LODGE AND NATURE PARK

16942 RR2341, Burnet, Texas 78611 (800) 977-0081, (512) 756-8787 Website: www.canyonoftheeagles.com

Migrating bald eagles, black-capped vireos, and golden-cheeked warblers stop to winter in the wooded area around Lake Buchanan in the Hill Country. At the Canyon of the Eagles Lodge, visitors can reserve a spot on the **Vanishing Texas River Cruise**. The seventy-foot, 200-passenger cruise boat is launched November through March, daily except Tuesday, in search of the bald eagle. The 2.5-hour trip goes through scenic wilderness areas up the Colorado River Canyon. In case of bad weather, the boat has an all-weather deck. The tour leaves from the Canyon of the Eagles Park Store. You may want to bring binoculars, a movie camera, and a camera with a telephoto lens. A small concession is aboard the boat. Wildflower Cruises are offered in April and May. For reservations, call the Canyon of the Eagles Lodge.

Near Burnet, the **Canyon of the Eagles Lodge and Nature Park** is on 940 wooded acres along Lake Buchanan. Forty-four lodge rooms, twenty cottages, and RV and camping facilities are available for guests. Attractions include a preserved wildlife habitat, twelve miles of nature trails, a fishing pier, a five-mile lakeside beach, the Eagle Eye Observatory, which has two telescopes and an Observing Salon, the Bedrock Grill Restaurant, and the Park Store, which rents kayaks, canoes, and small sailboats. For more family fun, visit www.lakebuchananadventures.com for wilderness and waterfall guided paddle trips up the Colorado River Valley.

Fairfield Lake State Park has a bald eagle sighting tour from November through February. The migrating eagles like to eat tilapia, which grows near the power plant hot-water discharge. The park is about 100 miles south of Dallas, 15 miles east of I-45 at Fairfield. Approximately twenty eagles migrate through the area. Visitors may go out on a forty-foot boat on Saturdays. Call (903) 389-4514 for reservations.

BOLIN WILDLIFE EXHIBIT

1028 N. McDonald, McKinney, Texas 75069 (972) 562-2639

Located inside the Bolin Oil Company, this exhibit of preserved animals from Africa and other areas of the world is a delightful surprise. Perry Bolin, rancher and oil distributor, collected these animals on big-game hunts and organized them in the museum as an educational experience. As visitors enter the large exhibit room, the push of a button begins an audio tape that explains the nature and habitat of each group of animals as you go around the exhibit.

Across the hall from the wildlife exhibit is a collection of vintage cars and oil-related items, and upstairs are displays of furniture and other items from life in Collin County in the early 1900s. Admission is free. Take US 75 to Exit 40/Virginia St. in McKinney and go east to McDonald. Turn left, and the oil company will be on the right. It is open Monday to Friday, 9 AM to 4 PM, and closed for lunch from 12 PM to 1 PM. It's about a forty-minute drive from Dallas. The lower floor is wheelchair accessible, and the stairway to the second floor has a lift chair attached to the stairway.

INTERNATIONAL EXOTIC FELINE SANCTUARY

This big-cat sanctuary cares for lions, tigers, cougars, and leopards. It's located west of Dallas/Ft. Worth International Airport off Hwy. 114. Take the Bridgeport exit at Boyd. Reservations for ages seven and older may be made for tours on Saturday and Sunday. Call (972) 235-0192 or visit www.bigcat.org. Another sanctuary is **In-Sync Exotic Wildlife Rescue and Education Center** located in Wylie. Call (972) 442-6888 or visit www.insyncexotics.com.

WILDSCAPES

Texas Parks and Wildlife offers suggestions for creating a landscape in your yard that will attract wildlife. Patterned after the National Wildlife Federation's Backyard Wildlife Habitat program, the Texas Wildscapes information packet includes lists of native plants, brochures on butterfly and hummingbird gardening, information on feeders and nest boxes, and an application. Send in the completed application after implementing your habitat design, and Texas Parks and Wildlife will send you an achievement certificate and a sign designating the site.

Address inquiries to Nongame and Urban Program, 4200 Smith School Rd., Austin, Texas 78744, or call (512) 389-4974. You may also find details and register online at www.tpwd.state.tx.us/nature/wildscapes.

Demonstration sites in the area include Cedar Hill State Park on Joe Pool Lake and White Rock Lake. For information about the sites, call the Urban Fish and Wildlife Program Leader at (972) 293-3841.

WILDLIFE SUCCESS STORIES

Wildlife Success Stories and Endangered Species is a popular wildlife program used by elementary schools. Developed by the Texas Agriculture Extension Service, the interactive computer program and accompanying exhibit include four Mac computers and an 8 × 10 display board. Something's Fishy is an aquatic science module that is available. Call (214) 904-3051 for information about scheduling or visit www.texasextension.tamu.edu.

CRITTERMAN

Denton, Texas (940) 365-9741 Website: www.critterman.com

Critterman and Safari Sue will bring part of their menagerie of more than sixty varmints to your location. The collection includes tarantulas and snakes, a beaver, a gray wolf, a hedgehog, and more. This traveling safari costs about $200 to $400.

HISTORY AND POLITICS

HISTORIC ARLINGTON

ARLINGTON HISTORICAL SOCIETY

1616 W. Abram, Arlington, Texas 76013 (817) 460-4001

The **Fielder House Museum** and the M. T. Johnson Plantation Cemetery and Historic Park are operated by the Arlington Historical Society, which is dedicated to preserving the historic landmarks of Arlington and educating the public about their heritage. In early December, the museum usually hosts a tree lighting, which includes carriage rides, a bake sale, Santa, and a home tour.

Built as a private residence in 1914, the home has served since 1978 as the Fielder House Museum, a place where the history of Arlington comes to life through exhibits such as Treasures of Native Americans and Metroplex: Then and Now. The quilt exhibit is a favorite annually, as are exhibits of other Arlington crafters and artists. The upstairs rooms are furnished to represent an early barbershop and a bedroom and nursery. A general store is downstairs. The basement houses a collection of irons and other tools of daily life, a root cellar, and a steam engine train handcrafted to 1/12 scale. Tours are available. Children who are about eight or older will probably enjoy the museum the most. Three picnic tables are outside. Hours are Wednesday to Saturday, 10 AM to 2 PM; Sunday, 1:30 PM to 4:30 PM. It may be open on Saturday during the summer. Call for information about special events. The museum is located at 1616 W. Abram at Fielder.

The **M. T. Johnson Plantation Cemetery**, which has Texas State historical markers, is located at 621 Arkansas Ln. in Arlington, on the northeast corner of Arkansas and Matlock.

Contact the historical society before going because the gate is usually locked.

The gravestones date from about 1831. At **Knapp Heritage Park** visitors may tour, by appointment, a 1910 North Side School, which is furnished with school desks, the Joplin-Melear cabin, and the P. A. Watson cabin, which is a dogtrot house with a furnished kitchen on one side and bedroom on the other. While in Arlington, visitors may want to drive by the **Stallions at Lincoln Square** sculpture located at Hwy. 157 and I-30 in North Arlington.

HISTORIC CARROLLTON

A. W. PERRY HOMESTEAD MUSEUM AND BARN

1509 N. Perry, Carrollton, Texas 75006 (972) 446-0442

Traveling in a covered wagon from Illinois to Texas in 1844, the Perrys were some of Carrollton's earliest settlers. This ten-room home built in 1909 is furnished with antiques and interesting memorabilia to remind us of the way we were and to share this history with children. Children will like the old farm tools in the barn. The homestead is open Wednesday to Saturday, 10 AM to 12 PM and 1 PM to 5 PM; tours are available. Admission is free, but donations are accepted. Website: www.cityofcarrollton.com/leisure/parksrec.

OLD DOWNTOWN CARROLLTON SQUARE

The Old Downtown Square in Carrollton is bordered by Broadway and Main streets and centered around a gazebo, which serves as a focal point for festivities during special events and on holidays, such as the Carrollton Christmas Parade and the October Country Fair. On the square, visitors shop for antiques. Just a little north of the square at Main and Carroll is a historical marker. Call the Carrollton Convention Center and Visitors Bureau for more about the square.

HISTORIC CEDAR HILL

PENN FARM AT CEDAR HILL STATE PARK

1570 F. M. 1382, Cedar Hill, Texas 74104 (972) 291-3900
Website: www.tpwd.state.tx.us/park/cedarhil

Overlooking Mountain Creek Valley in southwest Dallas County, Penn Farmstead is located in Cedar Hill State Park. In 1859 John Wesley Penn settled here and his descendants owned the family stock farm for more than a century. The original farm was about 1,100 acres, and some of the original structures, built of local oak and eastern red cedar, still survive. Both reconstructed and historic buildings from the mid-1800s through the mid-1900s serve as an educational resource and setting for demonstrations, special events, and displays. Self-guided tours are available daily. Groups should make reservations for guided tours.

HISTORIC DALLAS

Dallas's forefather **John Neely Bryan** (1810–1877) was a Tennessee lawyer and adventurer who heard about the Three Forks area of the Trinity River and decided to see what was there. Around 1841, he staked a claim on a bluff overlooking the Trinity and went about the business of negotiating with the local Indians, farming, and planning a town, which he named Dallas. A replica of his cabin is located at Dallas County Historical Plaza.

In addition to **Old City Park**, the **Hall of State**, **Age of Steam Railroad Museum**, **African American Museum**, **Dallas Firefighter's Museum**, **Dallas Museum for Holocaust Studies**, **American Museum of the Miniature Arts**, **Frontiers of Flight Museum**, **The Sixth Floor Museum**, **Telephone Pioneer Museum of Texas**, and **West End Historical District** mentioned in **Places to Go**, Dallas has many other landmarks worth visiting that are still very active.

The Dallas County Heritage Society is located at Old City Park, (214) 421-5141, and the Dallas Historical Society is located in the Hall of State at Fair Park, (214) 421-4500. The Historical Society offers tours of the Dallas area, often lead by historians. **Preservation Dallas** offers tours of the Wilson Historic District and information on historic sites. Call (214) 821-3290.

DALLAS CITY HALL

1500 Marilla (Ervay and Young), Dallas, Texas 75201 (214) 670-3011 Website: www.dallascityhall.org

The four-acre plaza surrounding City Hall with its imaginative sculpture by Henry Moore will first catch the interest of youngsters. The plaza is the setting of festivals during the year and the site of the city Christmas tree and its annual lighting ceremony. Architect I. M. Pei designed the ten-level cantilevered building, which opened in 1978. Inside, a view of the levels is good from the seventh floor, and there are usually art exhibits. Tours may be arranged by calling your local councilman or (214) 939-2701. The Dallas Police and Fire Communication Center is located here. While you are in the neighborhood, visit the historic Pioneer Park Cemetery about a block west at Griffin and Young, where many early Dallasites are buried. The Dallas Convention Center is also nearby on Griffin. See **Tours of the Working World** for more details about City Hall.

Outdoors, between the cemetery and Convention Center, are the seventy bronze longhorn steers and watchful bronze cowboys erected to commemorate the cattle drives of the Old West.

DALLAS COUNTY HISTORICAL PLAZA

The Dallas County Historical Plaza is a memorial to Dallas history. Located in the center of Elm, Houston, Commerce, and Market streets, the plaza is home for a representation of the **John Neely Bryan log cabin** built before 1850. A historical marker explains the contribution of the Log Cabin Pioneers of Dallas County. On the southwest side, the **Old Red Courthouse**, a sandstone, Romanesque Revival structure completed in 1891, allows a tour of the lobby area. The **John F. Kennedy Memorial**, a white cenotaph, is in front of Dallas's current courthouse. **Dealey Plaza**, located one block west, was the actual site of the assassination.

DAUGHTERS OF THE
AMERICAN REVOLUTION HOUSE

Open to the public during the State Fair of Texas, the Daughters of the American Revolution Continental DAR House is a colonial, white house located at the north end of Fair Park. The Jane Douglas Chapter houses a library of 3,500 genealogical books and bulletins, as well as 19th-century memorabilia, such as furniture, dishes, campaign buttons, and tools used in everyday life. The displays change each year. It is free to the public and handicapped accessible by the side door. Call (214) 670-8400 for more information.

DEALEY PLAZA

Bordered by Houston, Elm, and Commerce, Dealey Plaza is dedicated to George B. Dealey, who founded the *Dallas Morning News*, but its location near the Texas School Book Depository, now the Dallas County Administration Building, has also made it the site of a memorial plaque to John F. Kennedy. **The Sixth Floor Museum** is located in the Dallas County Administration Building.

HALL OF STATE AT FAIR PARK

The Hall of State described in **Places to Go** reflects the history of both Dallas and Texas through murals, statues, and exhibits. Through the Dallas Historical Society, programs about history for school and other groups are scheduled two weeks in advance for a small fee. Tours have names like "Texas History Tour," "Historic Character Programs," and "A Cowboy's Chuckwagon." The Hall of State also offers historical tours of Dallas, such as the "Downtown Dallas Tour" and the "Bonnie and Clyde Tour."

Often, the docents dress in historical costumes. Some programs may travel to a school.

Call the Hall of State at (214) 421-4500 for more details or visit www .dallashistory.org.

INTERNATIONAL MUSEUM OF CULTURES

7500 W. Camp Wisdom Rd., Dallas, Texas 75236 (972) 708-7341
Website: www.internationalmuseumofcultures.org

Opened in 1981 on the International Linguistics Center campus in southwest Dallas, the International Museum of Cultures has four permanent exhibits that display contemporary cultures of Ecuador, Papua, New Guinea, and Amazonian Peru. The museum focuses on the indigenous peoples of existing communities in remote locations of the world, as well as our own communities. There are some hands-on exhibits and an International Expressions gift shop, and tours are available. The museum is handicapped accessible, and there are picnic tables outside the dining hall.

From I-20, take the Cedar Ridge Rd. exit and go 1/2 mile south to Camp Wisdom Rd. Turn right and go one mile west to the International Linguistics Center entrance, and then turn west to the museum parking area. The museum is near Joe Pool Lake and Cedar Ridge Preserve. Admission is free, but donations of $2 for adults and $1 for children are accepted. Hours are Monday to Friday, 10 AM to 5 PM; Saturday, 1:30 PM to 5 PM; and closed Sunday.

JUANITA J. CRAFT CIVIL RIGHTS HOUSE
2618 Warren Ave., Dallas, Texas

Tours: (214) 670-8637

A leader in the Dallas Civil Rights Movement beginning in the 1930s, Juanita Craft became the first black woman to vote in a Dallas County primary in 1944, when Texas black residents were first allowed to participate in the Democratic primary. She helped organize more than 100 NAACP chapters in Texas and became a leader in the desegregation of the University of Texas Law School, the University of North Texas, and the state fair. Ms. Craft served as a Democratic precinct chairwoman for twenty-three years, and she became the second black woman elected to the Dallas City Council in 1975 at seventy-three years of age. She died in 1985 at age eighty-three. A recreation center and post office are named for her.

Black Dallas Remembered was very influential in preserving the house as a Dallas Historic Landmark and a memorial to the civil rights ideals for which Juanita Craft stood. In 2003, the organization received a donation of the $1 million Hill-Smith house and property in the State-Thomas neighborhood, which it plans to use for a museum and research center. They opened the **Hill-Smith Family Heritage Library and Research Center** in the historic neighborhood.

PEGASUS PLAZA

The theme of this beautiful plaza, located at Akard and Main, is based on the Greek myth of the flying horse Pegasus. This symbol is particularly meaningful to Dallasites because of Mobil Oil Company's flying red horse, which has resided on top of downtown's Magnolia Building for more than sixty years. The fountain is fed by a natural underground well. Trees, walkways, and boulders carved with symbols of the nine muses provide a pleasant refuge from city traffic.

SWISS AVENUE AND WILSON HISTORIC DISTRICTS

Butcher Pen Road was the original name of Swiss Ave., which connected Jacob Nussbaumer's farm to the city of Dallas. He changed the street's name to Swiss Ave. to honor his Swiss relatives and friends who settled nearby. In their glory days, the mansions along Swiss Ave. were owned by wealthy Dallas merchants and physicians, but now they are mainly used as offices for Dallas organizations. The neoclassical house at 5303 Swiss, built in 1905, is the oldest along the area between Fitzhugh and LaVista, which has been designated as a historic district. Children can see the differences in architecture from their own homes to those of the early 1900s. Some of these homes are usually featured on tour at

Christmas or Mother's Day. At **Central Square** on Swiss Ave. just west of Hall St. near Baylor Hospital is a unique preschool playground with swings, slide, and little structures to climb in and on. Azaleas bloom here in the spring, and there are picnic tables and a Victorian gazebo. While on Swiss Ave., you may also want to visit **Dallas Center for Contemporary Art** at 2801 Swiss. Call (214) 821-2522.

Frederick Wilson married a niece of the Nussbaumers and built Queen Anne–style houses on the block to rent or sell. His family home, built in 1899, was at the corner of Swiss and Oak, and it was kept in the Wilson family until 1977. The Meadows Foundation renovated a block of these historic homes and offers rent-free office space to nonprofit community agencies. Free forty-five-minute tours of the district are offered for individuals and for groups with a reservation. The tours begin at the Wilson House at 2922 Swiss Ave. Inside the Wilson House is **Preservation Dallas's In-Town Living Center**, which offers a storehouse of information about older neighborhoods in Dallas. The interactive kiosks feature sites within Loop 12 and include pictures, historical background, and special information about what makes that neighborhood particularly worthwhile. Center hours are Monday through Friday, 10 AM to 4 PM, and Saturday, 10 AM to 2 PM. Call (214) 821-3290.

THANKS-GIVING SQUARE

P.O. Box 1777, Dallas, Texas 75221 (214) 969-1977 Website: www.thanksgiving.org

Located downtown at the intersections of Akard, Pacific, Bryan, and Ervay streets, Thanks-Giving Square is a symbol of and a home for America's most beloved tradition, according to former president George H. W. Bush. In 1961, Dallas civic leaders decided to design a place of daily spiritual significance within the busy downtown area, a place of tranquility where citizens can reflect, pray, and count their blessings as Americans have been doing since before the Revolutionary War period.

Entering from Pacific, the three Bells of Thanksgiving ring out at noon on weekdays and every half hour on the weekends. Children are drawn to the courtyard with the rushing waters in the fountains. A good view of the fountains is from the ramp above. In the exhibit room is a series of photographs, taken by students at Texas A&M Commerce, that illustrate the three truths: We love God, God loves us, and we serve God singing. In the **Hall of World Thanksgiving** is the history of the American tradition of Thanksgiving, beginning with Samuel Adams's original proclamation of 1777 and continuing with presidents since then. Visitors will see a life-sized figure of George Washington kneeling in prayer next to the circular river of life.

The **Chapel of Thanksgiving** is a place for prayer and reflection. The spiraled ceiling with its ring of bright lights and stained glass causes visitors to look upward in praise. Upon leaving, visitors are reminded, "Love your neighbor." Sam Houston, president and later governor of Texas, recommended that Texans celebrate two Thanksgiving Days, one in the spring on March 2 for political independence and another in the fall to express thankfulness to God as Americans have been doing since the 1600s.

In 1997 a fifteen-ton monolith was dedicated to the Texas tradition of Thanksgiving. Four hundred years of celebration in Texas are outlined on the stone slab, the last of three monoliths that have been placed at the perimeter of the square. The first words of thanks came from Coronado's exploration of Texas in 1541: "It is right to give Him thanks and praise."

Thanks-Giving Square is free and open Monday to Friday, 9 AM to 7 PM, and on Saturday, Sunday, and holidays from 1 PM to 7 PM. Donations are appreciated. You may want to combine a visit here with a tour of the **underground walkway**, which may be entered from Thanksgiving Tower on the Pacific Ave. side. See **Tours of the Working World**.

UNION STATION

400 S. Houston St., Dallas, Texas 75202 (214) 746-6603

Built around 1914, Union Station was a center of rail activity in the area but now handles DART's Trinity Railway Express, which goes to Ft. Worth, and the Amtrak passenger trains. See **Transportation** for trips from Dallas. A tunnel connects Union Station to the Hyatt Regency Hotel and the fifty-story Reunion Tower.

HISTORIC FARMERS BRANCH

FARMERS BRANCH HISTORICAL PARK

2540 Farmers Branch Ln., Farmers Branch, Texas 75234
(972) 406-0184

Farmers Branch Historical Park is the site of the oldest rock structure on its original foundation in Dallas County. This home originally belonged to one of Dallas County's first doctors, Samuel Gilbert, and is furnished and open for tours. Within this twenty-two-acre park are a church, the original Farmers Branch train depot, the home of William Dodson, who was the first mayor of Farmers Branch, an 1856 dogtrot stone house, a single and a double crib barn, and an 1847 log house. The single crib barn has a blacksmith shop.

The park is located near the intersection of I-35 and I-635 on Farmers Branch Ln. at Denton Dr. Christmas is a special event here, with Dickens in the Park, which includes bell choirs, carolers, and horse-and-buggy rides, as well as the Christmas Light Drive Through on weekends and scheduled evenings. The buildings are handicapped accessible, and picnic tables are available. Winter hours are Monday to Thursday, 9:30 AM to 6 PM; Saturday and Sunday, 12 PM to 6 PM. During Daylight Saving Time in summer, the park is open until 8 PM. It is closed Fridays and major holidays. Groups by appointment may take guided tours on Tuesday and Thursday. Admission is free to the grounds, but the buildings are locked except at tour times. A small fee is charged for tours.

Mustang Trail is a 9.37-mile historic sight-seeing trail following city streets and beginning and ending at Farmers Branch Historical Park. For details, call (972) 406-0184.

HISTORIC GARLAND

LANDMARK MUSEUM

4th St. and State, Garland, Texas 75040 (972) 205-2749
Website: www.ci.garland.tx.us

Located behind Garland City Hall in Heritage Park, the Landmark Museum is in a three-room Santa Fe railroad depot, which houses many interesting artifacts dating from the late 1800s. Visitors may also look over a 1910 Santa Fe Pullman car and two homes (unfurnished) built at the turn of the century. Admission is free, and the depot is open Monday to Friday, 8:30 AM to 12 PM and 1 PM to 4:30 PM. Please call first for group tours. The Historic Downtown Square is recognized as a Main Street City.

HISTORIC GRAND PRAIRIE

A tour of historic Grand Prairie, which was named after the wide area of grasslands bordered on two sides by lines of timber, should include a look inside two historic homes.

The **Copeland Home**, 125 S.W. Dallas St., is the recently renovated 1904 home of a former physician, which houses antiques of old Grand Prairie families and tools of a physician's office of that period. The **Bowles Home**, 700 N.E. 28th St., is a dogtrot log cabin from 1845 that was covered with boarding and then siding. The siding has been removed, and the boarding recently repainted. Another small building nearby is called the Scout Hut because it may be rented for meetings.

The Copeland and Bowles homes may be seen by calling the Grand Prairie Parks and Recreation Department at (972) 237-8100. If visitors would like a docent to lead a tour, call the Grand Prairie Historical Commission or the Grand Prairie Historical Organization. The latter organization has a museum at 1516 W. Main St. Call 237-0389. Also, you might drive by City Hall Plaza for a look at the replica of the **Liberty Bell**, which was hung there during the bicentennial. For further information about Grand Prairie, contact Visitor Information at (972) 263-9588.

Grand Prairie Western Days celebrate the Old West with a parade, rodeo, county fair, and more family fun.

HISTORIC GRAPEVINE

The earliest settlers came to Grapevine by wagon train in 1844. Its name comes from the wild mustang grapes that once grew on the Grape Vine Prairie, which is now the location of the Dallas/Ft. Worth International Airport. Grapevine has seventy-five historic homes and buildings dating from 1865, and the Visitors Bureau can provide visitors with a list of homes and addresses. Liberty Park Plaza includes the Visitors Bureau and Torian Log Cabin. Another place of historical interest is Heritage Center, which has the Historical Museum in a 1901 depot, a railroad section farmer's home, and a tenant farmer's home. The museum is open from Monday to Saturday, 9 AM to 5 PM, and Sunday, 12 PM to 5 PM. The **Grapevine Opry** is also nearby for a Saturday evening of family entertainment. Main Street Days, held the third weekend in May, is a celebration of Grapevine's heritage. Grapefest is held in September, and Whistle Stop Christmas is held during the first two weekends in December.

The *Tarantula* train leaves from the Cotton Belt Depot at 707 S. Main on its way to the stockyards in Ft. Worth. Call (817) 625-RAIL for hours, rates, and type of engine.

Grapevine is in the midst of a continuing preservation effort downtown. Architexas has recreated the 1891 Wallis Hotel, a drummers lodging on the south side of Liberty Plaza across Main from the Opry. Look on S. Main by the funeral home for the glass-enclosed hearse, which was horse-drawn around 1900. Check with the Visitors Bureau for more information: 1280 S. Main, Ste. 103, Metro (817) 410-3185, (800) 457-6338 Website: www.grapevinetexasusa.com.

HISTORIC IRVING

Designated a historical landmark, the restored and furnished **Heritage House Pioneer Home** located at 303 S. O'Connor is open on the first Sunday of each month from 3 PM to 5 PM or by appointment. One of their special events is a **Valentine Tea** on the Sunday closest to Valentine's Day. Admission is adults, $1; children, free. Tours are available by appointment, and the fee is adults, $1; children, 50 cents. The house is not accessible by wheelchair. Call (972) 438-5775.

Details about historic trails in Irving are in the book *Irving: A Texas Odyssey*, and the trails map is the model for the mosaic tile map in the DART station in the Downtown Heritage District on Rock Island at Main.

MCDONALD'S FRIENDLY RED CABOOSE

301 W. Irving Blvd., Irving, Texas 75060 (972) 259-7881

Within three blocks of Heritage Park is an unusual McDonald's restaurant. On the walls and on the tabletops inside is memorabilia about trains and Irving's early days. In addition to a playground is the Missouri–Pacific Friendly Red Caboose, which is used for birthday parties. The restored caboose has booths on both sides of a center aisle.

NATIONAL SCOUTING MUSEUM

**1329 W. Walnut Hill Ln., Irving, Texas (800) 303-3047,
(972) 580-2100 Website: www.bsamuseum.org**

In addition to scouting artifacts, the 50,000-square-foot museum has a Cub Scout fort, a knot-tying wall, and animatronic characters that tell scouting and campfire stories. The most impressive exhibit is a mountainlike structure that has a screen on which visitors can simulate mountain-bike racing and kayaking. Kids can identify animal tracks on one wall and then visit the Norman Rockwell Gallery. Hours are Tuesdays, Wednesdays, and Fridays, 10 AM to 5 PM; Thursdays and Saturdays, 10 AM to 7 PM; and Sundays, 1 PM to 5 PM. Admission is adults, $10; seniors, $8; Scouts, $5; ages 3 and under, free.

HISTORIC LANCASTER

Located about twelve miles south of Dallas, Lancaster's town square was platted in 1852, modeled by a settler named Bledsoe after his hometown of Lancaster, Kentucky. The Visitors Bureau can give you a brief walking-tour map pointing out historical buildings as well as a driving-tour map of historic Lancaster. The driving tour includes an MKT Railroad depot, the site of a Confederate gun factory, and the Lancaster Airport, which was home of the Ghost Squadron of the DFW wing of the Confederate Air Force from 1939–1945. World War II artifacts and airplanes include the Coursair, which was used in the Pacific and the L-5/0Y1, which is painted in Marine livery and was used in Okinawa. The **American Airpower Heritage Museum**, located at 650 Ferris Rd., is open on Saturdays from 8 AM to 5 PM. Call (972) 227-9119 for information. Admission is $1. Website: http://dfwwing.natca.org.

Favorite events include the Second Saturday on the Square, town square's Halloween Pumpkin Festival, and the Christmas parade and lighting of the square. For more information, contact the Lancaster Chamber of Commerce at (972) 227-2579 or visit www.lancastertexas.org.

HISTORIC MCKINNEY

Both the county and town were named after a member of the Committee of Five who drafted the Texas Declaration of Independence, Collin McKinney. The town square, framed by Virginia, Tennessee, Louisiana, and Kentucky Streets, is dominated by the **Old Collin County Courthouse** (1876). Visitors browse in the antique stores along the square, and a favorite place to eat is the Pantry on Louisiana, well-known for its home cooking and fabulous pies, or you might try Herby's Soda Fountain at 210 Tennessee. Just northeast of the square is the renovated **Collin County History Museum** on E. Virginia at Chestnut, which houses memorabilia of Collin County and the world wars, such as an 1891 typewriter and a mill wheel. As you enter the museum, look up to the right at the 1934 triptych mural done by Frank Klepper of an 1862 Civil War scene in McKinney Town Square. The museum is open on Tuesdays from 1 PM to 5 PM.

Favorite festivals include Mayfair, October's Collin County Fall Festival, Dickens of a Christmas, and Tour of Homes. The Chamber of Commerce has a walk/ride tour map available, which points out historic sites, such as the Old Collin County Jail and the Heard Opera House. Contact the Chamber of Commerce at (972) 542-0163. **Chestnut Square** includes seven restored properties dating back to 1854. Four houses, a chapel, one cottage, and Dixie's Store may be toured on Tuesday, Thursday, and Saturday at 11 AM. It's located at 315 Chestnut near the town square. Call (972) 562-8790 or visit www.chestnutsquare.org.

West of McKinney is the **Collin County Youth Park and Farm Museum** located on eighty-three acres. This developing museum houses agricultural artifacts such as early tractors and other farm machinery. Acquisitions include a boll weevil machine, a windmill, and a 1936 International truck. In addition to the museum, the park has an indoor arena/show barn, a horse stall barn, a home-economics building, and Myer's Woods, which is thirty-five wooded acres with hiking trails. It's a favorite campsite for Scouts. The Collin County 4H hosts an annual chili cook-off here in February. The museum is open Monday to Friday, 8 AM to 5 PM, and on weekends by appointment. For directions, call Metro (972) 424-1460 ext. 4792 or (972) 548-4792.

While in McKinney, you may also want to visit the **Heard Museum** mentioned in **Places to Go** and the **Bolin Wildlife Exhibit** discussed earlier in this chapter. Additional entertainment might include some peddling in the swan boats on Towne Lake in warm weather (1400 Wilson Creek Pkwy.) and some skateboarding at Cyclone Indoor Skateboard Park (975 S. Central Expwy.). To reach McKinney, go north on Central Expwy. (US 75). Exit 40 (Louisiana) will take you to the square. Website: www.mckinneycvb.org.

HISTORIC MESQUITE

In Mesquite, the Florence Ranch Homestead operates as a home museum and community park. Donated by the Florence family, the homestead was built in 1891 and was surrounded by 160 acres. Today it is located on five acres at 1424 Barnes Bridge Rd. Most of the furniture is circa 1891 or earlier. The grounds are the site of community meetings and festivals, and tours may be arranged by calling Historic Mesquite at (972) 216-6468. The house is open on the second Saturday of each month from 10 AM to 1 PM. Free. The Lawrence House near downtown is being renovated and will be open for tours upon completion. You may wish to stay in Mesquite for a performance at the **Mesquite Arts Center** located at 1527 N. Galloway. The facility includes a concert hall, art gallery, black box theater, puppet theater, and courtyard. For a calendar of events, call (972) 285-0211 or visit www.mesquitechamber.com.

HISTORIC PLANO

Traveling north on Central Expwy. just past Richardson takes visitors to Plano. An exit east on 544, 15th St., leads from pavement to a redbrick road, taking you back in time to historic Plano. Old Downtown Plano offers shops, tearooms, services, a theater, a skate park, and restaurants. The Queen of Hearts Costume Shop at 15th St. and Avenue K is a favorite of all ages. The antique/craft mall on the north side of 15th St. houses interesting shops and a tearoom. Cobwebs Antique Mall and Tearoom is located just off 15th St. at Avenue J and 14th St. On the first Friday evening in December, the downtown streets are closed, and downtown is transformed into a Dickens-style English village that includes costumed characters and entertainment.

Settled by farmers from Kentucky and Tennessee in the 1840s, Plano survived two fires that devastated the downtown area, the last one in 1897. Since 1979, thirteen structures have acquired recognition as historic landmarks, and the Chamber of Commerce can provide visitors with background and maps of both the downtown area and other points of historic interest. A favorite stop is Haggard Park on 15th St. at Avenue H, which has a gazebo, fountain, and the **Interurban Railway Station Museum**, as well as picnic facilities.

The Texas Electric Railway Car once ran from Denison through Plano on its way to Waco, and it has been restored. The Railway Station Museum contains artifacts of the railroad and early Plano and pictures of area settlers. Operated by Plano Parks and Recreation, it is free and open to the public on Saturdays from 1 PM to 5 PM. For more information or to arrange a tour, call (972) 516-2117.

While in Plano, remember the **Heritage Farmstead** mentioned in **Places to Go**. For more information, contact the Plano Chamber of Commerce at (972) 424-7547.

HISTORIC RICHARDSON

In pre–Civil War days, this community was called Breckenridge, but this changed when a farmer gave free right of way to entice the railroad to come up from Dallas. The railroad accepted his offer, and the town was named after the railroad contractor, E. H. Richardson, in the 1870s.

While in Richardson, remember the **Owens Spring Creek Farm's** museum, with its collection of artifacts from the turn of the century, introduced in **Places to Go**. Two favorite annual events are the Wildflower Festival and the Cottonwood Art Festival. Call the Richardson Visitors Bureau at (972) 234-4141 or visit www.telecomcorridor.com/cvb.

HISTORIC ROCKWALL

Rockwall was named for an ancient stone wall running under the town. Some scientists believe it to be part of the Balcones Fault, but some of its characteristics lead others to speculate that it may have been built by a prehistoric civilization. A small replica of the wall is outside the courthouse in the middle of the downtown square.

While in Rockwall, relax at Lake Ray Hubbard on the *Texas Queen* riverboat or shop at **Goliad Place**, a cluster of small stores in quaint yellow houses. Eloise's Gifts and Antiques has collectible gnomes, PenniBears, and more. The Wedding Cottage is open Monday to Friday at lunch for hungry shoppers. The address is 722 S. Goliad (FM 740), two miles north of I-30. **The Rockwall County Historical Foundation Museum**, located at 901 E. Washington, is open Wednesdays and Saturdays, 10 AM to 2 PM. To reserve guided tours, call (972) 722-1507. No fee. Call the Chamber of Commerce at (972) 771-5733 for more information.

HISTORIC TERRELL

Located thirty-five miles east of Dallas on US 80, Terrell is another Texas town that grew up along the railroad. The attraction for the railroad was a large underground lake that would provide water for the trains. Terrell was established in 1873. The history of the town is preserved in the artifacts housed in the **Terrell Heritage Museum** in the Carnegie Building at 207 N. Francis St. Historical items, such as a 1912 Estey pipe organ and Texas–Midland Railroad memorabilia, are on display. Go east on US 80, take the Business US 80 exit, and turn north on N. Francis St. to reach the museum. Call Metro (972) 524-6082 for more information or visit www.terrellheritagesociety.org. Located at Terrell Airport, the **British Flight Training School Museum** features a No. 1 British Flying Training School Association display of newspaper and magazine clippings, model aircraft, WWII uniforms, navigation equipment, and a plaque given in gratitude for the kindness shown to trainees in the flight school. Terrell was home base for about 2,200 British and 138 American cadets in flight training school from 1941–1945. In 2006, the museum plans to move to a new location on the west side of the Terrell Airport. Open Wednesday to Saturday, 10 AM to 5 PM, and Sunday, 1 PM to 5 PM. Admission is adults, $3; seniors, $2; and students, $1. From I-20, exit north at Texas 34. Turn right on Airport Rd. and go right onto Silent Wings Blvd. The museum is located at 119 Silent Wings Blvd. From Business 80 in Terrell, go south on Texas 34 (S. Virginia) and east on Airport Rd. Call (972) 524-1714. Memberships are available.

While in Terrell, visitors may also want to stop by the **Tanger Factory Outlet** located along I-20. A favorite festival in Terrell is the April Heritage Jubilee. Call the Terrell Chamber of Commerce at (972) 563-5703 for information about Heritage Tours of Terrell and a copy of the historic trail map, or visit www.terrelltexas.com.

TOURS OF THE WORKING WORLD

Just as children love to go to their dad's and mom's offices to see what kind of work they do, family or group tours of the working world outside of their immediate family expand their horizons and begin the process in their minds of selecting careers for themselves. Many of these tours satisfy natural curiosity about how products are made or how services are performed. Most of the businesses that conduct tours ask that families and groups call ahead for appointments and remember to cancel the appointments if they cannot come, and the very popular ones often require reservations months in advance. If there is a minimum number for a tour, a family can sometimes join in a larger group. One other delightful aspect of taking tours is that most of them are free!

Tours listed in other locations in this guide are **Ameriquest Field, Legends of the Game Museum, Lone Star Park, Texas Motor Speedway, SPCA,** and **The Movie Studios at Las Colinas.**

Some businesses are reluctant to advertise tours to the public because they do not have staff to guide tours on a regular basis, but if they were approached individually, they might consider it. Many of the tours listed below are for children who are at least school age because they have longer attention spans and will understand more of what they see than preschoolers would. Suggestions for younger folks include local spots, such as a restaurant, post office, bank, veterinarian's office, hospital, police substation, fire department, grocery store, bakery, donut shop, pet store, dog groomer, pharmacy, and nurseries or florist's shops. Some of the **pick-your-own farms** listed will lead tours of their trees, fruits, and vegetables.

CARTER BLOODCARE

2205 Hwy. 121, Bedford, Texas 76021 (800) DONATE-4 Website: www.carterbloodcare.org

Groups who tour Carter BloodCare learn how vital it is for the public to donate blood. Each component can help different patients with various needs; your single donation can help save three lives! Visitors see the journey that each unit of blood takes to get to the patient and see the separation of red blood cells, platelets, and plasma.

Tours are given by request for groups who are in the seventh grade or older; large groups may be divided into smaller groups for touring. The tour takes about an hour, and reservations must be made in advance.

There is time for questions and discussion about career opportunities at Carter BloodCare. Because blood components are so perishable, life-saving blood donors are needed every day to ensure an adequate supply for patients in need. Contact Carter BloodCare to schedule the outing. Free.

CHANNEL 8/WFAA-TV

606 Young St., Dallas, Texas 75202 (214) 748-9631 Website: www.wfaa.com

Although it does not include live broadcasts, a tour of Channel 8 does take visitors through the familiar newsroom as the guide explains how assignments are made, through their broadcasting studios, and into the control room. The one-hour tour, scheduled on Tuesday, Wednesday, or Thursday, requires three weeks' written notice. Groups may choose 10:30 AM or 1:30 PM and should range from five to fifteen people who are twelve years old or older. The tour info line is (214) 977-6020. Free.

CHILDREN'S MEDICAL CENTER

1935 Motor St., Dallas, Texas 75235 (214) 456-6280

The two-story layout of tracks for the **miniature trains** that wind through tunnels and around mountains is always a favorite stop on a tour of Children's Medical Center. Children can watch the trains run from the first or second floor. Preschoolers on the tour go to Admitting, where they get a visitor's pass and see medical instruments, such as a stethoscope. Then they go on to Radiology, where they may see an X-ray machine and learn about the process of taking X-rays. Older children also visit a treatment room and surgery if available. No one under sixteen is allowed on patient floors.

Call the Education Office at least two weeks in advance to schedule a tour. One tour is scheduled on Thursday at around 10 AM for ages four to nine. Tours are arranged through the Children's Medical Center's Pathways Program, which comprises both child life specialists and volunteers. Group size may range from six to thirteen children, and the length of the tour is about forty-five minutes. Free.

DALLAS CITY HALL

1500 Marilla, Dallas, Texas 75201 (214) 939-2701

Tours of the impressive Dallas City Hall begin on the first floor and continue up to the sixth floor in City Council chambers. It may include a peek in the mayor's office if it is not occupied. Tours usually last about forty-five minutes. Your **local councilman** can take you on a tour. There are tables on the outside plaza, and a cafeteria on the seventh floor. See the section on **History and Politics** for more about City Hall.

DALLAS/FT. WORTH INTERNATIONAL AIRPORT

(972) 574-6701, (972) 574-8083 Website: www.dfwairport.com

A tour of the second most active airport in the world allows guests to see the inside operations, ride on the air trans system, and tour facilities. Make reservations at least four to six weeks in advance for groups no larger than thirty-five people. The tours, which last 1.5 hours, are conducted Monday to Friday at 10 AM for ages five and older. Families may join a group. One tour a month is given to Scout groups. Admission is free. The airport is located between Dallas and Ft. Worth, north of Hwy. 183 on the western edge of Irving. When you make a tour appointment, the guide will help with directions.

THE DALLAS MORNING NEWS

Communications Center, P.O. Box 655237, Dallas, Texas 75265
(214) 977-7257

The *Dallas Morning News* offers tours of the North Plant for children ages ten (fifth grade) and older. The Plano North Plant tour can accommodate groups numbering up to thirty-five. It may be possible to split and stagger larger groups into a double tour. The free tour needs to be reserved at least three weeks in advance, and hours are between 9 AM and 3 PM on Monday to Friday.

DALLAS PUBLIC LIBRARY

1515 Young St. at Ervay, Dallas, Texas 75201 (214) 670-1400
Website: www.dallaslibrary.org

The best place for information about the programs of the Dallas Public Library is in the monthly *Bookmark* published by the library and its website. The downtown J. Erik Jonsson Central Library and all branches are listed in this chapter, and announcements about special tours, exhibits, and educational classes are available through each library's activity sheet.

Tours of the downtown Children's Center for groups of children through sixth grade may be arranged by calling (214) 670-1671, and tours of the Central Library for older students may be arranged by calling (214) 670-1789. User Education Tours for students in grades four through eight may also be arranged through the Children's Center. Free.

DALLAS THEATER CENTER

3636 Turtle Creek Blvd., Dallas, Texas 75219 (214) 526-8210
Website: www.dallastheatercenter.com

The behind-the-scenes tour of the Dallas Theater Center (Kalita Humphreys Theater) is led by volunteers of the guild. They explain the history of the theater and its famous architect, Frank Lloyd Wright. Very casual clothes and flat shoes are recommended for this tour that takes visitors into the theater if there is no play or rehearsal, behind the stage, and into the Lay and Wynne Studios. On weekdays, tours go into the Heldt Building and see the rehearsal hall, if it is not being used, and the costume shop. Here, there are pictures of the theater being built. Because of the stairs and narrow aisles backstage, much of the tour is not wheelchair accessible. A forty-five-minute theater tour and forty-five-minute theater workshop may be arranged for school groups by calling (214) 252-3917. The fee for this is $5 per student.

The theater is located on beautiful Turtle Creek, and there are two picnic tables on the grounds if the group wants to have a picnic, or they can bring blankets and have a picnic down by the creek.

Tours: A family or group (usually not more than twenty-four) may call in advance for a tour appointment with a volunteer guide any day. If a volunteer is available, a tour may be scheduled on the weekend, but the Heldt Building may not be open. Free.

DR PEPPER BOTTLING COMPANY

2304 Century Center Blvd., Irving, Texas 75062

Tour line: (972) 721-8394

Dr Pepper originated in Texas, and Waco even has a Dr Pepper Museum. The tour of the plant near Texas Stadium begins in the lobby and goes throughout the plant, so visitors can see how the drink is made and put into bottles and cans. A video that explains operations is shown in the tour room, and each guest receives a free Dr Pepper and a pencil.

Tours: This forty-five-minute tour is best for ages six and older, and reservations should be made about six months in advance if you are planning a summer tour. Tours begin at 10 AM on Wednesday mornings and are limited to under forty people. A family may join a tour if there is space available. Free.

GENERAL MOTORS ASSEMBLY PLANT

2525 E. Abram, Arlington, Texas 76010 (817) 607-6571

Visitors to the General Motors Assembly Plant see how an automobile is mass-produced from assembly in the body shop to the final product. Tours enter at the road test area and proceed on to see stacks of fenders, trunk carpet, and hundreds of other parts being attached to painted and unpainted frames moving on conveyers. The only thing visitors don't see is painting. Those living in the Metroplex area hope that this plant making American cars continues to operate, but groups must call ahead to see if the plant is currently in production. The **Fielder Museum** is also on Abram St. Children should be at least ten years of age to get the most benefit from the tour, which lasts two hours and involves lots of walking. The group size should be about ten to thirty people. Sometimes families can join small groups. Call far ahead to make reservations for tours on Tuesday through Thursday. From Abram (at Hwy. 360), go to the southeast corner of the building through Gate 6, and parking is on the right. Free.

KLIF/KPLX RADIO STATION

3500 Maple St., Ste. 1600, Dallas, Texas 75219 (214) 526-2400

The walk through the station for a behind-the-scenes look at the production of radio shows is limited to sixth graders and up or college students who have an interest in communications. However, each Christmas the station participates in a toy drive for children, and families who bring donations are allowed to look around.

MARY KAY COSMETICS

Museum at corporate office: 16251 Dallas Pkwy., Addison, Texas (972) 687-6300

Manufacturing plant: 1330 Regal Row at I-35, Dallas, Texas

Website: www.marykay.com

The history of Mary Kay Cosmetics is showcased at the **Mary Kay Museum**, which is open for one-hour tours Monday to Friday, 9 AM to 4:30 PM, with reservations made at least two business days in advance. Visitors must be age ten or older. One-hour tours of the manufacturing plant are held Mondays at 2 PM, Tuesdays and Thursdays at 10:30 AM, and Fridays at 2 PM. These tours must be reserved two months in advance, and visitors must wear closed-toed shoes. Small children must be accompanied by parents.

MCKINNEY AVENUE TROLLEY

3153 Oak Grove Ave., Dallas, Texas 75204 (214) 855-0006
Website: www.mata.org

The historic McKinney Avenue Trolley Barn tour is given by volunteers who explain the history of electric transit and basically what makes the trolley run. Visitors usually then take a 2.8-mile round-trip run along McKinney Ave. through the Arts District to the Dallas Museum of Art and back to the barn. Sometimes this is included in a **birthday party** tour for which a trolley is rented and decorated for the birthday person and from six to thirty-two of his or her friends. There is a shop at the barn that has souvenir T-shirts, visors, caps, and bumper stickers.

Anyone who comes in is welcome to a tour. Group tours should be scheduled in advance. Tours are at 10 AM on Monday, Tuesday, Wednesday, and Friday. Call for hours and days of trolley operation. The trolleys are heated in winter, and a round-trip takes about thirty minutes. Barn tours are free, but there is a small fee for the trolley ride tour: Adults, $1.50; children under 12, $1; seniors, 50 cents.

MORTON H. MEYERSON SYMPHONY CENTER

2301 Flora, Ste. 100, Dallas, Texas 75201 (214) 670-3600
Website: www.dallassymphony.com

Tours of the majestic symphony center, located near the Dallas Museum of Art and the Arts District Theater, include a close look at the concert hall, Betty B. Marcus Park with its water-wall fountain, and the Wall of Honor.

Public tours are held at 1 PM on selected weekdays, and they last about one hour. Both families and school groups are welcome. Public demonstrations of the **Lay Family Concert Organ** are given once a month. Private tours should be scheduled at least six weeks in advance for groups of fifteen or more who are in the sixth grade or older. Call (214) 670-3600. Free.

TEXAS STADIUM

2401 E. Airport Fwy., Irving, Texas 75062 (972) 785-4780
Website: www.dallascowboys.com

Best known as the football field for the **Dallas Cowboys**, Texas Stadium is also the site of concerts and other exciting events. It has 63,855 covered seats and 296 skyboxes. Tours usually begin at the Pro Shop at Gate 8 below Jerry Jones's suite for some information about the stadium, then go out onto the field if it is not being used for an event. Guests may bring a football to throw around and a camera to record their day on the turf. Next, visitors go up the ramp into the locker room and take the coaches' elevator to the second floor to see a suite and the press box. Then the glass elevator takes them back to Gate 8 and the Pro Shop. Walk-up tours are given to the public on Monday to Saturday every hour from 10 AM to 4 PM and on Sunday each hour from 11 AM to 3 PM. The trip takes about an hour. Call for the schedule of private tours. One-hour birthday-party tours of the field and locker room may be arranged for children.

Admission: Public tours: Adults, $10; children 6–12 and seniors, $6; ages 5 and under, free. Private tours may be arranged by calling (972) 785-4850.

UNDERGROUND DALLAS/DOWNTOWN

Although children will not find any Ninja Turtles in the two miles of **underground tunnel** networks, they will still enjoy the adventure of seeing how the buildings downtown are connected and eating at one of the many restaurants provided for the working world. The Dallas Convention and Visitors Bureau may be able to help with the three main areas of connected buildings. Call (214) 571-1000 or visit www.visitdallas.com or www.downtowndallas.org.

One good place to start would be Thanksgiving Tower, which is right by **Thanks-Giving Square** on Pacific; underground parking is available (fee). Take the elevators to the underground. Various shops and restaurants are open during business hours. Children might enjoy lunch at one of the restaurants. Visitors can travel on to the NationsBank building and to One Dallas Center. Enter the tunnel system again at Lincoln Plaza at 500 N. Akard, where the steps down are by cascading water-wall fountains. This tunnel passes Dakota's restaurant and the Ross Garage before turning right to the Fairmount Hotel, where your group might go up for a look around. Going back into the tunnel again will take you to **Fountain Place**, located at 1445 Ross Ave. Children will love this, especially on a warm day. Tiered fountains and waterfalls surround shaded tables, and trees rise from the middle of the pools. A favorite fountain is the one with dancing waters that shoot one- to six-foot sprays up from the ground. Three hundred sixty high-pressure geysers shoot from holes in the concrete. Watch out because the temptation to run through it may be too great to resist. Website: www.fountainplace.com.

Families could combine a weekday trip to see a play at El Centro with a trek through the tunnels that begin at NationsBank Plaza on Lamar at Elm, then go on to One Main Place, Elm Place, Renaissance Tower, and the Holiday Inn Building at Griffin and Elm. You will also be near the Kennedy Memorial Plaza and the West End. Free.

TRANSPORTATION

The primary means of transportation in Dallas for many years has been the family car. However, with rising costs, overcrowded freeways, fitness awareness, and conservation efforts, other forms of transportation, ranging from bicycles to rail lines, are gaining in popularity. Some are here as pleasant reminders of bygone days, such as trolleys, paddle wheelers, steam engine–driven trains, and surrey rides. Children love vehicles, beginning with the ones that they power with their feet moving along the sidewalk. They like to ring the bells on the boats and honk the horns on the motorcycles at the amusement parks. A wide variety of transportation is available around Dallas, from a short bus ride to a hot-air balloon ride. Some conversation about what causes the vehicle to go makes any trip as educational as it is entertaining.

Several museums in the area are dedicated to preserving and informing the public about various types of transportation. Such museums listed in this guide are the **Age of Steam Museum at Fair Park**, **Interurban Railway Museum**, **Frontiers of Flight Museum**, **Cavanaugh Museum**, **Ennis Railway Museum**, **Confederate Air Force Museum**, **British Flight Training School Museum**, **C. R. Smith Museum**, and **Pate Museum of Transportation**.

AIRPLANES, SHUTTLES, HELICOPTERS, AND HOT-AIR BALLOONS

Even though most of today's parents have grown up accepting airplanes as part of daily life, most of us will still pause to watch an airplane take off and ascend to unknown destinations. Children love to spot airplanes and helicopters and are intrigued by all the contraptions at an airport, from the revolving luggage conveyors to moving sidewalks. A leisurely trip to the airport when no one is in a hurry to check luggage and catch a flight is an inexpensive and entertaining way to introduce a child to aviation.

Most commercial flights in Dallas leave from **Dallas/Ft. Worth International Airport** or **Love Field**, but some of the smaller airports will allow tours. Shuttle services are available for families who do not wish to drive in airport traffic or leave cars at the airport. Those who would like a simulation of flying a jet fighter should look under **More Amusements** in this chapter for Arlington's **Air Combat School**.

Helicopters are often kept at the smaller airports, and some owners offer rides to the public for a bird's-eye view of landmarks and homes. Expensive, but fantastic, hot-air balloon rides are also available. A favorite annual event is the **hot-air balloon festival** in Plano. Museums devoted to the history of aviation are located at Love Field, Dallas/Ft. Worth International Airport, Addison Airport, Terrell Airport, and Lancaster Airport. See **History and Politics** for more details.

The first two discussed below are the major airports in Dallas, but the ones listed after also contribute a great deal to the community and would be worth a visit.

DALLAS/FT. WORTH INTERNATIONAL AIRPORT

DFW Airport, Texas 75261 (972) 574-6000
Website: www.dfwairport.com

Dallas/Ft. Worth International Airport (DFW), aptly named for its location between the two cities, offers about 2,000 flights daily to almost 200 destinations. It has numerous stores and restaurants and lots of activity for children to watch. At **Founder's Plaza**, 2829 30th and Carbon, is an **observation park** with picnic benches and control tower conversation. To get there, follow the signs located on both the northbound and southbound service roads at DFW. They will take you to E. Airfield Dr. Turn west onto Carbon Rd. (30th Ave.) and look for the plaza flags. See **Tours of the Working World** in this chapter for more information.

The **C. R. Smith Museum**, which has a restored DC-3 at its entrance, is located adjacent to the AA Flight Academy at the intersection of 4601 Hwy. 360 and FAA Rd., southwest of DFW Airport in Ft. Worth. This **American Airlines** museum shows visitors what is needed to conduct a worldwide aviation system through interactive displays, hands-on exhibits, and video presentations on a thirty-foot-tall screen. Summer day camps may be available for children entering the fourth through seventh grades. Group tours are available, and admission is free. Hours are

Thursday to Saturday, 10 AM to 6 PM. Call Metro (817) 967-1560 or visit www.crsmithmuseum.org.

DALLAS LOVE FIELD AIRPORT

Cedar Springs at Mockingbird Ln., Dallas, Texas 75235 (214) 670-6080

Designated as a World War I training base in 1917, Love Field began its first passenger service in 1927 and has been an integral part of aviation in Dallas ever since. Until the Dallas/Ft. Worth International Airport was built, it was the major airport in Dallas. It still serves airlines such as Southwest, and it has food service and the **Frontiers of Flight Museum**. Look under **Places to Go** for more information about the museum.

ADDISON AIRPORT

4572 Claire Chennault Dr., Addison, Texas 75248 (972) 380-8800 Website: www.cavanaughflightmuseum.com

Addison Airport is the home of the **Cavanaugh Flight Museum**. Aviation history from World Wars I and II and Korea is brought to life through more than thirty-five refurbished aircraft such as the Fokker D VII, P51 Mustang, and MIG 15. Housed in airplane hangers, these planes are polished, kept in flyable condition, and used in air shows. An aviation art gallery and gift shop are at the entrance. For special occasions, such as Father's Day, pilots may offer Warbird Rides. Some of these planes are flown at Addison's Third of July fireworks celebration called Kaboomtown.

Also at the Addison Airport, **Discovery Flight** will take you up to see some of the best views in downtown Dallas. Call (972) 931-0345 or visit www.monarchair.com.

Museum hours: Monday to Saturday, 9 AM to 5 PM, and Sunday, 11 AM to 5 PM.

Admission: Adults, $6; children ages 6–12, $3.

LOCAL AIRPORTS

Alliance Airport 2250 Alliance Blvd., Ft. Worth, Texas 76177, Metro (817) 890-1000.

Mesquite Airport 1130 Airport Blvd., Mesquite, Texas 75149 (972) 222-8536.

Lancaster Airport 730 Ferris Rd./P.O. Box 551, Lancaster, Texas 75146 (972) 227-5721.

A shuttle service that serves both DFW and Love Field is **SuperShuttle**. Call Metro (817) 329-2000. The following are businesses that offer helicopter and hot-air balloon rides. To ride hot-air balloons, it is recommended that children be at least ten years old.

Airventure Balloonport 1791 Millard, Ste. D, Plano, Texas 75074 (972) 422-0212.

Zebra Air Helicopters Dallas Love Field, 7515 Lemmon, Bldg. J, Dallas, Texas 75235 (214) 358-7200.

BUSES, TRAINS, AND TROLLEYS

While DART buses and rail lines are taking families downtown and out to Plano and McKinney Ave., trolleys are taking them uptown, and Trinity Railway Express, Amtrak trains and Greyhound buses are taking them out of town. Any of these modes of transportation are going to delight and entertain children. Why not leave the car at home and hop on a bus downtown to see a play at El Centro's theater? You might discover the Underground and Fountain Place while downtown. Your family could park the car at the trolley barn on Oak Grove and ride the trolley to the Dallas Museum of Art or the Meyerson Symphony Center for a performance or tour and then eat at one of the fantastic restaurants on McKinney Ave. before riding back to the trolley barn. You could catch the DART rail line and ride to the West End, the zoo, or Reunion Arena.

Both native Dallasites and out-of-towners will enjoy sightseeing excursions around Dallas on commercial tour buses because often we never take the time to see the sights closest to home and know little of the history of our own hometown. For families who would like to vacation and leave the driving to someone else, Greyhound would be happy to escort you to a number of exciting cities in and out of Texas.

If your family has been to the Age of Steam Museum at Fair Park, and the children really want to experience travel by rail, plan to catch Amtrak at Union Station going either east or west daily, or drive down to Palestine to ride the Texas State Railroad round-trip. Look under **Day Trips** for passenger trains in Ft. Worth and Palestine. Six Flags Over Texas has a passenger train that takes visitors around the perimeter of the park. Visitors in Grapevine enjoy rides on the *Tarantula* train that boards at the depot and travels to the Ft. Worth Stockyards.

AMTRAK

Union Station, 400 S. Houston St., Dallas, Texas 75202 (214) 653-1101, (800) 872-7245 Website: www.amtrak.com

ALL ABOARD! Amtrak's passenger train service departs daily from historic Union Station, travels to Ft. Worth, and connects with a daily train that departs for Oklahoma City, stopping at five cities in between. The daily service heading west out of Dallas goes all the way to San Antonio, and three times a week, you can ride all the way to Los Angeles. The daily train going east from Dallas travels to Chicago. Reservations may be made online or by calling the 800 number. Call the 800 number for a copy of the national timetable and for copies of their magazines, *Amtrak's America* and *Amtrak Vacations*.

DALLAS-AREA RAPID TRANSIT

(214) 979-1111 Website: www.dart.org

The wheels on the DART buses go all over Big D and around thirteen other communities, providing inexpensive transportation and saving an estimated 24 million pounds of carbon monoxide from polluting Texas's blue skies. Students, RideShare commuters, senior citizens, and mobility-impaired passengers take advantage of DART's special programs. Cash fares for ninety minutes are adults, $1.25; students with ID, disabled passengers, and children (ages 5–11), 50 cents; and seniors (65+), 50 cents. Transfers are free. Call (214) 979-1111 or use the website for information about day and monthly passes, routes, schedules, and fares. Weekend service is limited.

The DART **red rail line** makes stops from Plano's Parker Road Station and passes Northpark Center, Mockingbird Station, City Place, the West End, Union Station, Reunion Arena, and the zoo on its way to the end of the line at Westmoreland in Oak Cliff. The ride from the Park Lane Station to the West End takes about thirty-five minutes. The **blue line** goes from Ledbetter through downtown and on to the city of Garland. The **Trinity Railway Express** leaves from Union Station on its route through Irving, by **Dallas/Ft. Worth International Airport** (DFW), and on to **Ft. Worth**. It takes seventy minutes to travel from Union Station to Ft. Worth's Texas and Pacific Station. To get to DFW, take a shuttle that connects DART's Centreport/DFW Airport Station to all airport terminals, Monday to Saturday. Note the interesting art at many of the stations. The design reflects the neighborhood where the station is located. For more information, call DART at (214) 979-1111.

DART offers Handiride buses, which have wheelchair lifts, and special DART Flyers, which are buses to sporting events, such as Dallas Cowboys games.

Presently, DART is carrying out its twenty-year plan to include both a light rail system and commuter rail service. DART also plans to expand the High Occupancy Vehicle (HOV) lanes and begin special transit circulator systems connecting heavily occupied centers. As each of these develops, families will enjoy trying them out and appreciate the efficiency of the transit options as compared to time wasted on overcrowded freeways. DART offers guest speakers, audiovisual presentations, and special exhibits for groups and school classrooms.

GREYHOUND

205 S. Lamar, Dallas, Texas 75202 (214) 655-7082

There are some suburban stations with bus service, but most Greyhound buses leave from Lamar to destinations such as Austin, San Antonio, Ft. Worth, Houston, Corpus Christi, Shreveport, Wichita Falls, and Amarillo. It is recommended that passengers arrive at least thirty minutes early. Call for fares and schedule information.

IDLE TIME TOURS, INC.

P.O. Box 610423, Dallas/Ft. Worth, Texas 75261-0423
(817) 790-7909, (800) 929-8015 Website: www.idletimetours.com

This company offers guided tours of the Metroplex and special packages for other Texas destinations.

MCKINNEY AVENUE TROLLEY: M-LINE

3153 Oak Grove Ave., Dallas, Texas 75204 (214) 855-0006
Website: www.mata.org

Clang! Clang! The bells of the free McKinney Ave. trolleys ring as passengers stop at exciting sites and tempting restaurants, such as the Hard Rock Cafe, all along the 3.6-mile route, which begins near the Oak Grove/McKinney Ave. trolley barn and goes on by the Crescent, the Dallas Museum of Art, the Nasher Sculpture Center, and the West Village. At St. Paul and Ross (by the Museum of Art), the streetcar system connects with a free M-line trolley bus, which proceeds down Ross to the West End and up Main St. and then returns to the Arts District streetcar. The trolley connects to the DART light rail system at City Place. The trolleys, operated by volunteers, are beautifully restored and are heated in winter. Ninety-year-old *Rosie* is the oldest operating streetcar in North America. A trolley may be rented for birthday parties and other occasions. M-line service operates seven days a week, running every fifteen minutes during peak and lunch hours, every twenty minutes during off-peak hours and weekends. Hours are weekdays, 7 AM and 10 PM, Saturdays, 10 AM to 10 PM, and Sundays, 12:30 PM to 10 PM. See **Tours of the Working World** for more information.

TEXAS TRAILS

1609 Trinity Hill, Mesquite, Texas 75181 (972) 222-5838

Even native Dallasites might like to lean back in a comfortable coach seat and let Texas Trails do the driving to sites such as Ft. Worth Stockyards, Waxahachie Gingerbread Trails, and Granbury, especially Dad, who misses a lot because he is keeping his eyes on the road, or Mom, who would like to leave the planning and navigation to someone else.

BOATS

Texas is well known for its large lakes and water sports. See Chapter Four, Sports and Recreation, for areas to ski, fish, and sail and for boat and water-bike rentals. One very tranquil boat ride is aboard the *Texas Queen* riverboat on Lake Ray Hubbard in Rockwall. The paddle wheeler usually casts off from the landing at Elgin B. Robertson Park just off I-30 at the Dalrock Rd. exit. Call (972) 771-0039 for information about excursions and dinner cruises or visit www.texasqueenriverboat.com.

A popular event in January is the **Dallas Boat Show** held at the Dallas Convention Center at 650 S. Griffin for ten days. More than 200 colorful fishing boats, water-ski boats, and yachts drop anchor here for all to admire whether interested in buying or not. Children enjoy workshops on topics such as necessities for tackle boxes, and some participants give away items to the first 500 children in the door. Dropping a line into the trout tank is another favorite of young, hopeful anglers. Watch the newspapers for announcements. The summer boat show is also very popular with local mariners.

CARS, CAMPERS, AND CARRIAGES

For a teenager living in Dallas, getting a driver's license is the number-one rite of passage. Most Texans are accustomed to driving their own cars and transporting large groups of children, as evidenced by the soaring numbers of minivans and Suburbans in the carpool lines, beside soccer fields, and on Scout field trips. Dallas does have several **taxi and limousine services** for visitors. Two taxicab services are Cowboy Cab at (214) 428-0202 and Yellow Cab Company at (214) 426-6262. A wide variety of cars may be rented from Budget Car Rental at (800) 527-0700 and the Hertz Corporation at (800) 564-3131. Campers may be rented from Longhorn Sales and Leasing at (972) 272-9363 or www.longhornrv.com.

Children who are fascinated with driving at an early age will enjoy cars designed with them in mind at amusement parks, such as the antique cars at Six Flags, the minivirage race cars at Speedzone, and go-carts at Mesquite Go-carts and Batting Cages and Celebration Station.

Families can step back in time with a **surrey ride** through the West End. Dallas Surrey Services offers carriage rides during good weather. They also offer ponies for parties. Call (214) 946-9911 for schedules and fares. Usually during Christmas, the Arboretum at (214) 515-6500, Highland Park Village at (214) 559-2740, and Old City Park at (214) 428-5448 offer tours of lights in **carriages**.

Each April, the Dallas Convention Center is filled with all kinds of new cars, ranging from sports cars and luxury sedans to cars of the future, in the **Dallas Auto Show**. Families enjoy radio personalities and exhibits, which include car-care products, car phones, and automobile memorabilia. Elementary school students participate in the exhibit of the Car of the Future in a display of their ideas of what cars will look like. The auto show lasts five days, and children twelve and under are admitted for free. Discount coupons are available at car dealerships. For more information, call the New Car Dealers Association at (214) 637-0531. Another very popular annual car show is held at the **Automobile Building** at the state fair in early October.

STORYTELLING, LIBRARIES, AND BOOKSTORES

Some people express fear that the magic of storytelling is disappearing with the onset of video games and a bumper crop of TV tater tots, but the art really is alive and well in many homes where parents still read to their children nightly, recite ageless nursery rhymes, and relate favorite tales heard in childhood from their parents and grandparents. Children love this tradition and the cozy, undivided attention of their parents.

Stories are woven weekly in area libraries as children's librarians sit before a semicircle of preschoolers and guide them through exciting tales. The rapt audiences cry for more.

Those who love folk humor and recounting stories have formed at least three guilds in the North Texas area. The **Dallas Storytelling Guild** meets each second Wednesday at 7 PM to share stories at the Churchill Recreation Center. On the Saturday before Thanksgiving, they sponsor **Tellabration**, an evening concert of storytellers in which four or five members tell favorite stories. Occasionally, members present workshops, and they have a list of storytellers and the types of stories they like to tell if an individual or group contacts them. Storytelling is popular at children's birthday parties. Call (214) 692-5355 or visit www.geocities.com/tellastory.geo/storytellers.

One very active storyteller is **Elizabeth Ellis** who tells stories for both adults and children at a wide variety of occasions. To reach Elizabeth Ellis, call (214) 381-4676.

Tsagoi is the founder of Tipi Tellers, and he tells his stories in a full-size Tipi. Contact him at (817) 320-5048 or Tsagoi@tipitellers.org. Educator and early childhood specialist Mary Ann Blue tells stories in both Spanish and English and fosters an appreciation of Mexican culture. She may be reached by e-mail at mabstories@home.com. The teller with a banjo, Dan Gibson, includes traditional folktales and ghost stories as well as tall tales and cowboy poetry in his repertoire. Contact him at dan.gibson@juno.com.

A popular annual event is the **Texas Storytelling Festival** in March in which storytellers gather at Texas Women's University in Denton for a weekend of folktales, fantasy, and music. Workshops for the storytellers are combined with storytelling sessions that the public may attend. At Friday evening's Olio, participants tell stories to introduce themselves, and on Saturday afternoon, a Family Olio and Traditional Texas tales are also open to the public. Some performances are interpreted for the deaf. For details, write the Tejas Storytelling Association, P.O. Box 2806, Denton, Texas 76202, call (940) 387-8336, or visit www.tejasstorytelling.com.

LIBRARIES

DALLAS PUBLIC LIBRARY

Twenty-two branches stem from the J. Erik Jonsson Central Library to form the Dallas Public Library system. Daily, children discover a love of reading from the story times, educational user classes (including free computer classes), reading clubs, and special events designed to inspire and encourage them. Patrons who live in Dallas may apply for a free library card, but those who live outside the city limits must purchase a fee card: $20 for five items checked out, $50 for fifteen items, $75 for twenty-five items, and $175 for unlimited check out for one year. Most books and magazines may be checked out for three weeks and may be renewed. Videos, DVDs, books, and music on cassette tapes and CDs, large print books, ESL tapes, and paintings may be borrowed for one week. To renew by phone, call (214) 670-1735 on weekdays. Free Internet access is available at all locations. The Dallas Public Library's home page is http://dallaslibrary.org.

J. ERIK JONSSON CENTRAL LIBRARY

1515 Young St. at Ervay, Dallas, Texas 75201 (214) 670-1400

Information and reference: (214) 670-1700

Families who make regular trips to the downtown library like the exhibits, usually displayed on the lobby level, in the fourth-floor gallery, and in the seventh-floor O'Hara exhibit hall, as well as the multitude of books from which they may choose their favorites. The best guide to special exhibits, programs, tours, and events is the *Bookmark* or the individual library's calendar. Families who are puzzled by a subject at home should call Information and Reference. An annual program greeted with enthusiasm each year is the **Summer Reading Club**. Certificates and rewards are given for the number of hours a child reads or is read to, and the summer is climaxed with a recognition party. Upper elementary students could combine this program with reading the year's new Bluebonnet book selections and vote for their favorites during the school year if their school library participates.

The imagination of children is stimulated by the second-floor **Children's Center** with its storytelling forest, a "village" to read in, and the Kahn Pavilion used for plays, puppet shows, films, and story times. The microcomputer area contains educational software, and the Writing to Read computer program has been implemented to help fight illiteracy in children. Microcomputer orientation classes are scheduled regularly to familiarize children with the computers. They cannot use the computers until they take the course, and preregistration is required. Preschool stories in both English and Spanish are offered regularly. Call (214) 670-1671 for information about children's activities. See **Tours of the Working World** for information about special tours and user-education classes for both children and adults.

Annually, the library sponsors a **Youth Poetry Competition** for Dallas students in grades two to twelve. Call (214) 670-1671 or visit www.dallas library.org and click on "Kids' Page." The **Dallas Children's Book Fair and Literary Festival** usually takes place in the fall at the Central Library.

Consider a family ride on a DART bus to the library for an outing. Be sure to browse in **BookEnds: Used and Rare Books** at (214) 670-1727 for great bargains on books, audio books, and magazines. The downtown library is open daily: Sunday, 1 PM to 5 PM; Monday to Thursday, 9 AM to 9 PM; and Friday and Saturday, 9 AM to 5 PM. Some branches are open on Sunday.

The following are the twenty-two branches of the Dallas Public Library. Regularly there is discussion at City Hall about cutting back branch-library services as a way to save money. If you enjoy the service of your branch library, please let your local representative know how vital its services are to you and your neighborhood. Contact each library for days and hours of operation.

All libraries have the 214 area code:

Audelia Rd., 10045 Audelia Rd., 670-1350
Casa View, 10355 Ferguson Rd., 670-8403
Dallas West, 2332 Singleton Blvd., 670-6445
Forest Green, 9015 Forest Ln., 670-1335
Fretz Park, 6990 Belt Line Rd., 670-6421
Hampton-Illinois, 2210 W. Illinois Ave., 670-7646
Highland Hills, 3624 Simpson Stuart Rd., 670-0987
Kleberg-Rylie, 1301 Edd Rd., 670-8471
Lakewood, 6121 Worth St., 670-1376
Lancaster-Kiest, 3039 S. Lancaster Rd., 670-1952
MLK Library, 2922 Martin L. King Blvd., 670-0344

Mountain Creek, 6102 Mountain Creek Pkwy., 670-6704
North Oak Cliff, 302 W. Tenth St., 670-7555
Oak Lawn, 4100 Cedar Springs Rd., 670-1359
Park Forest, 3421 Forest Ln., 670-6333
Pleasant Grove, 1125 S. Buckner Blvd., 670-0965
Polk-Wisdom, 7151 Library Ln., 670-1947
Preston Royal, 5626 Royal Ln., 670-7128
Renner-Frankford, 6400 Frankford Rd., 670-6100
Skillman/Southwestern, 5707 Skillman, 670-6078
Skyline, 6006 Everglade Rd., 670-0938
Walnut Hill, 9495 Marsh Ln., 670-6376

BOOKSTORES

Children love to read their favorite books over and over. Being able to write your own name and the date that you acquired the book is a special pleasure. Some of the most unique collections of books for children are not housed in a bookstore but in a museum gift shop specializing in science or nature.

Many of the retail chain bookstores house wonderful collections of fiction and nonfiction books, CDs, and tapes for children of all ages. These include **B. Dalton, Bookstop, Borders, Barnes & Noble, and Waldenbooks. Half Price Books,** which has multiple locations, and **75% Off Bookstore,** located in Dallas, Mesquite, and Plano, save families some dollars. Bookstores with a Christian family emphasis are **Deeper Life Bookstore, Logos, Family Christian Bookstores, Lifeway Christian Stores,** and **Mardel Christian and Educational Supply.** Imported **Books** offers books in Spanish and other foreign languages. Large discount warehouses like Sam's or department and grocery stores, such as Target, Wal-Mart, and Tom Thumb, often carry entertaining children's books and tapes at reasonable prices. The addresses and phone numbers for these bookstores are listed under "Book Dealers Retail" in the *Yellow Pages.* On a visit to a neighboring junior college or university, stop by the college bookstore for a look at its children's books. For announcements about local literary events, look each Sunday in the *Dallas Morning News* "Books" section for the literary calendar. The Friday "Guide" section lists literary events at bookstores and library events for children.

Summer reading clubs are a traditional form of summer entertainment. These clubs often offer prizes for a designated number of books read or hours spent in reading or being read to. Look for these clubs at bookstores, public libraries, church libraries, and movie theaters.

Earful of Books is an audio book retailer that carries children's books for purchase or rental. This is a real nerve saver on long car trips. The store is located in Plano at 3033 W. Parker Blvd. Call (972) 985-6447. **Premiere Video**, 5400 E. Mockingbird, also has an extensive selection of audio books as well as classic videos. Call (214) 827-8969. **Half Price Books** stocks used books-on-tape.

A LIKELY STORY

4801 Park Blvd. at Preston Rd., N.E. corner, Plano, Texas 75093
(972) 964-8838

A Likely Story is a very kid-friendly bookstore. A Brio Train area is available to give children something to do while parents browse. Children also like to have their favorite editions autographed by guest authors. In addition to a wide variety of books, there are educational toys, crafts, games, science and art projects, puppets, and much more for infants and children through age fourteen. This bookstore also has gift wrapping. A Likely Story is open Monday to Saturday, 9:30 AM to 6 PM, and Sunday, 12 PM to 5 PM.

SMALL ART MUSEUMS, GALLERIES, AND ART CENTERS

Artists agree that the earlier children are exposed to art, the more they will appreciate it throughout their lives. They are attracted to the colors and designs at a very early age, and a home with easy access to crayons and watercolors and art paper encourages creativity in budding artists.

Art is all around you in Dallas. It's hanging in the halls in school buildings, in the sculptures in the parks, in the center aisles at the malls, and in the gallery at City Hall. Sometimes a small art center or gallery is just the right speed for younger children who do not have long attention spans or like to walk long distances. Most of the area community colleges and universities have small galleries that feature local artists, and personnel will be happy to mail information about the exhibits scheduled. Many city halls, libraries, community cultural centers, performing-arts centers, and museums display changing exhibits regularly, and local art groups regularly sponsor art exhibits and offer classes for both children and adults. Many art museums and community colleges hold summer art classes and day camps.

The Friday "Guide" section of the *Dallas Morning News* lists museums and galleries and their current exhibits, and many of these also have mailing lists. See Chapter Five, Festivals and Special Events, for Artfest and Imagination Celebration, two popular family art festivals. Richardson's

Cottonwood Art Festival is another favorite event. More art fun is listed under **Hobbies and Collections**.

ARLINGTON MUSEUM OF ART

201 W. Main at Pecan, Arlington, Texas 76010 (817) 275-4600
Website: www.arlingtonmuseum.org

Throughout the year, exciting permanent and changing exhibits focusing on contemporary regional art are on display. On selected monthly Saturday afternoons are **family art days** and activities that are coordinated with the Arlington Public Library. Call about special events, summer day camps, gallery tours, birthday parties, and children's classes. Parking is available at nearby City Hall.

Hours: Wednesday, 10 AM to 8 PM; Thursday to Saturday, 10 AM to 5 PM.

ARTCENTRE OF PLANO

1039 E. 15th St., Plano, Texas (972) 423-7809
Website: www.artcentreofplano.org

The galleries and classrooms of ArtCentre of Plano are dedicated to promoting art and art education in both visual and performing arts. Business hours are Tuesday to Saturday, 10 AM to 6 PM.

BATH HOUSE CULTURAL CENTER

521 E. Lawther Dr., Dallas, Texas 75218-0032 (214) 670-8749
Website: www.bathhousecultural.com

Located on the eastern shores of White Rock Lake in northeast Dallas, the Bath House beach was a popular place in the 1930s for swimming. Chain-link fences ran on both sides of the building and down into the water to mark off a swimming area. Today, no swimming is allowed in the lake, and the Bath House has been converted into a cultural center that fosters the growth, development, and quality of multicultural arts within the city of Dallas. It also houses a lake museum.

Part of the City of Dallas Office of Cultural Affairs, the Bath House includes a 105-seat theater, the Main and Hall galleries, and several workshops. Plays, concerts, art exhibits, and workshops for both children and adults are regularly scheduled. Classes for children include printmaking and weaving, and student art exhibits are often displayed in the galleries. Write or call the center to be on their mailing list for advance notice of activities.

You might like to bring a picnic lunch and plan to spend some time on playground equipment at White Rock Lake while there. To reach the Bath House from N. Buckner Blvd., turn west on Northcliff. Signs are there to guide you.

Hours: Office hours are Tuesday to Saturday, 12 PM to 6 PM.

BIBLICAL ARTS CENTER

7500 Park Ln., P.O. Box 12727, Dallas, Texas 75225 (214) 691-4661 Website: www.biblicalarts.org

A feeling of stepping into Biblical times is evoked at the limestone entrance modeled after Paul's Gate in Damascus at the nondenominational Biblical Arts Center. Its focus is to help all people better understand the places, events, and people of the Bible through artwork and historical artifacts, theater, music, and film.

The *Miracle at Pentecost* mural, measuring 124 × 20 feet and featuring more than 200 characters from the Bible, is unveiled once each hour on the half hour, with a thirty-minute light and sound show based on Acts 2.

A life-size replica of Christ's Garden Tomb at Calvary is featured in the atrium. Galleries display both permanent and changing exhibits. A gift shop carries books and collectibles. Call or write to be added to the mailing list. The center offers children's programs and summer art camp to help them develop an appreciation of art.

Admission is free to the galleries. Admission to *Miracle at Pentecost* is $7 for ages six and up. Ages five and under are free. A Passport admission for all events is $12. Group rates are available. The museum is located west of Northpark Center. Hours are Tuesday to Saturday, 10 AM to 5 PM, except Thursday when it is open until 9 PM, and Sunday, 1 PM to 5 PM. Closed major holidays.

CRAFT GUILD OF DALLAS

14325 Proton, Dallas, Texas 75244 (972) 490-0303 Website: www.craftguildofdallas.org

Classes for children and adults in fiber arts, book binding, paper art, jewelry making, ceramics, surface design, and other media are offered by the Craft Guild of Dallas. Fees vary, with discounts available to members. A family membership is $70, and a student membership is $25. Classes in clay throwing and hand building are open for ages three to twelve. The Saturday Morning Art Camp is fun for young artists. A holiday craft fair is offered in December, and children's camps are offered in the summer. Shop for great gifts at the Craft Guild Store.

CROW COLLECTION OF ASIAN ART

Trammell Crow Center, 2010 Flora at Olive, Dallas, Texas (214) 979-6430 Website: www.crowcollection.org

Located by the Dallas Museum of Art, the Crow Collection of Asian Art includes more than 300 pieces from Japan, China, India, and Southeast Asia, dating from 3500 B.C. to the early 20th century. A sculpture garden surrounds Trammell Center. On the website is "Passport to Asia for Kids." Two pictures are available to print out and then color. Schedule group tours two weeks in advance. Call (214) 979-6435 for reservations.

DALLAS CENTER FOR CONTEMPORARY ART

2801 Swiss Ave., Dallas, Texas 75204 (214) 821-2522 Website: www.thecontemporary.net

Dallas Center for Contemporary Art is a nonprofit agency that exists to provide community access to and education about the art and artists of Texas. Located in the **Wilson Historic District**, the center provides year-round exhibitions, art classes, and a resource room of art-related periodicals and art-organization materials. Information concerning the center's latest exhibition may be found on the center's website and in the "Art Centers: Openings" listing in the newspaper each Friday. The gallery plans to expand its youth programs, family days, and tours.

The center offers fifteen exhibition opportunities throughout the year. Following a visit to the center, children might enjoy a picnic at the scenic **Central Park Square** and a stroll down Swiss Ave. along the row of Victorian- and Queen Anne–influenced houses in the Wilson Historic District. Hours are Tuesday to Saturday, 10 AM to 5 PM.

CAPERS FOR KIDS

12306 Park Central Dr., Dallas, Texas 75251-1801 (972) 661-2787 Website: www.capersforkids.com

Capers for Kids is a creative-arts school and outreach program that provides classes in creative drama and visual arts to more than 2,500 children and adults weekly. Classes are provided to more than twenty public and private schools as supplements to existing curricula and as after-school programs.

JESUIT DALLAS MUSEUM

12345 Inwood, Dallas, Texas 75244 (972) 387-8700

Housed in Jesuit College Preparatory School, the museum's collection includes 375 pieces by artists such as Henry Moore, Joan Miró, and Eduardo Chillida. Call for information about viewing the exhibit, and the school office will give you the name of a docent who can lead a tour.

J'S ART STUDIO

17822 Davenport, Ste. C, Dallas, Texas 75252 (972) 931-1933

Art classes for ages four through adults are offered at J's Art Studio. They use multimedia projects, which include painting, drawing, sculpture, pottery, and printmaking, as well as alternative approaches to art, such as collage and assemblage. Classes meet once each week beginning in mid-August, and summer camps are also offered. The studio is located between Campbell and Frankfort, east of Preston.

THE BLACK ACADEMY OF ARTS AND LETTERS, INC.

Dallas Convention Center Theater Complex, 650 S. Griffin, Dallas, Texas 75202 (214) 743-2440

Dedicated to promoting and preserving the works of black Americans, the academy presents workshops, exhibitions, and seminars. It is located near City Hall. Call for a brochure of events and concerts.

Hours: Monday to Friday, 9 AM to 5:30 PM, and Saturday, during events. The gallery stays open on weekends.

SOUTH DALLAS CULTURAL CENTER

3400 S. Fitzhugh, Dallas, Texas 75210 (214) 939-2787 Website: www.dallasculture.org/sdcc/index.html

The South Dallas Cultural Center is a multipurpose arts venue in South Dallas by Fair Park. It has a visual arts gallery and studios for two-dimensional art, ceramics, printmaking and photography. Also, it features a 100-seat black box theater and studios for dance, as well as classes in digital recording technology for youths and adults.

Summer Arts at the Center is a five-week arts institute for school-aged kids, taught by local and visiting artists.

LAKEWOOD ARTS ACADEMY

1911 Abrams Pkwy., Dallas, Texas 75214 (214) 827-1222 Website: www.lakewoodarts.com

Classes for ages two through teens are planned according to the age and needs of each student in a studio environment. Creative opportunities are offered in two- and three-dimensional art. Summer camps, some of which include field trips to locations such as the arboretum, and birthday parties are also offered.

KID ART

3407 Milton Ave., Dallas, Texas 75205 (214) 750-7118 E-mail: kidartdallas@hotmail.com

Located in Snider Plaza, Kid Art offers art classes and summer camps for children age three to sixth graders. They have lots of registration policies and procedures. Read carefully; tuition is about $80 or more per month.

KIDSARTS

Irving Arts Center, 3333 N. MacArthur Blvd., Ste. 300, Irving, Texas 75062 Website: www.ci.irving.tx.us.org

Workshops, performances, and camps related to art, photography, music, theater, weaving, and storytelling are popular at the Irving Arts Center. The center has art exhibitions in its galleries. KIDSarts participants may have their art on display in the New Talent Gallery.

LATINO CULTURAL CENTER

2600 Live Oak, Dallas, Texas (214) 670-3320
Website: www.dallasculture.org/latinocc/index.html

Opened in 2003, the Latino Cultural Center has galleries for art exhibitions and workspace for artists. The center presents opportunities for education and experience in visual, literary, media, performance, and traditional arts.

THE ICE HOUSE CULTURAL CENTER

1000 W. Page St., Dallas, Texas 75208 (214) 670-7524
Website: www.dallasculture.org/icehouse/index.html

Providing a Latino-focused venue to promote the arts and cultural events that reflect the diversity of Oak Cliff and nearby areas, the Ice House Cultural Center works with the Dallas Museum of Art and provides visual art exhibitions and workshops as well as theater and dance workshops.

MEADOWS MUSEUM

Southern Methodist University, 5900 Bishop Blvd. at Schlegel St., Dallas, Texas 75275 (214) 768-2516
Website: http://meadowsmuseum.smu.edu

The Meadows Museum houses the most comprehensive collection of Spanish art in the United States, including paintings, sculpture, and works on paper from the tenth through the twenty-first centuries. Artists represented in the collection include Velázquez, Murillo, Goya, Picasso, and Miró. The museum offers a variety of programs for visitors of all ages, including docent-led tours, art classes, and Family Days. Free public gallery tours are offered on Thursdays at 6 PM and Saturdays and Sundays at 2 PM. Private tours of the museum's permanent collection and special exhibitions may be scheduled for groups of ten to sixty people by calling (214) 768-2740. Group tours are available for ages five to adult, and reservations must be made at least three weeks in advance.

The Meadows Community Education Program hosts children's art classes throughout the year to introduce students to a variety of media and techniques. **Family Days** are scheduled regularly in conjunction with special exhibitions or events. Family Day activities and programs are designed especially for children and include live performances by musicians, dancers, or performing artists; studio-art activities; and storytelling in the galleries.

Visit the Meadows Museum store for a wide selection of books, gifts, and educational materials with a Spanish flair. Admission to the museum is free; special exhibitions, group tours, and classes may incur additional fees.

Hours: Monday, Tuesday, Friday, and Saturday, 10 AM to 5 PM; Thursday, 10 AM to 8 PM; Sunday, 1 PM to 5 PM. Closed Wednesday. **The Gates** restaurant is open Monday to Friday, 11 AM to 2 PM. Free parking is available in the museum garage.

PAN AMERICAN ART GALLERY

3303 Lee Pkwy., Ste. 101, Dallas, Texas 75219 (214) 522-3303
Website: www.panamericanart.com

The Pan American Art Gallery specializes in the art of the Americas, featuring work from Canada, the United States, the Caribbean, and Latin America. They have a large collection of Cuban, Haitian, and Jamaican art. The gallery includes avant-garde and contemporary works, as well as ceramics, photography, folk art, and sculpture.

MADI MUSEUM AND GALLERY

Kilgore Law Center, 3109 Carlisle, Dallas, Texas 75204 (214) 855-7802 Website: www.madimuseumandgallery.org

Kids are immediately attracted to the bright green, red, blue, and yellow facade of the building. Dedicated to a movement founded in Argentina in 1946, the MADI collection is distinguished by asymmetrical geometric influences, polygonal forms, and contoured surfaces. It includes bright visual art, music, poetry, and three-dimensional parts that move. Hours of operation are Tuesday, Wednesday, Friday, and Saturday, 11 AM to 5 PM; Thursday, 1 PM to 8 PM; Sunday, 1 PM to 5 PM. Closed Monday.

OUTDOOR SCULPTURE AND MURALS IN DALLAS

Visitors to downtown might want a copy of the Dallas Convention Center's guide to the thirty-two sculptures located there. They include some lifelike pieces, such as the elderly lady who is knitting while sitting on a park bench at Olive and Ross. Many other pieces located throughout the Dallas area are also cataloged. Call (214) 751-1300 for details.

Other sections of the guide list Metroplex outdoor sculpture, such as the garden at the Dallas Museum of Art, Dallas City Hall, the Pump

House at White Rock Lake, the Dallas Zoo (tallest in Texas), the Natural History Museum, the Mustangs at Las Colinas, and the Meadows Museum.

Northpark Center developer Raymond Nasher constructed a two-acre sculpture garden on land across Harwood from the Dallas Museum of Art. The **Nasher Sculpture Garden** is the setting for 30 to 40 sculptures at a time from his collection, which consists of more than 250 masterworks. See Chapter One for more details.

In the Quorum Business Center in Addison is a sculpture that marks the equinox twice yearly when fall and spring begin. The sun shines through the metal arch and aligns with marks on a metal ball below it. John V. House's sculpture is located west of the Tollway and south of Belt Line Rd. in a traffic circle at the Quorum.

Huge **murals** are being painted in downtown Dallas by artists from Eyecon Inc. Some are painted on the sides of parking garages and may take up a city block. Three locations and titles are *Mass Transit* at Griffin and Pacific, *Resources* at St. Paul and San Jacinto, and *The Storm* (twelve stories high) at San Jacinto and Leonard. *Whaling Walls* by Wyland is located at 505 Akard St. near San Jacinto. On the nine-story brick wall of the old Sanger Building section of El Centro College is *We Are One*, depicting a Native American pipe smoking ceremony that includes the points of the compass, Mother Earth and Father Sky, animal symbols, and the four elements: earth, fire, air, and water.

TRUETT HOSPITAL/BAYLOR

On permanent display at Baylor's Truett Hospital are more than eighty-six casts of hands, which are the work of orthopedic surgeon Dr. Adrian Flatt. Famous hands in the display are those of U.S. presidents, actors, athletes, writers, and more. The hands of Nolan Ryan hold a baseball.

DALLAS CONVENTION CENTER

650 S. Griffin, Dallas, Texas (214) 658-7000

The $9 million Pioneer Plaza includes a 19th-century cattle drive with a herd of forty bronze longhorns and attending cowboys on horseback heading downhill to water. The historic Shawnee Trail ran through the area near today's Reunion Arena, and the sculptures celebrate it as well as the introduction of longhorn cattle to our land more than 500 years ago. This is a definite photo opportunity.

TRAMMEL CROW CENTER

2001 Ross Ave. at Olive, Dallas, Texas 75201 (214) 979-6430

Located near the Dallas Museum of Art downtown, the Trammel Crow Center includes the Crow Collection of Asian Art. Children especially like the sculptures that surround the building. Call for information about current exhibits or read the gallery listing in the Friday newspaper.

FREEDMAN'S MEMORIAL CEMETERY

Central Expwy. (US 75) at Lemmon Ave., S.W. corner, Dallas

The cemetery, which is more than 135 years old, is the burial ground for about 7,000 former slaves. Sculptor David Newton designed the twenty-foot marble-and-stone entry arch and the bronze sculptures. On the left of the entrance is a bronze African warrior who protects those who are buried there; on the right is an African historian/storyteller called a *griot*. A sculpture of an African couple who are comforting each other following enslavement is located at the reflection area. A male in chains and a sorrowful woman, the "Struggling Soul" and the "Violated Soul," are at the back of the arch. Erykah Badu performed a song she wrote for Freedman's Cemetery when the new memorial was dedicated in 1999.

HORSES

Dallas Soars! is the Pegasus art project based on the Dallas landmark **Flying Red Horse** on the Magnolia Building in downtown Dallas. About eighty Pegasus sculptures, decorated by both professional and amateur artists, can be spotted around Dallas. One is in front of the Dallas Children's Theater. Other horse art includes the following:

Colts in Motion by Anna Debska, 2001 Bryan at San Jacinto, Maxus Energy Tower Garage
Freedom Horses a stallion and a mare by Veryl Goodnight, Dallas North Tollway and Loop 12
Pegasus by Booker T. Washington Art Students, 2501 Flora, Dallas
Traveler and Robert E. Lee, Lee Park, Dallas

TEXAS SCULPTURE GARDEN

Hall Office Park, 6801 Gaylord Pkwy., Frisco, Texas (after Hwy. 121 on the Dallas North Tollway) Website: www.texassculpturegarden.org

Outdoors are seventeen of the thirty-seven contemporary sculptures by Texas artists, while the remaining ones are in the lobby. Guided tours are available for groups of fifteen or more. Call (972) 377-1152. It's located near Stonebriar Centre. Open dawn to dusk; lobby hours are weekdays, 9 AM to 5 PM.

SHOPPING AND HOBBIES

SHOPPING

Shopping is such a favorite pastime in Dallas that the city is able to claim more shopping centers per shopper than any other city in the United States. "Shop till ya drop" is more than a motto. However, this is accurate only for teenage mall dwellers on up. Most five-year-olds would not place a trip to the mall as a top-ten activity, but there are usually some shops at the malls or centers that focus on the younger set and some fast food restaurants that are just their speed. Many shopping centers have fountains and displays with flags that catch the eye of little ones, especially during holiday seasons.

Check with the malls near you for a calendar of special events. Health fairs, children's art exhibits, puppet shows, petting zoos, Santa, and the Easter Bunny are often part of mall activities. The mall or a particular restaurant may offer breakfast and photos with the latter two. Valley View Mall has a Kid's Club and Northpark has High Tech Kids.

Hobby shops are great places to spend time with your young shopper. Starting a collection at an early age makes a real adventure out of shopping as kids try to find a certain baseball card or add to their dollhouses.

One of the most entertaining family shopping days can be found at local flea markets and trade days, such as the one in Canton.

Listed below are only some of the Metroplex area's malls and their shops and fast food restaurants that would appeal to children. Look under "Hobbies" and "Toys" in the *Yellow Pages* for additional shops. Near to most of the wonderful shops is sure to be a place to make the necessary stop for ice cream or other rejuvenating snacks.

SHOPPING MALLS

COLLIN CREEK MALL

811 Central Expwy.,
Plano, Texas (972) 422-1070

Children's Place Clothing
Disney Store
Gap Kids
Gymboree
Picture People

Soft Play Area
Waldenbooks

GALLERIA

I-635 (LBJ) at Dallas Pkwy.,
Dallas, Texas (972) 702-7100

Adopt-a-Bear
BabyGap and GapKids
Children's Place

Discovery Channel Store
Disney Store
Ice-Skating Center
Limited, Too
McDonald's
Noah's Ark
Slappy's Puppet House

GRAPEVINE MILLS OUTLET CENTER

Hwy. 121 North and 3000
Grapevine Mills Pkwy.,
Grapevine, Texas (972) 724-
4900 Website:
www.grapevinemills.com

Build-a-Bear Workshop
Candy Hqtrs.
Carters
Children's Place
Cowboys Pro Shop
Dallas Dancewear
Disney's Rainforest Cafe
EB Games
Games Workshop
GameWorks Arcade
Gap
The Icing
JC Penney
Kiddie Kandids
Old Navy
Oshkosh B'Gosh
Sanrio
Sports Authority
Tommy Kids Company Store
(on perimeter)
AMC Movie Theater
Bass Pro Shops Outdoor World
Dr Pepper Stars Center
ESPN X Games Skatepark
Polar Ice-Skating Arena

NORTHPARK CENTER

Northwest Hwy. and Central
Expwy., Dallas, Texas (214) 363-
7441

AMC Movie Theater
Charlotte Russe
Corner Bakery
Disney Store
GapKids
High Tech Kids of the Science
   Place
Model train display in December
Museums and More
Playhouse Parade in May, SPCA
   in December

RICHARDSON SQUARE MALL

501. S. Plano Rd. at Belt Line,
Richardson, Texas
(972) 783-0117

Arcade
Barnes and Noble Bookstore
Dillard's
Food court
Old Navy
Oshman's

STONEBRIAR CENTRE

Hwy. 121 and Preston Rd.,
Frisco, Texas (972) 668-6255
Website: www.shopstonebriar.com

abercrombie
AMC 24 Movie Theater
Baby changing areas
BabyGap and GapKids
Build-a-Bear Workshop
Carousel at the food court
Charlotte Russe
Chick-Fil-A
Claire's
Co-Serv KidZone
Discovery Channel Store
Family restrooms
Gymboree
Ice-skating rink
Limited, Too
Noah's Ark

Nursing rooms
Sonic
Stride Rite Shoes
Stroller rental

TANGER OUTLET MALL

I-20 and Hwy. 34, Exit 501, 301
Tanger Dr., Terrell, Texas
Website: www.tangeroutlet.com

Bass Company Store
Book Warehouse
Claire's
Gap
Levi's
OshKosh B'Gosh
Reebok

TOWN EAST MALL

Town East Blvd. at LBJ Fwy.
(I-635), Mesquite, Texas
(972) 270-2363
Website: www.towneast.com

abercrombie
BabyGap and GapKids
B. Dalton Bookseller
Champs
Charlotte Russe
Children's Place
Claire's
Cyber Zone
Dallas Cowboys Pro Shop
Disney Store
Game Stop

Gymboree
Journeys Kidz
Kid's Foot Locker
Limited, Too
Pet Depot
Picture People
Stride Rite Shoes
Wacky Bear Factory

VALLEY VIEW CENTER

Preston Rd. at LBJ Fwy. (I-635),
Dallas, Texas (972) 661-2424
Website: www.shopvalleyview
center.com

AMC Movie Theater
Animal Krackers
Camp Valley View Kid's Club
Camp Valley View Soft Play Area
Champs
Claire's
Cyber Zone Arcade
Dallas Children's Museum
Disney Store
Food court
Game Stop
Gameworks
Kid's Foot Locker
Old Navy
Spotlight on Karaoke
Stride Rite
Surprise Gifts
Teddy Bear Depot
Waldenbooks

HOBBIES AND COLLECTIONS

In addition to the hobby and collection shops in the malls, some very
interesting and helpful shops are located all around the city. Two stores
with multiple locations that specialize in craft and hobby items but also
carry toys, party supplies, and a variety of other items are **Michaels** and
Hobby Lobby. Below are some more popular shops that have personnel
who are very interested in your hobby or collection and have some gen-
uine expertise to offer.

COLLECTIBLE TRAINS AND TOYS
10051 Whitehurst, Dallas, Texas
(214) 373-9469
 Trains and related items

DISCOUNT MODEL TRAINS
4641 Ratliff Ln., Addison, Texas
(972) 931-8135
 Trains and related items

BP'ERS CERAMICS
731 S. Sherman, Richardson,
Texas (972) 705-9754

ART-A-RAMA
1610 Avenue J, Plano, Texas
(972) 423-4554
7158 Main St., Frisco, Texas
(972) 423-4554
Website: www.art-a-rama.com

HOBBYTOWN USA
N.E. corner of Central (US 75)
and 8041 Walnut Hill, Dallas,
Texas (214) 987-4744
N.E. Corner of 3033 W. Parker
and Independence, Plano, Texas
(972) 758-7875

LONE STAR COMIC BOOKS, GAMES & TOYS
11661 Preston Rd., Dallas,
Texas (214) 373-0934 Website:
www.mycomicshop.com

MAGICLAND
11888 Marsh Ln., Dallas, Texas
(972) 241-9898

QUEEN OF HEARTS COSTUME & MAGIC SHOP
1032 E. 15th St. and Avenue K,
Plano, Texas (972) 578-1969

TEXAS R/C MODELERS
230 W. Parker, Ste. 180, Plano,
Texas (972) 422-5386

PAINT YER POTTERY
17194 Preston and Campbell,
N.E. corner, Dallas, Texas
(972) 248-0001 Website:
www.paintyerpottery.com

PURPLE GLAZE, INC.
6128 Berkshire, Preston Center,
Dallas, Texas (214) 987-1440

THE PURPLE CRAYON
Children's Art Studio, 1108 W.
Parker #130, S.W. corner of
Parker and Alma, Plano, Texas
(972) 516-4915

ARTZY SMARTZY
8440 Abrams Rd., #404 at
Royal, Dallas, Texas
(214) 341-0053
Website: www.artzysmartzy.com

THROUGH THE KEYHOLE
Miniatures and Dollhouses, 625
Preston Forest Shopping Center,
S.E. corner, Dallas, Texas
(214) 691-7467

FOR THE LOVE OF DOLLS
Madame Alexander, Play Dolls,
Collectibles, Furniture, and

Clothing, 4359 Lover's Ln.,
Dallas, Texas (214) 528-5683

Richardson, Texas
(972) 234-5500

THE ENCHANTED COTTAGE

Dolls, Bears, and Surprises, 202
N. Greenville at Tyler,

HOME DEPOT KIDS WORKSHOP

Saturdays; multiple locations

COOKING CLASSES

Central Market, Dallas (214) 361-5754
Sur la Table, Dallas (214) 219-4404
Viking Culinary Arts Center, Dallas (214) 526-3942

TOY STORES AND LEARNING STORES

Most children are willing to take time out from whatever they are doing for a trip to the toy store. The aisles of Toys R Us are almost over-
whelming with their array of games, dolls, skates, books, bicycles,
school and party supplies, and other toys, as well as many items for ba-
bies and preschoolers. Toys R Us has several locations around Dallas.
Some of the other toy stores listed below are also not located in the
malls and often carry popular toys, as well as some challenging and educational toys, collectible items, and nature-related projects. Nature
stores, museum gift shops, and bookstores listed earlier in this chapter
often have some fascinating toys to help children learn more about the
world around them.

US TOY

1927 E. Belt Line at Josey,
Carrollton, Texas
(972) 418-1860

LEARNING EXPRESS

6818 Snider Plaza, Dallas, Texas
(214) 696-4876

Willow Bend Market, 5964 W.
Parker Rd. #120, Plano, Texas
(972) 473-8697

4760 Preston Rd. #226, Frisco,
Texas (214) 387-8697

4900 Eldorado Pkwy. #148,
McKinney, Texas
(972) 542-8697

Website:
www.learningexpress.com

LAKESHORE LEARNING STORE

13846 Dallas Pkwy., Dallas,
Texas (972) 934-8866 Website:
www.lakeshorelearningstore.com

TOYS UNIQUE

5600 W. Lover's Ln. #130,
Dallas, Texas (214) 956-8697

PARTY SUPPLIES

Sometimes nothing else will do for your child's birthday but the face of his or her favorite character on invitations and party plates. A wide assortment of paper goods, decorations, party favors, and invitations may be found at the area's stores devoted solely to helping you organize a fun and hassle-free party. Party Universe, Party City, Michaels, and Hobby Lobby have multiple locations around the city. Other favorite party suppliers are listed below.

PAPERIE & COMPANY

5331 E. Mockingbird #170, Mockingbird Station, Dallas, Texas (214) 821-8811

PARTY BAZAAR

4435 W. Lovers Ln., Dallas, Texas (214) 528-4795

THE PARTY PLACE

Preston Center, Dallas, Texas (214) 696-4550

THE SOCIAL BEE

5960 W. Parker Rd. #256, S.E. corner at Tollway, Plano, Texas (972) 781-0151

FLEA MARKETS AND TRADE DAYS

CANTON FIRST MONDAY TRADE DAYS

P.O. Box 245, Hwy. 19, Canton, Texas 75103 (903) 567-6556
Website: www.firstmondaycanton.com

The tradition of trading and swapping goods and animals began at the turn of the century in Canton around the courthouse in the square. Farmers and vendors would come on the first Monday when the court was in session. The popularity of the trade day outgrew its surroundings, so in 1965 it was moved to a location a little north of town that could accommodate the crowds and provide 100 acres for vendors. Be prepared for a great deal of walking. Mobility scooter rentals: $7/hour. No admission fee. Parking fee.

Hours: Canton Trade Days are Thursday to Sunday before the first Monday of every month, 7 AM until dark, rain or shine. Some of the vendors are covered.

Directions: Take I-20E about sixty miles. Exit on Hwy. 19 or FM 859 and go about one mile south.

THIRD MONDAY TRADE DAYS

4550 University Dr., McKinney, Texas (972) 562-5466
Website: www.tmtd.com

Both indoor and outdoor treasures abound at the nearly 800-booth flea market in McKinney. This market is smaller than Canton. No admission fee. Parking fee.

Hours: Friday, Saturday, Sunday preceding the third Monday of each month, 9 AM to 4 PM.

Directions: Hwy. 380 (W. University), two miles west of Hwy. 75.

TRADERS VILLAGE AND RV PARK

2602 Mayfield Rd., Grand Prairie, Texas 75052 (972) 647-2331
Website: www.tradersvillage.com

More than 1,800 dealers set up shop in the 106-acre flea market every Saturday and Sunday. Traders Village also has great festival foods, kiddie rides, and arcade games. Special events include the Prairie Dog Chili Cook-off in April and the National Championship Indian Powwow on the weekend after Labor Day, as well as other family activities. This market is not like Canton. Most of the vendors sell new, inexpensive products. There are few craft items. No admission fee. Parking fee.

Hours: 8 AM until dark.

Directions: Traders Village is located just off Hwy. 360 on Mayfield, one mile north of I-20 or five miles south of I-30. RV Park: (972) 647-8205.

HOTEL HIATUS

If your family enjoys staying in hotels, letting someone else cook and make beds, and lounging by the pool (or splashing wildly in it) but hates the long rides in the car that it often takes to reach vacation spots, try a weekend at one of our local hotels. Sometimes discount rates are available because the business folks have flown home and the rooms are empty and waiting. If it is winter, pick one with an indoor pool, such as the Embassy Suites Hotel–Market Center or the one by Dallas Love Field, both of which also have rooms with refrigerators, ranges, and two televisions. Others with indoor pools include Intercontinental Dallas, Adam's Mark Hotel, Holiday Inn Select North Dallas, Sheraton Suites Market Center. Many even offer complimentary breakfast.

Some are within walking distance of major attractions, and others, like the Westin by the Galleria, are attached to shopping centers. The Galleria has an ice rink and wonderful shops, and the Crescent is on the trolley line to the Arts District. In Las Colinas, the Omni Mandalay is on the canal, which winds by the famous Mustangs sculpture. Not far away are the Las Colinas Equestrian Center and the Movie Studios at Las Colinas.

Sunday brunch at the hotels is a family treat. What appears to be acres of beautifully displayed breakfast and lunch dishes are bound to encourage even the pickiest eaters.

Hotels with scrumptious Sunday brunch include Wyndham Anatole, the Crescent Court, Doubletree Hotels at Campbell Center and at Lincoln Center, the Mansion on Turtle Creek, and Antares in the tower at Hyatt Regency Reunion. Watch the weekend newspapers around holidays for other special meals and surprise visits from characters like the Easter Bunny.

HYATT REGENCY AT REUNION

300 Reunion Blvd., Dallas, Texas 75207-4498 (214) 651-1234
Website: www.dallasregency.hyatt.com

One of the favorite landmarks of the downtown skyline that children love to spot, especially at night, is the ball atop Reunion Tower. The multifaceted glass facade of the hotel reflects the growing downtown area and fantastic Texas's sunsets. Children enjoy riding the glass-fronted elevator up fifty stories whether or not they are treated to lunch at **Antares**, the revolving restaurant with a panoramic view of the city. At night the dome dances in a computer-operated light show. Inside the hotel is an eighteen-story atrium, an interesting mineral ball, and more glass elevators. Just outside the hotel are fountains cascading into a serene pool. Those staying at the Hyatt have access to the outdoor swimming pool, three tennis courts, the jogging track, the health club, and four restaurants. Reunion Arena, which is also part of the complex, is home to the Dallas Sidekicks, ice-skating performances, concerts, circuses, and a variety of other entertainment. Reunion is so named because of its location at the sight of an early settlement, so it is part of a historic district that includes Union Station next door. Union Station, once a thriving railway station, now is the site of a DART rail stop, Trinity Railway Express, and Amtrak.

GAYLORD TEXAN RESORT AND CONVENTION CENTER

1501 Gaylord Trail, Grapevine, Texas 76051

Toll free: (866) 782-7897

Website: www.gaylordhotels.com/gaylordtexan

Opened in 2004 by the owners of Nashville's Opryland Hotel, the Gaylord Resort, located on the southern tip of Lake Grapevine, is a $328 million luxury hotel. A striking four-acre indoor atrium features familiar elements of the Texas landscape, such as Texas limestone and lush native plants, as well as waterfalls and a babbling brook. A Lone Star, which can be seen from airplanes flying over, tops off the atrium. Amenities include an indoor lap pool and an outdoor pool, four restaurants, shops, jogging and biking trails, workout facilities, and an indoor entertainment complex. Sections of the hotel have different Texas themes, such as the oil boom. A nine-story oil derrick is the showpiece of that area. Visitors also have access to the Cowboys Golf Club and water sports on Lake Grapevine. Nearby are Dallas/Ft. Worth International Airport, Grapevine Outlet Mall, and Bass Pro Shops.

RESTAURANTS WITH MORE

Dallas has so many restaurants that a family could easily eat out every night without dining in the same restaurant twice. The staple foods for children, such as pizza, hamburgers, and fried chicken strips, are readily available as are Dallas's famous Tex-Mex and many other delicious ethnic foods. But some of the area restaurants don't just satisfy hunger; they also entertain with the addition of small rides, music, arcades, play areas, and costumed characters.

When asking the very young where they would like to go for lunch, the first reaction is likely to be McDonald's, Braum's, or Burger King because of the soft-floored play areas with slides and other toys to play on, as well as little prizes to take home if you buy the child's meal. Some Burger Kings and McDonald's also have indoor play parks. However, as children grow older, they notice that in addition to these great restaurants, Dallas has many others designed with their entertainment in mind. They also are good places for birthday parties.

PIZZA AND MORE

CHUCK E. CHEESE'S PIZZA

Arlington (817) 861-1561

Garland (972) 681-1385

Irving (972) 256-1600

Richardson (972) 234-8778

Dallas (972) 392-1944

Rides, video games, music

CRYSTAL'S PIZZA

930 W. Airport Fwy., Irving, Texas (972) 579-0441

Arcade, room to show a team video

MR. GATTI'S PIZZA

5941 Greenville Ave., Dallas, Texas (214) 691-2222

1305 Promenade Center, Coit at Belt Line, Richardson, Texas (972) 783-2222

Video games

PETER PIPER PIZZA PARLOR

951 W. Centerville Rd., Garland, Texas (972) 279-0200

729 W. Jefferson, Oak Cliff, Dallas, Texas (214) 943-6582

9480 Webb Chapel Rd., Dallas, Texas (214) 366-2600

Video games

PLANET PIZZA

3000 Custer Rd., S.E. corner, Plano, Texas (972) 985-7711

Indoor rides, soft play

HAMBURGERS, CHICKEN, STEAKS, AND MORE

BALL'S HAMBURGERS

4343 W. Northwest Hwy. at Midway, Dallas, Texas (214) 352-2525

3404 Rankin in Snider Plaza, Dallas, Texas (214) 373-1717

Sports theme, TV, video games

BENIHANA

7775 Banner Dr., Dallas, Texas (972) 387-4404

Food cooked at your table with a flourish, pricey

DAVE & BUSTER'S

10727 Composite, Dallas, Texas (214) 353-0620

Walnut Hill at Central Expwy., Dallas, Texas (214) 361-5553

1202/2220 Stonebriar Centre, Frisco, Texas (214) 387-0915

Large arcade; redeem prizes; they insist that you accompany each child

THE DREAM CAFE

2800 Routh St. at the Quadrangle, Dallas, Texas (214) 954-0486

5100 Belt Line Rd., Addison, Texas (972) 503-7326

Small playground area

FUDDRUCKER'S

5500 Greenville, Dallas, Texas (214) 360-0146

4520 Frankford Rd., Dallas, Texas (972) 818-3833

Video games

HARD ROCK CAFE

2601 McKinney Ave., Dallas, Texas (214) 855-0007

Rock memorabilia, loud music, souvenir store

JOE'S CRAB SHACK

10250 E. Technology Blvd., Near Loop 12-35E split and Lombardy, Dallas, Texas

(214) 654-0909

2001 No. Lamar, West End,
Dallas, Texas (214) 220-0404

Locations in Addison, Mesquite, Lewisville, and Plano. Outdoor playground, loud music; go early to avoid a large crowd

MAGIC TIME MACHINE

5003 Belt Line, Addison, Texas
(972) 980-1903

Costumed waitpersons, unique dining rooms

THE PURPLE COW

110 Preston Royal Shopping
Center, Dallas, Texas
(214) 373-0037

Famous for purple milkshake, hot pimento cheese sandwich

SLIDER AND BLUES

8517 Hillcrest at Northwest
Hwy., Dallas, Texas

(214) 696-8632

3033 W. Parker Rd., Plano,
Texas (972) 696-8632

Video games

TRAIL DUST STEAKHOUSE

10841 Composite, Dallas, Texas
(214) 357-3862

21717 LBJ Fwy. (I-635),
Mesquite, Texas
(972) 289-5457

Casual family-style seating, country music, no ties, long slide; bring socks

WHITE ROCK YACHT CLUB

7530 E. Grand at Gaston,
Dallas, Texas (214) 328-FUNN

Video games, playground, volleyball, very casual

WILD ABOUT HARRYS

3113 Knox St., Dallas, Texas
(214) 520-3113

Great hot dogs, cold custard

COOK YOUR OWN

MELTING POT

4900 Belt Line, Addison, Texas
(972) 960-7027

Fondue

SIMPLY FONDUE

2108 Lower Greenville, Dallas,
Texas (214) 827-8878

Older children cook chicken, dip fruit at table, pricey

DINNER THEATER

MEDIEVAL TIMES DINNER TOURNAMENT

2021 Stemmons at Market Center, Dallas, Texas (214) 761-1800

Return to the age of chivalry and knighthood as you come to Medieval Times Dinner & Tournament. As you feast on a sumptuous four-course banquet, you will witness feats of skill and daring adventure. See the beautiful Andalusian stallions dance and the graceful falcon soar. Cheer as six brave knights compete in the Tournament Royale, a joust and combat to determine the true champion of the castle. Call for reservations or group discounts.

THE POCKET SANDWICH THEATER

5400 E. Mockingbird, east of Central Expwy., Dallas, Texas (214) 821-1860 Website: www.pocketsandwich.com

Dine on sandwiches, nachos, and so forth, while watching the fun at Pocket Sandwich Theater. A variety of performances are scheduled, but the favorites seem to be the melodramas (popcorn available to throw at the villain) and spoofs. Thursdays through Sundays.

COMMUNITY COLLEGES

The Dallas County Community College District offers both credit and noncredit courses for adults, but it is also a place for children. Each college has a different program, but most offer a few classes during the school year and a wide variety of classes and day camps in the summer. The classes vary according to interest and the availability of instructors. If the college has a drama department, there will probably be some plays for the family included, and some of them are free. Each campus also has literary and music festivals, art exhibits, guest lecturers, and sports events. Some campuses have mailing lists to which community members may be added by calling Student Programs or Continuing Education. If the college that you are interested in does not mail out, then stop by those offices and pick up their schedule of events periodically. Listed below are the colleges and numbers to call for continuing education classes and camps for kids. Most classes are during the summer months.

BROOKHAVEN

3939 Valley View Ln., Farmers Branch, Texas 75244 (972) 860-4600

Theater box office: (972) 860-4118

CEDAR VALLEY

3030 N. Dallas Ave., Lancaster, Texas 75134 (972) 860-8210

EASTFIELD

3737 Motley, Mesquite, Texas 75150 (972) 860-7113
   Theater

EL CENTRO

Downtown: Main and Lamar, Dallas, Texas 75202 (214) 860-2147
   Some children's theater productions

MOUNTAIN VIEW

4849 W. Illinois Ave., Dallas, Texas 75211 (214) 860-8680

NORTH LAKE

5001 N. MacArthur Blvd., Irving, Texas 75038 (972) 273-3360

RICHLAND COLLEGE

12800 Abrams Rd., Dallas, Texas 75243 (972) 238-6144
   Pretty trail around pond, ducks, tree farm, horticulture area, theater

3. PERFORMING ARTS FOR CHILDREN

Although all of us are not blessed with a beautiful singing voice, an unfailing sense of rhythm, limber joints, and the ability to convincingly assume the personality of a character in a play, we are able to sit back at a performance and appreciate the talents of others and leave with the feeling that we are better for it whether the music is opera or opry, the play *Romeo and Juliet* or *Snow White*. Encouraging creative expression in children is an important part of parenting. The arts in the Dallas area have numerous avenues to help parents introduce their children to many types of theater, music, and dance. Opportunities for children to attend stimulating classes and become performers themselves are available in all of the arts to help children develop skills and self-confidence. Performing-arts festivals held throughout the year enable families to relax together and to be thoroughly entertained by live performances, far away from televisions and video games.

In the Friday "Guide" section of the *Dallas Morning News*, notices are given of performances, visual arts presentations, and festivals for families. The website, www.guidelive.com, gives the name, location, phone, price, and date of current productions. A very similar site, www.kidsmetroplex .com/theculart.html, is tailored for local kids.

Also a good source for Dallas arts and cultural organizations is the website of the **Dallas Office of Cultural Affairs** at www.dallasculture .org, which lists links for public art, cultural centers, performance organizations, and events. The **Sammons Center for the Arts** is home to various nonprofit performing-arts groups, and www.sammonsartscenter.org provides helpful links. The downtown **Arts District Friends** provide an Events Calendar at www.artsdistrict.org, or you may call (214) 953-1977. A very useful site for teachers, schools, and parents is **Dallas ArtsPartners** at www.dallasartspartners.org, a collaboration between Dallas Independent School District, Dallas Office of Cultural Affairs, Young Audiences of North Texas, Jewish Community Center FamiliArts, A.R.T.S. for People, and more than sixty additional cultural and community arts agencies.

If parents are not sure if a performance is appropriate for their children, they should call the performing-arts group and ask what ages would most enjoy the performance. Many arts organizations and performing-arts centers have mailing lists and websites that can keep you up to date on their schedules. Usually discounts are given for children, students with ID, and groups. Some performances are free. A matinee is a good time to introduce younger children to classical music and dance because the atmosphere is more informal. Shorter performances are often presented at the Dallas Museum of Art, Texas Discovery Gardens, and libraries. Many of the performing-arts groups have outreach programs that allow them to perform in schools, and some of the Dallas County Community Colleges and other area colleges include children's theater in their season. Listed below are some of the major performing-arts centers in the area that include performances for families. Your chamber of commerce or visitors center can give you the phone numbers of performing-arts groups in your community.

Tickets for many performances may be purchased through **Ticketmaster** at (214) 373-8000 or Metro (972) 647-5700, through Arts Line at (214) 631-ARTS or (817) 467-ARTS, or by visiting www.ticketmaster.com.

ADDISON THEATRE CENTRE

15650 Addison at Mildred, Addison, Texas
(972) 450-6232 Website: www.watertowertheatre.org

ARTS DISTRICT THEATRE

2401 Flora, Dallas, Texas
(214) 922-0427 Website: www.dallastheatercenter.org

ARTCENTRE THEATRE

1039 E. 15th St., Plano, Texas
(972) 423-7809

DALLAS CONVENTION CENTER

650 S. Griffin, Dallas, Texas
(214) 939-2700

GRANVILLE ARTS CENTER

Garland Performing Arts Center, 300 N. 5th St., Garland, Texas
(972) 205-2780
Tickets: (972) 205-2790

DALLAS THEATER CENTER

3636 Turtle Creek Blvd., Dallas, Texas (214) 526-8210 Website: www.dallastheatercenter.org

SAMMONS CENTER FOR THE ARTS

3630 Harry Hines, Dallas, Texas
(214) 520-7788 Website: www.sammonsartscenter.org

MAJESTIC THEATRE

1925 Elm, Dallas, Texas
(214) 880-0137 Website: www.dsmmanagementgroup.com

MEYERSON SYMPHONY CENTER

2301 Flora, Ste. 300, Dallas, Texas (214) 670-3600 Website: www.dallassymphony.com

IRVING ARTS CENTER

3333 N. MacArthur, Irving, Texas (972) 252-ARTS, (972) 252-7558
Website: www.ci.irving.tx.us/arts

LATINO CULTURAL CENTER

2600 Live Oak, Dallas, Texas
(214) 670-3320

MEADOWS SCHOOL OF THE ARTS

SMU Hillcrest and Binkley,
Dallas, Texas (214) 768-2880
Tickets: (214) 768-ARTS
Website: www.meadows.smu.edu

MUSIC HALL

Fair Park, 1st St. and Parry,
Dallas, Texas (214) 565-1116
Website:
www.dsmmanagementgroup.org

POCKET SANDWICH THEATER

400 E. Mockingbird, Dallas,
Texas (214) 821-1860 Website:
www.pocketsandwich.com

NOKIA LIVE!

1001 Next Stage Dr., Grand
Prairie, Texas (972) 854-5050
Website: www.nokialive.com

THEATRE ARLINGTON

305 W. Main, Arlington, Texas
(817) 275-7661 Website:
www.theatrearlington.org

MESQUITE ARTS CENTER

1527 N. Galloway, Mesquite,
Texas (972) 216-8122, (972)
216-6444

SMIRNOFF AMPHITHEATER

Fair Park, Dallas, Texas (214)
421-1111

THEATRE THREE

2800 Routh St. at the
Quadrangle, Dallas, Texas (214)
871-3300 Website:
www.theatre3dallas.com

EISEMANN CENTER FOR PERFORMING ARTS

2351 Performance Dr.,
Richardson, Texas (972) 744-
4600 Website:
www.eisemanncenter.com

DALLAS CHILDREN'S THEATER

Rosewood Center for Family
Arts, 5938 Skillman, Dallas,
Texas (214) 740-0051 Website:
www.dct.org

AMERICAN AIRLINES CENTER

2500 Victory Ave., Dallas, Texas
75207 (214) 222-3687,
(214) 665-4200

DANCE

One good source for keeping up with dance-related activities in the Metroplex is through the Dance Council publication *Dance* and their at www.thedancecouncil.org. The Dance Council number is (214) 219-2290. Memberships are available.

ANITA N. MARTINEZ BALLET FOLKLORICO DANCE STUDIO

4422 Live Oak, Dallas, Texas 75204 (214) 828-0181
Website: www.anmbf.org

The performance season for this professional Hispanic dance company runs from May through September and includes both public and private performances. Some dancers also teach in the Anita M. Martinez Ballet Folklorico Academy and train children six years of age and up to perform regional folk dances of Mexico.

DALLAS BLACK DANCE THEATRE

2627 Flora St., Dallas, Texas 75201 (214) 871-2376

The Dallas Black Dance Theatre, a modern contemporary dance company, has entertained local, national, and international audiences since 1976. During each performance season, they schedule three major concerts at the Majestic Theatre. It also performs in the September *Dallas Morning News* Dance Festival and the Imagination Celebration and for Young Audiences. As part of an outreach program, the company presents school-day matinee performances for area schools and other groups. In their **Dallas Black Dance Academy**, students age four to adult study dance on site at the Arts District facility; classes are offered off site for DISD, private schools, and other youth centers. Their repertory consists of jazz, modern, ethnic, and spiritual works by well-known choreographers.

Boys and girls ages nine to sixteen are offered the opportunity to audition for their summer dance program, providing the dancers have had some experience.

TEXAS BALLET THEATER

6845 Green Oaks Rd., Ft. Worth, Texas 76116
(817) 763-0207 Website: www.texasballettheater.org

This dance company, formerly the Ft. Worth Dallas Ballet, presents its season from October through May at both Ft. Worth Bass Hall and Dallas Music Hall. **Texas Ballet Theater School** enrolls students, age four and up, at its Ft. Worth location.

TITAS

3101 N. Fitzhugh Ave., Ste. 301, Dallas, Texas 75204
(214) 528-5576 Website: www.titas.org

TITAS is a nonprofit organization dedicated to bringing the best performances in **dance** and **music** to the Dallas area. To encourage families to attend performances together, TITAS offers $5 youth tickets for grades K through twelve, as well as 50-percent-off Student Rush tickets for college-age youths. Call the box office for details on these programs as well as series subscription information.

MUSIC AND CHORUS

TEXAS CHAMBER ORCHESTRA

P.O. Box 111333, Carrollton, Texas 75011-1333, Metro (817) 461-0318 Website: www.texaschamberorchestra.org

The Texas Chamber Orchestra is a nonprofit chamber symphony with a core group of seventeen professional string musicians. It performs four subscription concerts in the cities of Carrollton, Farmers Branch, and Addison. In the city of Farmers Branch, the orchestra performs free concerts annually at the Christmas Tree Lighting Ceremony at City Hall and Dickens in the Park at the Historical Park. It also performs Kinder Concerts with backstage visits at the Farmers Branch Manske Library and at the Frankford Village Branch Library in Carrollton. There is no charge for these family concerts or for the annual Outdoor Labor Day Concert at the Perry Homestead Museum, 1509 N. Perry, Carrollton. Call the above number or check the city calendars to learn the dates and times of these family concerts.

THE CHILDREN'S CHORUS OF GREATER DALLAS

1928 Ross Ave., Dallas, Texas 75201 (214) 965-0491 Website: www.thechildrenschorus.com

The Children's Chorus of Greater Dallas offers Metroplex children the opportunity to experience musical artistry and excellence through choral singing in a group that reflects Dallas's diversity. This tuition-based ensemble includes fourth- through eighth-grade girls and boys with unchanged voices. Qualifications are a good voice, a good sense of pitch, and a commitment to regular attendance at rehearsals and performances. Auditions are held in March. Current membership is 250 children singing in four choirs. The chorus performs extensively in the area and tours both regionally and nationally.

DALLAS CHAMBER ORCHESTRA

P.O. Box 600954, Dallas, Texas 75360 (214) 321-1411 Website: www.dallaschamberorchestra.org

An award-winning orchestra of fifteen strings, the Dallas Chamber Orchestra presents a diverse repertoire and highlights local soloists and world-class artists in a comfortable and less formal atmosphere. The orchestra presents two concert series each season: the Traditional Series of five concerts and the Sunset at the Lake Series of six concerts. The Lake series is held at White Rock Lake's Dreyfus Club. Check the website for other North Dallas locations of the concerts.

DALLAS CLASSIC GUITAR SOCIETY

P.O. Box 190823, Dallas, Texas 75219 (214) 528-3733 Website: www.dallasguitar.org

Concert presenters of classical guitar and related forms, the Dallas Classic Guitar Society offers a Tuesday-evening series at Caruth Auditorium (tickets, $25; students $19), but the most family-oriented performances are their Saturday-afternoon concerts at the Dallas Museum of Art. About five or six of these 3 PM performances are held each year at $6 for adults, $4 for students. The outreach program for schools, nursing homes, and churches, called Guitar in the Community, reaches more than 50,000 people yearly. It also performs at festivals, such as the Imagination Celebration and Artfest. The society also presents concerts at the Meyerson and the Majestic, which cost from $25 to $75. A list of guitar teachers will be provided upon request. **GuitarZone** is a spring guitar competition for young artists age eighteen and under to display talents and be evaluated. Certificates are awarded with a grade that indicates achievement, similar to UIL (University Interscholastic League) competition.

DALLAS JAZZ ORCHESTRA

P.O. Box 743875, Dallas, Texas 75374 (214) 521-8816

Office: Sammons Center for the Arts, 3636 Harry Hines Blvd., Dallas, Texas 75219 Website: www.djo.org

The Dallas Jazz Orchestra, a twenty-piece big band, plays original and traditional big band jazz music. It performs regularly at The Village, 8310 Southwestern, and listeners high school age and older really enjoy attending. Once each July, the orchestra performs with DISD's Dallas Area Youth Orchestra and college groups at The Village. Families are more familiar with their free, summer, Sunday-afternoon performances at Lee, Samuell, and Kidd Springs parks. Several recordings are available.

A popular jazz event at the Sammons Center in the fall and spring is Sammons Jazz, the only regular, ongoing jazz performance series in the area featuring local jazz artists. Call ahead for tickets.

DALLAS/MUSIC

Snider Plaza, 3415 Milton, Dallas, Texas 75205 (214) 363-4980 Website: www.dallas-music.net

Dallas/Music has classes in piano, guitar, Suzuki flute, and Suzuki violin for ages four or five to adult. Classes for ages three months to kindergarten include Music, Mommy & Me, First Movement, and Wee Music Makers. Recitals, festivals, and other activities round out the music experience.

THE DALLAS SCHOOL OF MUSIC

2650 Midway Rd., Ste. 204, Carrollton, Texas 75006
(972) 380-8050 Website: www.dsminfo.com

The Dallas School of Music has been providing award-winning and innovative music education for both children and adults for more than a decade. Programs include voice, individual instruction on all instruments, infant and toddler classes, and group piano, as well as a variety of ensembles, Guitar Club, String Club, and Music League. These are a few of the courses designed by the staff of full-time, degreed music educators. Special summer camps, faculty concerts, art festivals, student showcases, and holiday recitals allow students and families to enjoy a wide variety of year-round activities. Many events are free and open to the public.

DALLAS SYMPHONY ASSOCIATION, INC.

Morton H. Meyerson Symphony Center, 2301 Flora St., Ste. 300, Dallas, Texas 75201 (214) 871-4000
Website: www.dallassymphony.com

The Dallas Symphony Orchestra (DSO) performs year-round in the internationally acclaimed Meyerson Symphony Center. In addition to Classical, Pops, and Summer Festival series, the DSO presents numerous concerts throughout the year for children and their families. The Ida M. Green Youth Concert Series features the DSO performing educational programs approximately forty-five-minutes in length. Sixteen daytime concerts are offered for children grades three to six. Eight concerts each year are presented for children in grades pre-K to two. The DSO also presents an annual high school concert featuring a side-by-side performance with the Greater Dallas Youth Orchestra.

In addition to the youth concert series, the Dallas Symphony offers numerous free concerts throughout the year. The summer concert series each April through June features free concerts in Dallas parks. Other free concerts in the Meyerson include the Sundayfest concerts as well as the annual Hispanic Festival Concert and the African American Festival Concert. For ticket information, please call (214) 692-0203 or check the website. The Kids Page of the website is audiovisual fun.

FINE ARTS CHAMBER PLAYERS

Sammons Center for the Arts, 3630 Harry Hines Blvd., Dallas, Texas 75219 (214) 520-2219 Website: www.fineartschamberplayers.org

The Fine Arts Chamber Players include musicians from the Dallas Symphony, the Dallas Opera, and music teachers who perform many free concerts annually. Several of these are in DISD elementary schools. Every Sunday afternoon in July, the players perform classical music designed for family entertainment at Fair Park's Texas Discovery Gardens. These free performances begin at 3 PM and end at 5 PM with one intermission.

A good format for children to be exposed to classical music in a more informal setting is the Bancroft Family Concerts Series in October and November and January through May. These concerts, held at the Dallas Museum of Art's Horchow Auditorium, begin at 3 PM and last for one hour. For the Love of Music is a twenty-minute preconcert that showcases young musicians. The doors open at 2:30 PM.

School children especially like the Dream Collectors, which is a performing group consisting of musicians and actors and featuring classical music, mime, masks, and storytelling in free forty-five-minute presentations for school groups.

GREATER DALLAS YOUTH ORCHESTRA ASSOCIATION, INC.

Sammons Center for the Arts, 3630 Harry Hines Blvd., Dallas, Texas 75219 (214) 528-7747 Website: www.gdyo.org

The Greater Dallas Youth Orchestra offers a wonderful opportunity for children to experience other children and youths performing music. The six orchestras perform a variety of concerts at various locations throughout the school year. Four concerts, performed at the Meyerson by the top orchestra, are two-hour symphony concerts similar to what you would experience in a Saturday-evening Dallas Symphony classical concert. They may be beyond the attention span of younger children but could be very inspiring for older elementary school–age children.

The afternoon concerts performed by the younger orchestras are accessible to all ages and can be "come and go" affairs depending on the child's attention span. Details about auditions and concerts are available on the website.

KINDERMUSIK, INTERNATIONAL

Changing locations in the Metroplex; Website: www.kindermusik.com

Kindermusik instructors lead a group of parents and children in fun, musical play that is designed to promote self-esteem, improve coordination and balance, and develop creative skills. Ages newborn to seven years old are included in Kindermusik classes. The classes may be held in private studios, music stores and studios, schools, community centers, churches, and other types of locations. Go to the website to find classes in your area.

MEADOWS SCHOOL OF THE ARTS

P.O. Box 750356, Southern Methodist University, Dallas, Texas 75275 (214) 768-ARTS Website: www.meadows.smu.edu

Meadows School of the Arts performances in music, dance, and theater are held at the Meadows School of the Arts. The *Dallas Morning News* Community Arts Calendar on Sunday lists performances, and Southern Methodist University has an arts line to call. Student presentations of classic, modern, and musical productions are usually held in the Caruth Auditorium, Bob Hope Theatre, and Margo Jones Theatre.

MUSIC MILL AMPHITHEATRE

2201 Road to Six Flags, Arlington, Texas 76010, Metro (817) 640-8900

Pop, country, gospel, and many other types of superstar concerts are enjoyed during Six Flags' summer season as well as throughout the year. Concert ticket prices are usually in addition to the park entrance fee.

RICHARDSON SYMPHONY ORCHESTRA

1131 Rockingham Ln., Ste. 110, Richardson, Texas 75080 (972) 234-4195 Website: www.richardsonsymphony.org

The Richardson Symphony Orchestra (RSO) usually holds six evening performances at Richardson's Eisemann Center. The orchestra also helps to sponsor the RSO/Lennox Young Artists Competition in January. Young musicians from all over the country come to compete in three categories, and the winners of the top honors perform with the RSO in the March concert. The Sounds of Freedom patriotic program is held annually in the spring in conjunction with the Richardson Wildflower Festival, and they also present Symphony Days for RISD third graders. The orchestra also offers free matinees for children and their families.

PLANO SYMPHONY ORCHESTRA

7317 Preston Rd., Plano, Texas (972) 473-7262 Website: www.planosymphony.org

The Plano Symphony Orchestra presents an orchestral series of four symphonies from January through March called Family Symphony Sundays at Plano's Courtyard Theater, 1509 Avenue H, and at the Eisemann Center for the Arts in Richardson. The symphony offers educational programs for elementary school–age children and supports the Collin County Young Artist Competition.

SMIRNOFF AMPHITHEATRE

3839 S. Fitzhugh at Fair Park, Dallas, Texas 75210 (214) 421-1111

The Smirnoff Amphitheatre presents concerts by popular musicians and singers year-round, but the summer season is a favorite. This outdoor theater can seat 20,000 people, and concessions are available. Tickets are available at Ticketmaster outlets or by calling (214) 373-8000 or (972) 647-5700; or call the Arts Line at (214) 631-ARTS or (817) 467-ARTS. Tickets may also be purchased on the web at www.ticketmaster.com.

SOUTH DALLAS CULTURAL CENTER

3400 S. Fitzhugh at Second Ave., Dallas, Texas 75210
(214) 939-2787

The South Dallas Cultural Center near Fair Park has a wide variety of activities for all ages and income groups. It provides a 100-seat black box theater; a visual arts gallery; studios for dance, two-dimensional arts, ceramics, printmaking, and photography; and a digital recording studio. Classes are available for children and adults. A summer program is included in the activities.

TEXAS BOYS CHOIR

3901 S. Hulen St., Ft. Worth, Texas 76109 (817) 924-1482
Website: www.texasboyschoir.org

Founded in 1946 in Denton, the Texas Boys Choir moved to Ft. Worth in 1957. The fifty-voice choir is the top-level choir of the Texas Boys Choir organization, and it performs both nationally and internationally. The Ft. Worth Academy of Fine Arts owns the campus, where both classes and some TBC performances are held. The academy has become a publicly funded charter coed school, with 350 students in grades three to twelve; it offers music, dance, and theater in conjunction with an academic core curriculum. The repertoire of the Texas Boys Choir includes early classical, sacred, folk, patriotic, international, and Broadway music.

TEXAS GIRLS CHOIR

4449 Camp Bowie, Ft. Worth, Texas 76107 (817) 732-8161
Website: www.texasgirlschoir.org

The 200-voice Texas Girls Choir has been an active performance group for more than thirty years. The talented girls, ages eight to twelve, audition to become members of the choir, which performs locally and also takes two tours each year, one primarily in the South and the other abroad. The concert choir includes approximately forty of the girls, and the remainder are in a preparatory choir. Choir members are drawn primarily from Tarrant, Dallas, Johnson, and Parker counties. Concerts are usually held in October, December, February, and May. Call for locations or look on the website.

OPERA

THE DALLAS OPERA
Campbell Centre 1, 8350 N. Central Exprwy., Ste. 210, LB 1-11, Dallas, Texas 75206 (214) 443-1043 Website: www.dallasopera.org

The Dallas Opera season, November through March, consists of approximately five operas with easy-to-read, English subtitles and an additional holiday presentation held at Fair Park's Music Hall. The Sunday matinee would be a good time for a family with older children to attend. One hour before the 2 PM performance on Saturday is Opera Overtures, in which background information about the opera is given. Call (214) 443-1000 for tickets, or visit the website. The **Puppet Opera Theater** visits more than sixty schools to present short puppet shows for students in grades K through three. Other school programs are offered to older students, such as the four student matinees each season, which introduce opera to more than ten thousand young people each year. The Dallas Opera also hosts two **summer opera camps** for kids who want to sing, write, design, or work in opera.

OPRY

The oprys in Texas should be on each country music lover's list of family entertainment. They are smaller but similar to Nashville's Grand Ole Opry. They provide great singers and bands and a wholesome, lively atmosphere, free from the smoke and liquor of honky-tonks. Concessions are provided, and some offer group rates and dinner and show combinations. Some recommend reservations. Dress casually and get ready for a toe-tappin' good time.

GARLAND OPRY
605 W. State St., Garland, Texas (972) 494-3835

The Big G Jamboree has been operating for more than twenty years. Eight bands rotate to provide country music entertainment on Saturdays at 8 PM. Occasionally, the opry performs at the Garland Granville Arts Center.

GRAPEVINE OPRY

300 S. Main St., Grapevine, Texas, Metro (817) 481-8733
Website: www.grapevineopry.com

Grapevine Opry, which has a lower floor and a balcony, is usually packed at its 7:30 PM. Saturday performance. Sometimes, talented youngsters appear to sing, clog, and fiddle. The second half of the program is often arranged around themes, such as Waltz Across Texas, gospel songs, and patriotic songs. Dinner and show combinations for groups are offered. Occasionally, the singers and musicians in Grapevine will rotate with performers from other oprys. Gospel music is presented on the fourth Friday of each month. A concession stand is available. Reservations are made by telephone. If you must cancel, do so twenty-four hours in advance, or the opry will keep your money.

PUPPETRY

The antics of puppets have entertained all ages for hundreds of years. In the Dallas area, the public libraries often present free puppet shows for children, and the Dallas Opera's Puppet Opera Theater performs for elementary school children at their schools. Shopping malls, such as Northpark, sometimes offer December puppet shows, and groups who offer series for children often include puppet shows. KIDSarts, the summer program of the Irving Arts Center, sometimes offers classes in puppetry.

Three companies are very active in the Dallas area, performing in theaters, cultural-arts centers, colleges, schools, and other private venues. **Slappy's Puppet Playhouse** is on the third level of the Galleria. Call (214) 369-4849 or look online at www.slappysplayhouse.com. **Dallas Puppet Theater** may be contacted at www.puppetry.org or (214) 515-0004. **Kathy Burks Theatre of Puppetry Arts** may be contacted at www.flash.net/~saltee. Puppet shows are sometimes held at the Rosewood Center for Family Arts, home of the Dallas Children's Theater.

THEATER

WATERTOWER THEATRE AT ADDISON THEATRE CENTRE

15650 Addison Rd., Addison, Texas 75001 (972) 450-6232
Website: www.watertowertheatre.com

The WaterTower Theatre offers a season of five productions and two holiday shows at the Addison Theatre Centre. A yearly favorite is the Out of the Loop Festival of theater, dance, music, and visual arts. For kids, they have a summer **musical theater camp**.

CAPERS FOR KIDS

12306 Park Central Dr., Dallas, Texas 75251 (972) 661-2787
Website: www.capersforkids.com

Capers for Kids, located just north of Medical City, is an educational creative-arts school that offers a faculty of degreed teachers who teach classes in drama and the visual arts Monday through Saturday for nine months to children ages three to eighteen. It also works in private schools in the area with mainstream students and also those with learning differences. The half-day summer arts camps are held in the morning and afternoon on Monday to Friday for two-week sessions.

THE CLASSICS: THEATER AND ART FOR CHILDREN

3013 W. 15th St., Plano, Texas 75075 (972) 596-8948
Box office: (972) 596-0055
Website: www.classicsplano.org

The Classics series features six performances by national and international companies for family audiences. The performances are usually held at the Eisemann Center on Sunday afternoons. Classes are offered in art, music, and theater for ages three to fourteen.

CREATIVE ARTS THEATRE AND SCHOOL

1100 W. Randol Mill Rd., Arlington, Texas 76012, Metro (817) 265-8512 Website: www.creativearts.org

The Creative Arts Theatre is a youth theater that includes classes for age four to grade twelve in dance, acting, creative dramatics, technical theater, and more. The theater presents Spotlight shows in the main season. Three shows plus a fundraiser are presented in the summer. A special two-week summer program is offered for out-of-town, gifted students. Regular summer classes are held in two-week sessions.

DALLAS CHILDREN'S THEATER, INC

5938 Skillman St., Dallas, Texas 75231 (214) 978-0110
Box office: (214) 740-0051
Website: www.dct.org

The Dallas Children's Theater presents exciting professional theater performances by actors with advanced degrees and extensive experience in its new home, Rosewood Center for Family Arts. The group also performs at El Centro College Performance Hall at Main and Market in downtown Dallas. Most of the plays have an intermission, and drinks and snacks may be purchased. Season tickets are also available. In addition, on the second Friday-night performance of each show, signing is offered for the hearing impaired. **School matinees** are available to area schools, and **year-round classes** are open to ages three and up. Three summer sessions last for two weeks each and feature a performance on Saturday. Group discounts for eight or more are offered on weekends.

The summer **Teen Conservancy** for ages twelve and up gives teens the opportunity to work with professional actors, directors, and teachers to improve their acting skills. Movie-making skills are also included in the lineup of courses. The conservancy usually offers a fun **Family Fall Festival** on a Saturday in October.

THE DALLAS SUMMER MUSICALS

The box office: 542 Preston Royal Shopping Center, Dallas, Texas 75230 (214) 691-7200 (no phone sales)

Ticketmaster phone orders: (214) 631-ARTS (2787) or www.ticketmaster.com

Administrative offices: The Music Hall at Fair Park, 909 First Ave., Dallas 75210 (Mailing address: P.O. Box 710336, Dallas, Texas 75371) (214) 421-5678 Website: www.dallassummermusicals.org

The Dallas Summer Musicals is a nonprofit organization dedicated to bringing the very best of American musical theater and Broadway shows to the Dallas area. Since 1941, it has produced a summer season of entertainment, performing outdoors for ten years, then moving indoors to the air-conditioned Music Hall in 1951. It also presents the **Broadway Contemporary Series** in the winter at both the Music Hall and the Majestic Theatre.

Ticketmaster outlets are located in Foley's and in the lobby of the Majestic Theatre.

Of special interest to children and parents is the **Kids Club**, a free-to-join club that rewards kids with free events and prizes for coming to the shows. Also, the **Dallas Summer Musicals School of Musical Theatre**, located in the Majestic Theatre, is a school for ages twelve to adult. It sometimes offers free special-showcase performances.

For more information about the school, call (214) 969-SHOW or visit the website above and click "DSM School of Musical Theatre."

DALLAS THEATER CENTER

3636 Turtle Creek, Dallas, Texas 75219-5598 (214) 252-3918
Website: www.dtcinfo.org

The Dallas Theater Center opened its doors in 1959, and it continues to hold performances in the Kalita Humphreys Theater, designed by Frank Lloyd Wright, and in the **Arts District Theater** at 2401 Flora. Usually, the theater center kicks off each season with an evening festival in late August called **Neighborhood Nights**. A family favorite during the regular season, which runs from September through April, is the annual performance of *A Christmas Carol*. See **Tours of the Working World** for information about touring the theater, rehearsal halls, and costume shop. The Dallas Theater Center also offers year-round classes in theater for children ages four to eighteen, which are taught by professional actors and teachers with extensive theater experience. In **The Lab**, these students have the opportunity to audition for children's parts in the professional productions, such as *A Christmas Carol*. The teen company does a summer production. Call (214) 252-3916.

HARTT AND SOUL STUDIO

4105 Brook Tree, Dallas, Texas 75287 (972) 788-1150 Website: www.harttandsoul.com

Located between the Dallas North Tollway and Midway, Hartt and Soul Studio offers exciting classes in acting, improv, on-camera/auditions, and master scene work for ages four to adult.

It offers one-on-one private coaching, small-group sessions, summer camps, and one- and two-day weekend workshops.

GARLAND CIVIC THEATRE'S CHILDREN ON STAGE

108 N. 6th St., Garland, Texas 75040 (972) 485-8884

Box office: (972) 487-2159

Website: www.garlandcivictheatre.org

Young people audition for and perform in the plays produced by Children on Stage. Two shows, such as *Dorothy Meets Alice* and *Joseph and the Amazing Technicolor Dreamcoat*, are presented in the summer, one in the fall, and another in the spring. These performances are at the Performing Arts Center in downtown Garland on the east side of the town square. Theater classes are offered for ages eight to eighteen in the fall and spring with two-week camps held during the summer.

The Garland Civic Theatre's main season is listed on the website, or you may call (972) 485-8884 for production titles and dates.

JUNIOR PLAYERS

4054 McKinney Ave., Dallas, Texas 75204 (214) 526-4076
Website: www.juniorplayers.org

The Junior Players is the oldest children's theater group in Dallas. Its goal is to introduce children ages seven to eighteen to theater arts and to help them develop self-confidence and self-esteem through after-school, Saturday, and summer programs. Junior Players holds free summer camps at recreation centers and other locations in the area. During the summer, it also works with high school actors and the Shakespeare Festival of Dallas to present a Shakespearean play in late July or early August at Samuell-Grand's amphitheater. Call its office for specific dates and times.

KD STUDIO ACTORS CONSERVATORY

2600 N. Stemmons # 117, Dallas, Texas 75207 (877) 278-2283
Website: www.kdstudio.com

KD Studio offers classes for teens and children who want to learn the fundamentals of acting for film, TV commercials, and theater. The studio schedules eight-week Saturday courses for ages four to eleven, as well as teen classes on Saturday and weekdays. In addition, it offers **fashion and image** Saturday classes for ages seven to twenty-one. Acting classes are also available for adults.

MEADOWS SCHOOL OF THE ARTS

Community education: P.O. Box 750356, Dallas, Texas 75275-0356 (214) 768-3343

Twenty-four-hour online registration: www.meadows.smu.edu/communityed

Community Education offers noncredit classes for children and adults in the arts. Workshops and classes for children ages seven to seventeen are offered in musical theater and creative dramatics and more.

PLANO CHILDREN'S THEATRE

1301 Custer Rd., Ste. 810, Plano, Texas 75075 (972) 422-2575Website: www.planochildrenstheatre.com

The Plano Children's Theatre (PCT) is an active, nonprofit, educational theater that offers skill classes for children and teens age three to grade twelve in acting, creative drama, art, voice, and musical theater. The PCT also has production classes in which every child in the class gets a part in a play that is produced as a finale. In addition, PCT has a touring performance series for children that is performed by adults, as well as workshops and special holiday shows that are performed by adults and children together. Performances are usually Thursday to Sunday.

POCKET SANDWICH THEATRE

5400 E. Mockingbird, Dallas, Texas 75206 (214) 821-1860
Website: www.pocketsandwichtheatre.com

Many of the performances by the Pocket Sandwich Theatre are suitable for families, but if you have a question, just call the theater, and someone who is familiar with the play can discuss it with you. Melodramas, in which the audience can hiss, boo, cheer, and throw popcorn, are favorites for families and birthday parties. Performances are held Thursday, Friday, Saturday nights at 8 PM with food service open at 6:30 PM, and Sunday at 7 PM with food service open at 5:30 PM. There is table seating, and the optional menu consists of sandwiches, soup, salads, nachos, and individual pizzas. Prices for the plays are $6 to $14 depending on the evening you attend. A $2 discount is offered for seniors and children. The theater is located in the corner of the L-shaped shopping village. Reservations are recommended.

REPERTORY COMPANY THEATRE

2100 Promenade Center #2176, Richardson, Texas 75080
(972) 690-5029 Website: www.rctheatre.com

Repertory Company Theatre (RCT) is a nonprofit theater that has been producing quality family theater for the Dallas area for more than seventeen years. Each season, special weekday-morning performances are offered at reduced rates for area school groups. Performances are held at the Eisemann Theatre Centre, UTD Theatre, and RCT Theatre. Repertory Company's **School of Musical Theatre** offers year-round theater-arts education for all ages. Classes focus on all aspects of musical theater from entry-level classes to advanced programs and are taught by professional performers. RCT's **Arts in Education Classes** are available for school field trips.

TEATRO DALLAS

1331 Record Crossing Rd., Dallas, Texas 75235 (214) 689-6492

Teatro Dallas is dedicated to the presentation of theater that reflects the culture of Latino communities. It presents works by classical and contemporary playwrights and hosts the International Theater Festival.

Classes, taught in both English and Spanish, include dance, theater, improv, theater crafts, and makeup. The programs end with two presentations. Children's summer theater classes are for ages six to fifteen. Adult classes for ages sixteen and older are held in summer and winter.

THEATRE THREE

2800 Routh St. at the Quadrangle, Dallas, Texas 75201
(214) 871-3300 Website: www.theatre3dallas.com

Theatre Three has some performances each season that are suitable for families with older children. The theater occasionally presents a play for younger children, particularly during the summer. Education Zone is an outreach program that provides teachers with study guides for the season's productions and group discounts for matinees.

YOUNG ACTORS STUDIO AND PERFORMANCE CENTER

11496 Luna Rd. #G, Dallas, Texas 75234 (972) 401-2090
Website: www.youngactors.org

For more than sixteen years, the Young Actors Studio (YAS) has been encouraging young actors and actresses through classes that have an emphasis in television, film, and commercials. YAS offers programs for ages six to nineteen year-round, including classes, workshops, summer camps, and much more. The YAS offers a large amount of on-camera experience. With a sitcom set located inside the studio as well as state-of-the-art production equipment, each child can develop his or her individual talents. Courses are divided into two semesters during the school year.

ANNUAL CONCERTS, PERFORMANCES, AND FILM FESTIVALS

JANUARY

KidFilm, Angelica Theater. KidFilm is a film and video festival for kids sponsored by the USA Film Festival. It includes features, shorts, and animation, and offers tributes to greats in children's arts. Selections are viewed on Saturday and on Sunday afternoons. Admission fee. Call (214) 821-6300.

SBC Cotton Bowl Parade of Bands. Fair Park. An annual parade of bands from U.S. Call (214) 634-7525.

Dallas Dance Gathering. Booker T. Washington High School. Concerts featuring many local, national, and international freelance dancers and choreographers. Call (214) 925-1226.

FEBRUARY

Dallas Black Dance Cultural Awareness Series. Majestic Theatre. Call (214) 880-0137.

MARCH

North Texas Irish Festival. Fair Park. Showcase of Irish cultural arts, including lively Irish dancing and music. Call (214) 823-4370.

Texas Storytelling Festival. Denton Civic Center Park. An annual event with family folio, master storytellers weave their tales for audiences. Workshops. Call (940) 387-8336.

Hispanic Concert and Festival. Meyerson Symphony Center. Celebration of Hispanic heritage, including music and activities for families. Call (214) 692-0203.

African American Concert and Festival. Meyerson Symphony Center. Features cultural music contributions of African Americans and includes family activities. Call (214) 692-0203.

Dallas Video Festival. Angelica Theater and Dallas Museum of Art. Features more than 250 screenings of local, regional, and internationally produced programs.

Katy Trail/Knox St. Arts Festival. Art festival on Katy Trail off Knox between Travis and Abbot. Call (214) 522-0123.

APRIL

Lee Park Annual Easter Concert. Corner of Lemmon Ave. and Turtle Creek Blvd. A Dallas Symphony Association free performance is held annually at Lee Park. Families are invited to the park on Sunday afternoon for a picnic and music. Call (214) 692-0203.

Deep Ellum Art Festival. Dallas Deep Ellum, downtown. Music, visual arts, food. Call (214) 855-1881.

North Texas Jazz Festival. InterContinental Hotel Dallas, Addison, and UNT. Jazz artists performing in the area for a week. Call (972) 450-6221.

Main St. Fort Worth Arts Festival. Main St. in downtown Ft. Worth. A celebration of visual and performing arts. Call (817) 336-ARTS.

Scarborough Faire Renaissance Festival. Waxahachie. Opening this month and held on weekends through Memorial Day. Includes music, dancing, short theatrical performances. Call (972) 938-3247.

Denton Arts and Jazz Festival. Denton's Civic Center Park. Call (940) 565-0931.

Folklorico Festival. Annette Strauss Artist Square downtown. Two days with multiethnic artists sharing dancing, music, art, and food. Call (214) 788-0604.

USA Film Festival. Held in several theaters. Screenings of films from around the world and discussions with those who are involved in filmmaking. Call (214) 821-6300.

Art in the Square. Southlake Town Square. Spring family festival in visual and performing arts. Call (817) 421-6792.

MAY

Memorial Day Concert. Flag Pole Hill, E. Northwest Hwy. at Buckner Blvd. Free outdoor concert by Dallas Symphony Orchestra. Bring kids and a picnic. Call (214) 692-0203.

Kennedy Center Imagination Celebration. Old City Park. More than thirty arts-related organizations bring activities for children to this free event. Call (214) 421-5141.

Cottonwood Art Festival. Cottonwood Park, Richardson. Includes more than 200 artists, music, and children's activities. Call (972) 638-9116.

Wildflower! Arts and Music Festival. Richardson's Galatyn Park. Spring festival with music acts, arts and crafts, and children's entertainment. Call (972) 744-4581.

Asian Festival. Annette Strauss Artist Square, downtown. Features cultural music, dance, art, and more. Call (972) 241-8592.

Jazz Under the Stars. Dallas Museum of Art. Series of outdoor jazz concerts on Thursday nights, beginning at 8 PM. Call (214) 922-1200.

Artfest. Fair Park. For more than thirty years, Artfest has entertained with hundreds of artists and included great music and food. Call (214) 565-0200.

Mesquite Music Festival. Civic Expressions, City Lake Park and Mesquite Arts Complex, Mesquite. Music and theater performances on Friday and Saturday nights and an art fair and children's festival on Saturday. Groups participating usually include the Mesquite Community Theatre, Mesquite Civic Chorus, Mesquite Symphony Orchestra, and Mesquite Community Band. Call (972) 216-6444.

McKinney Art and Jazz Festival. In McKinney on the downtown square. Call (972) 562-6880.

Musicfest Concerts. In Lancaster in Heritage Park. A series of May concerts. Call (972) 227-1112.

JUNE, JULY, AND AUGUST

Basically Beethoven. Texas Discovery Gardens at Fair Park. The Fine Arts Chamber Players perform selections from Beethoven and other composers every Sunday in July at 2:30 PM. Call (214) 520-2219.

Garden of Music Evenings. Dallas Arboretum. Music on Thursdays at 7 PM in July. Call (214) 327-4901. Admission fee.

Dallas Jazz Orchestra. City Parks. These free concerts are held on Sunday afternoons at 3 PM at various city parks. Call (972) 644-8833.

Dallas Summer Musicals. Music Hall at Fair Park. The Dallas Summer Musicals presents spectacular dramas, comedies, Las Vegas–type shows, and many others in both matinee and evening performances. There are usually five plays in the summer, one during the state fair, and one in March. Call (214) 691-7200.

Jazz Under the Stars. Dallas Museum of Art. For more than ten years, the museum has provided entertainment for visitors with concerts each Thursday evening at 8 PM at the Ross Avenue Plaza. Call (214) 922-1200.

Patriotic Pops Concert. Las Colinas, Irving. The Irving Symphony Orchestra presents this free evening concert in Williams Square, site of the famous Mustangs sculpture. Lawn chairs, blankets, and picnics are encouraged, and fireworks follow the concert held on July 4. Call (972) 831-8818.

Shakespeare Festival of Dallas. Samuell-Grand Park Amphitheatre. Three of Shakespeare's plays are performed each June and July. Families may bring picnics and have dinner before the performance. Those with blankets and sand chairs sit closer to the front, while those with lawn chairs are nearer the back, but the sound system is excellent, and you will be able to hear and see no matter where you sit. Older children will enjoy the play more if they are familiar with the characters and plot before they attend. The gates open at 7 PM, and the play begins at 8:15 PM. There is an intermission, and the play ends around 11:15 PM. Most people bring a picnic supper, but concessions are available, as are T-shirts and other souvenirs. The park is located at 5808 E. Grand. Restrooms are provided, and bringing insect repellent is recommended. The amphitheatre is located behind Samuell-Grand Recreation Center and across from Tennyson Golf Course. A $7 donation is appreciated. Call (214) 559-2778.

The Sounds of Freedom. Richardson Symphony Orchestra. Usually held on the grounds of MCI, 2400 N. Glenville in Richardson, The Sounds of Freedom celebration is an evening of music and fireworks in mid-June. The gates open at 5:30 PM for those with lawn chairs and picnic dinners. Activities are planned for children, and the free concert begins at 8 PM. Concessions are available. Call (972) 234-4195.

Festival of Drums and Bugles. Lake Highlands High School Stadium, 9449 Church Rd. This lively performance festival by high school players is sponsored by the Lake Highlands High School Band Club annually on an evening in later July. Around seven groups from throughout the United States compete, and a clinic is held earlier in the afternoon. All seats are reserved.

Texas Scottish Festival and Highland Games. UTA's Maverick Stadium. Dance competitions, Celtic music, and games. Call (817) 654-2293.

Tejano Wednesdays. Annette Strauss Artist Square, downtown. A series of about five free concerts in July at 8 PM. Call (214) 800-5220.

Annual Festival of Independent Theatres. Bath House Cultural Center at White Rock Lake. An ongoing theater festival in July that features smaller theater companies. Call (214) 528-5576.

Summer Music Concert Series. Vista Ridge Amphitheater in Lewisville. Four July concerts. Call (972) 219-3550.

Summer Music Fest. Armstrong Park, Duncanville. Four July concerts. Call (972) 780-5086.

Dallas Morning News Dance Festival. Annette Strauss Artist Square, downtown. Late August, early September, featuring a free program of local professional dance companies. Call (214) 953-1977.

SEPTEMBER

Dallas Symphony Orchestra's Annual Gala. Meyerson Symphony Center. Music and song. Call (972) 692-0203.

TITAS Music & Dance Series Kickoff. McFarlin Auditorium, Southern Methodist University campus. Music and dance artists featured. Call (214) 528-5576.

Addison Oktoberfest. Addison Conference and Theatre Centre. Recreation of the festival in Munich with German entertainment and food. Call (800) 233-4766.

Greek Food Festival. Holy Trinity Greek Orthodox Church. Greek dancing, arts, and food. Call (972) 991-1166.

OCTOBER

Deep Ellum Film and New Music Festival. Deep Ellum venues and Lakewood Theater. Features international filmmakers and musicians. Call (214) 752-6741.

Harambee Festival. Martin Luther King Jr. Center. All day family festival. Call (214) 670-8355.

Vistas Film Festival. Angelica Theater. Hispanic film festival. Call (214) 826-9560.

StageFest. Annette Strauss Artist Square, downtown. Fundraiser and celebration of the performing arts. Outdoor family festival. Call (214) 953-1977.

American Indian Art Festival & Market. Annette Strauss Artist Square, downtown. Includes more than 150 documented American Indian visual and performing artists from Texas and other states. Call (214) 891-9640.

NOVEMBER

Texas Stampede. American Airlines Center. Combination of country music and rodeo. Call (214) 520-8874.

Dallas International Festival. Annette Strauss Artist Square, downtown. A free festival showcasing world music performances and dance from cultures represented in North Texas. Call (972) 458-7007.

Family Day. Meadows Museum at Southern Methodist University. Storytelling, art, dancing. Call (214) 768-2516.

DECEMBER

A Christmas Carol, Dallas Theater Center. This family favorite is presented each year at the Kalita Humphreys Theater or the Arts District Theater. Call (214) 526-8210. Many Metroplex theater companies perform this annual favorite.

Christmas Celebration Concerts, Meyerson Symphony Center. The Dallas Symphony Orchestra presents **Deck the Halls**, a magical afternoon of family fun focused on ages three to twelve. They also present family-oriented Christmas concerts of a **pops** nature, which includes soloists and chorus. Call (214) 692-0203.

Christmas in the Branch. City Hall Plaza, Farmers Branch. The Farmers Branch Chamber of Commerce holds a free concert for families followed by Santa's arrival on Friday evening at City Hall Plaza on William Dodson Pkwy. at Valley View Ln.

Dallas Children's Theater. 5938 Skillman St. Each Christmas the Dallas Children's Theater presents a wonderful holiday program, such as *The Best Christmas Pageant Ever*. Call (214) 978-0110. Most of the **local children's theaters** and **choruses** have holiday performances.

The Night Before Christmas, McFarlin Auditorium at Southern Methodist University. Fanciful, full-length ballet performed by adults and children of the Dallas Metropolitan Ballet during two December weekends. Call (214) 361-0278 or (214) 631-2787.

The Nutcracker. Various groups perform this traditional favorite. One of the best ways to enhance its enjoyment by young children is to read them the story first so they are familiar with the story line and anticipate the entrance of the characters. Some of the performing companies are the Texas Ballet Theater, Tuzer Ballet, Ballet Ensemble of Texas, Garland's City Dance Theatre, Mesquite Repertory Ballet, and Dallas Ballet Center.

Greater Dallas Youth Orchestra. Meyerson Symphony Center. The orchestra is joined by the **Children's Chorus of Greater Dallas** to present holiday music. Call (214) 528-7747.

Texas Boys Choir. Check for location. Musical holiday performance. Call (800) 848-6443.

Holiday Sing. UTD, Campbell and University in Richardson. Annual sing with children's concert in the afternoon. Free. Call (972) 883-2787.

4. SPORTS AND RECREATION

Observing a generation of children often referred to as couch pota-toes or tater tots because of their sedentary lifestyle in which they are parked endlessly in front of TV sitcoms, rented movies, and video games, more and more parents are recognizing the need to get these children outdoors and moving. The Dallas area has abundant oppor-tunities for physical exercise and fun for individuals, teams, and fami-lies. Finding activities, such as hiking, bicycling, or fishing, that the family can enjoy will not only aid in physical fitness and an apprecia-tion of the world outdoors, but also create some wonderful memories as well.

Area sports information is available at www.dallasnews.com. For your particular community's sports on this website, choose "local news" and then select the "city-by-city" option. For recreation information in Dal-las, look online at www.dallascityhall.com.

SPECTATOR SPORTS

MAJOR LEAGUE SPORTS

Dallas Cowboys (National Football League). Preseason and regular season games for the silver and blue team begin in August and end in December. The Cowboys play home games in Texas Stadium, 2401 E. Airport Fwy., Irving. Subscribe to *The Dallas Cowboys Official Weekly* by calling (972) 556-9972. DART provides shuttles to the home games. For more information about the Cowboys, call (972) 556-9900. Ticket office: (972) 785-5000. Season tickets: (972) 579-5100. Group Tick-ets: (972) 785-4800. Fan Club Number: (972) 556-9978. Mailing address: 1 Cowboys Pkwy., Irving, Texas 75063 Website: www.dallas cowboys.com.

Dallas Mavericks (National Basketball Association). The Dallas Mav-ericks season runs from November through April. Home games are played at American Airlines Center, 2500 Victory Ave. For a schedule or ticket information, call (214) 747-MAVS. The Mavs also offer summer basketball camps to kids ages eight to eighteen. Join **Mavs VIP Fan**

Club online or at a game. Mailing address: 2909 Taylor, Dallas, Texas 75226 Website: www.dallasmavericks.com.

Texas Rangers (American League). This baseball team is now playing at The Ballpark in Arlington. See **Places to Go** for more information about the stadium and the season, which runs from April through October. Special promotion nights allow all children ages thirteen and under with a paid admission to receive items such as baseball gloves, backpacks, and jerseys. The Rangers usually hold an open house for fans during the winter. While at the park, visitors may want to see baseball memorabilia in the **Legends of the Game Museum** at (817) 273-5600 or have dinner at **Rawling's All-American Grille** located inside the stadium.

Half-price tickets for Tuesday and Thursday home games are available at Tom Thumb locations. For information about schedules, tickets, or membership in the **Junior Rangers Club**, call Metro (817) 273-5100. Mailing address: 1000 Ballpark Way, Arlington, Texas 76011. Phone: (817) 273-5222 Website: www.texasrangers.com.

FC Dallas (formerly **Dallas Burn**; Major League Soccer). The Dallas Burn soccer team wound up its last season before becoming FC Dallas in conjunction with the move to the new Frisco Soccer and Entertainment Center, located at Main St. and North Dallas Tollway in Frisco. Kids ages seventeen and under are eligible for the **Kids' Club**, and ages two to eighteen may be interested in the MLS soccer camps. For information, visit www.mlscamps.com. For tickets call Ticketmaster or call (214) 979-0303 to reach the club office. Mailing address: 14800 Quorum Dr., Suite 300, Dallas, Texas 75254 Website: fc.dallas .mlsnet.com.

Dallas Fury (National Women's Basketball League). The Fury plays a twenty-one-game season from January to April. Nancy Lieberman coaches the team at the University of Texas, Dallas, located at 2601 N. Floyd Rd. in Richardson. Another entrance is on W. Campbell, west of Central Expwy. Tickets are available online or at the UTD box office on game day. Call (214) 943-1559 with questions or visit www .nwbl.com/fury.

ARENA SPORTS

Dallas Desperados (Arena Football League). An expansion team of Dallas Cowboys owner Jerry Jones, the Desperados play at American Airlines Center on a hockey-rink-sized arena. Eight men play on each side. They offer special birthday packages. For information about their season and tickets, call (972) 785-4900. Mailing address: Cowboys

Center, One Cowboys Pkwy., Irving, Texas 75063 Website: www.dallas
desperados.com.

Dallas Dragoons (National Polo League). The Dragoons play arena
polo and give lessons for ages ten and up at Bear Creek Polo Ranch, 550
Bent Trail, Red Oak, Texas 75154. The Dragoons play eight matches in
the spring and eight in the fall. Call (214) 979-0301 for more information or visit www.dallaspoloclub.org.

Dallas Stars (National Hockey League). The Dallas Stars ice hockey
team plays home games at American Airlines Center during a season that
runs from October through April. Online, young fans may join the **Junior Stars Club** as well as do the weekly activities on the "Kid Page."
Fans may watch the Stars practice at the Dr Pepper Star Center in Valley Ranch (214-GO-SKATE). Summer camps are offered there. Call
(214) GO-STARS for information. Tickets may be purchased online, by
phone, at American Airlines Center, or at any of the five Dr Pepper Star-
Center locations. Mailing address: 211 Cowboys Pkwy., Irving, Texas
75063 Website: www.dallasstars.com.

COLLEGIATE SPORTS

Cotton Bowl. Fair Park. Annually the Cotton Bowl is the site for at
least three exciting collegiate football games, the Cotton Bowl Classic on New Year's Day, and the state fair matches between the University of Texas and the University of Oklahoma and between Grambling
University and their opponent. State high school playoffs are also
scheduled here.

Southern Methodist University (Conference USA). Mustang football is played at Gerald Ford Stadium on the SMU campus. Ages thirteen
and under are invited to join the **Junior Mustang Club**, and birthday
packages may be reserved. The Boulevard offers food and music during
games, as well as a kids' area with inflatables and other interactive games.
Call (214) SMU-GAME for tickets or purchase them online at www
.smumustangs.com. Other popular sports include men's and women's
basketball played at Moody Coliseum and swimming, baseball, track,
and soccer. Summer sports camps for youths are held on campus, as are
cheerleading camps and camps for talented and gifted students. Moody
Coliseum is the site for the annual SWC Women's Post-Season Basketball Classic and the SWC Post-Season Men's Basketball Classic, usually
held in March. The SMU Swim Center is the site for the *Dallas Morning
News* Swimming Classic held in late January. SMU invites the top five
finishers in the NCAA Swimming Championship to compete with the
SMU team.

Other College Sports. Many other colleges in the Metroplex have sporting events open to the public. Here are some phone numbers if the family is interested in going to cheer for them:

Dallas Baptist University (214) 333-5324
Dallas County Community College District: Eastfield, Brookhaven, Richland, Mountain View, North Lake, Cedar Valley
University of Dallas (972) 721-5009
University of North Texas, Denton, Metro (817) 267-3731
University of Texas, Arlington (817) 272-2261

AUTO RACING

Devil's Bowl. (972) 222-2421. This raceway is located at 1711 Lawson, off Hwy. 80, in Mesquite. Races are usually held on Friday night from March through October.

Texas Motor Speedway. (817) 215-8500. NASCAR racing is held here on a 1.5-mile track. The 150,000-seat facility is located on SH114 and I-35W in Roanoke. The cars average more than 180 mph. Track officials advise bringing sunscreen, earplugs, comfortable shoes, and plenty of liquids. Fans may bring a fourteen-inch cooler. The park also hosts concerts and other events. Tours are available daily, except during racing events. To make a reservation, call toll free at (888) 816-TMS1 or (817) 215-8565. Concessions and souvenirs are available. Traffic is usually awful, so leave very early. Website: www.texasmotorspeedway.com.

GOLF

GTE Byron Nelson Classic. (972) 717-0700. Held at the Four Seasons Resort and Club at Las Colinas, Irving, the activities in this May golf tournament usually extend for one week. A free youth clinic is usually scheduled on one afternoon, and there are door prizes and giveaways and a free golf club after the exhibition is over. Look for the statue of Byron Nelson.

Colonial National Invitational. The PGA tournament is held at Colonial Country Club in Ft. Worth on a 7,010-yard, par-70 course in May.

RODEOS, HORSE RACING, AND HORSE SHOWS

Rodeo events and horse shows, such as the **Texas Black Invitational Rodeo** (Fair Park Coliseum) and the **Big D Charity Horse Show** (Las

Colinas Equestrian Center), both in May, are annual events. The **Mesquite Rodeo** and Rodeo Parade are covered in **Places to Go**. Year-round indoor rodeo is held each weekend at **Kowbell Indoor Rodeo**, Mansfield, FM 157 and Business 287, Metro (817) 477-3092. See Ft. Worth in **Day Trips** for more rodeo events. The Collin County Youth Park and Farm Museum northwest of McKinney has a show barn with a complete rodeo arena, and various rodeos, horse and livestock shows, and team roping, cutting, and penning are scheduled here. Call Metro (214) 231-7170 ext. 4793. Horse shows and competitive exhibitions, such as the S.W. Classic Grand Prix, are held at **Las Colinas Equestrian Center**, 600 W. Royal, Irving, Texas (972) 869-0600.

Lone Star Park. 1000 Lone Star Pkwy., Grand Prairie, Texas 75050 (972) 263-RACE. The 315-acre Lone Star Park (LSP) has races for both quarter and thoroughbred horses in October. The thoroughbred horses race on Wednesday to Sunday from mid-April through July and again on Sunday to Thursday in October and November. Simulcasting is used the rest of the year. Up to 8,000 fans may sit in the grandstand and 1,500 in the Post Time Pavilion. A playground, picnic tables, petting zoo, and pony rides are offered in a family area. Dining is in the pavilion and outdoor patio. On the LSP grounds is **GPX Skate Park & Entertainment Center**. LSP is located 1/2 mile north of I-30 just off Belt Line Rd. in Grand Prairie. Website: www.lonestarpark.com.

HOT-AIR BALLOONING

A spectacular hot-air balloon festival is held each year in Plano's Bob Woodruff Park. Call (972) 422-0296. In late September, colorful hot-air balloons fill the skies over a weekend. In addition to the races, there are usually arts and crafts, exhibits, food, and carnivals. See the **Transportation** section of Chapter Two for information about taking private balloon rides.

TENNIS

The **Dallas Tennis Association** at (972) 387-1538 or www.dta.org and the **Dallas Professional Tennis Association** at www.dptatennis.org can provide information about tennis in Dallas. A Texas link can be found at www.usta.com.

Texas Open. National Hardcourt Tournament at Canyon Creek Country Club, Richardson. July or August. Call (972) 231-2881.

Irving Tennis Classic. Top-ranked male players on international circuit. Irving. September. Call (972) 252-7476.

ZATS zone qualifiers. January through June. Dallas usually hosts two, Plano hosts one. Ages fourteen to eighteen, boys and girls. Call Dallas Tennis Association for the schedule at (972) 387-1538.

MCB Indoor Tennis Classic Superchampionship Major Zone. December. Juniors and adults. Cotton Bowl. Call (972) 387-1538 or visit www.dta.org.

Little Mo (Maureen Connolly Brinker) Tournament. May. Juniors. Call Dallas Professional Tennis Association at (972) 931-9711 or visit www.dptatennis.org.

INDIVIDUAL, FAMILY, AND TEAM SPORTS

ARCHERY

The National Field Archery Association sponsors archery for youths. There are Cub (ages 4–10), Youth, and Young Adult levels in lessons and competition. In the *Yellow Pages*, look up "Archery Equipment and Supplies" for the location of outdoor and indoor ranges, and the proprietor can give you information about clubs near you. Also, on the Web, look up www.texasfieldarchery.org and www.nfaa-archery .org.

BASEBALL, SOFTBALL, AND T-BALL

Youngsters all over the Metroplex begin warming up in April for baseball season, which lasts into July. Recreation centers, churches, YMCAs, and athletic associations field hundreds of recreational teams with players ages four and up. Baseball camps are offered in the summer. Very popular with boys who are serious about the game is **Boys Baseball Inc.** for ages eight to eighteen. Call (972) 682-1444 or visit www.bbidallas.org. Baseball card collecting is a popular hobby for some fans. For a list of stores that sell cards, look in the *Yellow Pages* for "Baseball–Sports Cards and Memorabilia." All across town are batting cages so players can practice their swings, but some may have height requirements. Baseball camps in the area may be found on America's Baseball Camps website at www.baseballcamps.com.

Home Run Alley. 3221 Skylane Dallas, Texas 75006 (972) 447-9066 Website: www.homerunalley.org. Located in Addison at Midway and Skylane, Home Run Alley has a 15,000-square-foot indoor hitting area, nine indoor batting tunnels, an outdoor field for practices, five Iron Mike pitching machines, and a stocked Pro Shop. It offers lessons, clinics, and camps for baseball players to improve skills.

Celebration Station, 4040 Towne Crossing Blvd., Mesquite, Texas (972) 279-7888.

Carter Softball Complex, 440 Oates, Garland, Texas (972) 613-7729.

Mesquite Go-carts and Batting Cages, 1630 E. Hwy. 80, Mesquite, Texas (972) 288-4888.

Hank Haney, 8787 Park Ln., near Abrams Rd., Dallas, Texas (214) 341-9600.

Adventure Landing, 17717 Coit, Dallas, Texas (972) 248-4966.

The Zone Sportsplex, 5702 Alpha, Dallas, Texas (972) 701-8444.

BASKETBALL

Basketball is usually offered for third grade and up at recreation centers, YMCAs, athletic associations, and churches. Practice usually begins in December and play in January to early March. Basketball clinics are often advertised through the newspaper or athletic clubs, and summer camps are abundant. Look for camps sponsored by **Dallas Fury** women's team.

The **Hoop-It-Up** is a three-on-three street-basketball tournament held for children and adults at the West End on a weekend in late June. Wheelchair teams are included. Each team should play at least three games. Call (972) 392-5700. The Hoop-It-Up Winter Warmup takes place in March at Lone Star Park. Both are free for spectators.

BICYCLING

Bicyclists of all ages and skill levels enjoy Dallas-area bike trails. Covering more than 500 miles of city streets, the bike routes are marked by Pegasus on wheels signs. Bike-trail maps may be obtained from the Department of Transportation. Maps are also available at bike shops. The east-west routes are the three-digit even numbers, and north-south routes are two-digit odd numbers. A helpful bicycling book is *Bicycling in the Dallas/Ft. Worth Area* by Bill Pellerin and Ralph Neidherdt. Call your Parks and Recreation Department for bike routes in your area. Remember your helmet!

The **Greater Dallas Bicyclists** is an active club that sponsors more than sixty rides per month. For information, call (214) 946-BIKE or visit www.gdbclub.org. Monthly, they publish the *Spokesman* with information about rides, rallies, festivals, clinics, bike care, and trails. A family membership is $30.

Another local bicycling group is **Dallas Off-road Bicycling Association** at www.dorba.org. It has information on mountain biking at good beginner places, such as L. B. Houston Park, Cedar Hill State Park, and Dinosaur Valley State Park. May is National Bicycle Month, and special events are planned.

Dallas Bike Trails include the following:

Bachman Lake (3.08 mi.) 2750 Bachman
Glendale Park (1.7 mi.) 1300 E. Ledbetter

Juanita J. Craft Park (1.41 mi.) 4500 Spring
Kiest Park (2.4 mi.) 3000 S. Hampton
L. B. Houston (5 mi./mtn. bike) 1600 California Crossing
Samuell/Elam/Crawford (2.13 mi.) 8700 Elam
Trinity Park (.66 mi.) 3700 Sylvan
White Rock Cr. Greenbelt (7.5 mi.) 7000 Valley View
White Rock Lake (11.1 mi.) 8300 Garland Rd.

BOWLING

Children have become so much a part of bowling that most bowling lanes have designated youth directors, and young bowlers take lessons and play in leagues and tournaments under the leadership of the **Youth American Bowling Alliance**. The website is www.bowl.com/bowl/yaba. Youth leagues usually play two games on Saturday mornings in mixed leagues for ages six to eight and three games for ages nine to eleven and twelve to fourteen. The PeeWee bowlers may begin lessons and leagues as early as age two. Local winners play in a state tournament. Some centers have youth-adult leagues. Bowling is a great family sport, and children as young as three may play using six-pound balls. Bumpers may be added so that very young bowlers don't get discouraged. Birthday parties at the bowling lanes are great fun, and some lanes will take party members behind the scenes so they can see how the pins are loaded and balls returned. Some amusement centers, such as **Main Event** and **Fun-Fest**, have bowling lanes.

AMF Garland Lanes. 1950 Plaza Dr., Garland, Texas (972) 613-8100.

AMF Jupiter Lanes. 11336 Jupiter Rd., Dallas, Texas (214) 328-3266.

AMF Richardson Lanes. 2101 N. Central Expwy., Richardson, Texas (972) 231-2695.

Don Carter's All Star Lanes. 10920 Composite, Dallas, Texas (214) 358-1382.

Plano Super Bowl. 2521 Avenue K, Plano, Texas (972) 881-0242.

CHEERLEADING

Cheerleading is good fun and exercise for both girls and boys. Lessons and summer camps are offered through recreation centers, gymnastic centers, high school fundraisers, and private cheerleading schools. Some of the cheerleading schools also offer birthday parties. Area schools include Cheer Basics, 10137 Shoreview (214) 342-7770; NCA Supercenter, 2010 Merritt, Garland (972) 840-2282; ASI Gymnastics, 11835 S. Greenville (972) 671-5510; Dallas Gymnastics Center, 4350 Sojourn, Addison (972) 248-9950; and Metroplex Gymnastics, 9858 Chartwell (214) 343-8652 and in Allen (972) 727-9095.

DANCING

Dance lessons are a part of many young girl's and boy's education. Ballet, tap, modern, and jazz are all very popular with children. In the *Yellow Pages*, look under "Dancing" for schools near you. Some dance companies with classes for children are listed in Chapter Three. Dancing is also offered through recreation centers and some community colleges. A family place for country western dancing is the Trail Dust Steakhouse.

DISC GOLF

A Frisbee, a pretty day, and a good arm are all that are needed to participate in one of Dallas parks' disc golf courses. Call the Parks and Recreation Department for the location of one near you. Tournaments are sometimes scheduled. The following are some courses in the area: B. B. Owen Park, Kingsley and Plano Rd.; Shawnee Park, near Avenue P and Parker Rd., Plano; Fritz Park, Britain Rd. one block So. of Shady Grove, Irving; Victoria Park, Northgate at Pleasant Run, Irving; Greenbelt Area 2, Southern Oaks and Josey Ln., Carrollton.

FENCING

Fencing for youths usually begins at age six in a local fencing club. Classes are held for ages six through adult at the **Dallas Fencers Club**, Oak Hill Academy, 9407 Midway Rd., Dallas, Texas 75220 (214) 629-5358. Students may belong to the United States Fencing Association and compete on local, divisional, sectional, and then the National Junior Olympic Competition levels. Wheelchair tournaments are included. Contact www.dallasfencers.com and www.usfencing.org for more information.

FISHING

Look under **Lakes, State Parks, and Recreation Areas** in this chapter for some great fishing in the Metroplex and surrounding area, and see **White Rock Lake** in Chapter One for fishing in the city. Anyone seventeen years old or older is required to have a fishing license, which costs about $23, or a temporary fourteen-day license, which costs $15. Fishing supply stores usually have them. A *Texas Fishing Guide* may be obtained by calling (800) 792-1112. The first Saturday in June is the annual **Free Fishing Day**. Contact the Texas Parks and Wildlife Department online at www.tpwd.state.tx.us to find a park and learn about their facilities and events.

Information about lakes operated by the Ft. Worth District of the U.S. Army Corps of Engineers may be accessed online at www.swf-wc.usace .army.mil/index.htm. Texas lakes usually have fishing guides, such as G. A. Miller, Fishing Guide Service at (903) 786-9866, or look online at websites such as www.fishtexoma.com.

FOOTBALL

Youth football is offered through private associations, such as Spring Valley Athletic Association, for fourth, fifth, and sixth graders, and the teams play other teams at their grade level. Look under "Athletic Organizations" in the *Yellow Pages*. Football in school begins in the seventh grade, and many coaches feel that is soon enough. Some YMCAs offer flag football for elementary school grades. Youth teams in the area are organized by Pop Warner Football at www.popwarner.com and Texas Select Football League at www.leaguelineup.com or (469) 726-0958. Peewee football is played in suburban cities, such as Garland, Carrollton, Mesquite, and Grand Prairie. Sports International sponsors football camps for ages eight to eighteen that include NFL players. In the Dallas area, the player has been Jay Novacek of the Dallas Cowboys. To find out dates and locations, call (800) 555-0801 or look online at www .footballcamps.com.

An annual four-on-four Air-It-Out flag football competition that includes some youth activities is held by Dallas Cowboys NFL, usually in November.

GOLF AND MINIATURE GOLF

Northern Texas PGA Junior Golf Foundation. (972) 429-1111 ext. 110. The JGF sponsors the junior tours, the Texas State Junior Championship, PGA Junior Qualifying, and the Junior Tournament of Champions and Cup Matches. Many area recreation centers and country clubs offer lessons, youth rates, summer golf programs, and tournaments. Some driving ranges also offer lessons. A junior golf clinic is offered at the Byron Nelson each year. Community outreach includes a program called Golf-in-Schools. Contact the foundation at NTPGA, P.O. Box 2169, Wylie, Texas 75098, or online at www.ajga.org. The five public golf courses in Dallas that offer youth programs are listed below:

Cedar Crest, 1800 Southerland (214) 670-7615
Grover Keaton, 2323 N. Jim Miller (214) 670-8784
L. B. Houston, 11223 Luna Rd. (214) 670-6322
Stevens Park, 1005 Montclair (214) 670-7506
Tenison Park, 3501 Samuell Blvd. (214) 670-1402

The following are more family amusement parks and miniature golf parks:

Adventure Landing, 17717 Coit, Dallas (972) 248-4966
Celebration Station, 4040 Towne Crossing Blvd., Mesquite (972) 279-7888
Golden Bear Golf Center, 2538 Golden Bear Dr., Carrollton (972) 733-4111
Hank Haney Golf Park, 8787 Park Ln., Dallas (214) 341-9600
The Practice Tee, 2950 Waterview Pkwy., Richardson (972) 235-6540
Putt Putt, 1951 Summit, Lewisville (972) 317-7373 Website: www.puttputt.com
Sandy Lake Park, I-30E North at Sandy Lake Rd., Carrollton (972) 242-7449
Speedzone, 1130 Malibu Dr., I-35E and Walnut Hill, Dallas (972) 247-RACE

GYMNASTICS AND TUMBLING

Gymnastics and tumbling help children with flexibility, control, and confidence. Young gymnasts in Dallas take lessons through recreation centers, the YMCA, summer camps, and private gyms. Many offer USGF competitive teams, and some Dallas youths have national ranking. Mom and tot classes are available through these centers and the nationally known Gymboree (www.gymboree.com), The Little Gym, Gymstar, and My Gym. Three popular gymnastic centers with multiple locations are Texas Gymnastics (www.texasgymnastics.com), ASI Gymnastics (www.asigymnastics.com), and Metroplex Gymnastics (www.metroplexgymnastics.com). Some private gyms offer birthday parties and parents' night out. In the *Yellow Pages*, look under "Gymnastics Instruction."

HIKING AND VOLKSMARCHING

Look under **Nature** in Chapter Two for beautiful, woodsy places to hike in the Dallas area. Groups, such as the Sierra Club and Audubon Society, regularly publish calendars of hiking and backpacking adventures. A Texas Forestry Association brochure lists eleven East Texas trails maintained by timber companies; call (409) 632-8733.

Volksmarchers, who often trek through nature areas, belong to clubs that measure routes, set trail markers, bring water, sign walkers in and out, and give medals and stamps indicating completion of walks. Youths and adults earn special awards for participating together in volkssporting events, and special programs are designed for Girl Scouts. One Dallas

club is **Dallas Trekkers Inc.** at (972) 386-5922 or www.dallastrekkers
.org. Call (800) 830-WALK for American Volkssport Association's list of
Texas walks.

HUNTING AND SPORTING CLAYS

As a sideline of the Texas Wildlife Association, the **Texas Youth Hunting Association** serves children and teens ages nine to seventeen, who
pay a membership fee of $12. Other requirements include buying a hunt-
ing license, signing a medical release, and passing a hunter-education
course. The association tries to find a place for each young hunter to hunt
at least once a year. Sometimes this is before the official season begins.
For more information, call (800) 839-9453 or visit www.texas-wildlife
.org/tyhp.

Designed to stimulate different types of wild-bird hunting conditions,
sporting clays is a shotgun clay-target game. Target speeds, shooting positions, and angles change, unlike skeet and trap, where clay targets are
thrown from standardized speeds and positions. Subjunior and junior
competitions are held at various locations. A course in the area is Elm
Fork Shooting Park Inc., 10751 Luna Rd. Call (972) 556-0164.

ICE HOCKEY

Sign-up time for ice hockey for ages four to nineteen is in September.
Ice-skating lessons are not required for younger players but are recommended for older divisions. The season lasts from October to March. For
information about ice hockey teams in the area, contact the **Dallas Junior Hockey Association** at (972) 506-7825 or call the ice-skating rinks.

A hockey-only facility, which hosts leagues and camps, is Ice Training
Center–Richardson, 522 Centennial Blvd., Richardson, Texas. Call (972)
238-1803 or visit www.djha.com.

ICE-SKATING AND BROOMBALL

Ice-skating is fun any time of year, but in the heat of a Texas summer,
it is the coolest spot in town. Ice-skating rinks offer public skating, lessons and competition in the U.S. Figure Skating Association, ice hockey,
and broomball. Birthday-party packages and group rates are available,
and the rinks may be rented for broomball. The Galleria rink is particularly beautiful in December with a huge Christmas tree in the center.

The **Dr Pepper Star Centers** (www.drpepperstarcenter.com) offer
skate school, hockey academy, and figure skating. They also offer public skating, hockey leagues, laser tag, and an arcade. Look for them at the
following locations:

211 Cowboys Pkwy., Irving (972) 831-2453
1700 S. Main, Duncanville (972) 283-9133
1400 S. Pipeline Rd., Euless (817) 267-4233
4020 W. Plano Pkwy., Plano (972) 758-7528
PSA StarCenter, 6500 Preston Meadow, Plano (972) 208-5437

More area ice-skating rinks are listed below:

Americas Ice Garden, Plaza of the Americas, 700 N. Pearl at San Jacinto, Dallas (214) 720-8080

Blue Line Ice Complex, 8851 Ice House Dr., North Richland Hills (817) 788-5400

Galleria Ice-Skating Center, 13350 Dallas Pkwy., Dallas (972) 392-3363

Ice at the Parks, The Parks at Arlington Mall, 3815 S. Cooper St., Arlington (817) 419-0095

The Ice at Stonebriar Mall, 2601 Preston Rd., Dallas (972) 731-9600

Polar Ice, Grapevine Mills Mall, 3000 Grapevine Mills Pkwy., Grapevine (972) 874-1930

The Rink in Addison, 15100 Midway Rd. at Belt Line, Addison (972) 960-7465

KITE FLYING

Kiters in the **Dallas Area Kiteflying Association** meet monthly to share information about kite construction and flying techniques and to fly their extraordinary kites. Children are welcome with parental supervision. Three locations where they fly kites are Richardson's Breckenridge Park and Rockwall's Elgin B. Robertson Park at Lake Ray Hubbard. Contact them online at www.dako-club.tripod.com. Flag Pole Hill at Northwest Hwy. and N. Buckner is a favorite spot to fly kites.

LACROSSE

To locate a lacrosse team in the area, summer camps, and clinics for grades five to eight, look online at www.texasyouthlacrosse.org to contact the **North Texas Youth Lacrosse Association**. One very active association is Plano Junior Lacrosse at (972) 378-1745 or www.dallaslacrosse .com. In lacrosse, ten players in protective gear are on the field at a time, and they are trying to move the ball toward the opponent's goal by running with the ball in the basket of the stick. They run, pass, and change directions in this full-contact sport.

MARTIAL ARTS

Those who love karate and other martial arts believe that they foster not only physical fitness but also build a positive self-image, self-discipline, confidence, and respect for others. Classes are offered at recreation centers, YMCAs, and some schools. It's a good idea to observe a class before enrolling. Popular centers include Ahn's Tae Kwon Do Institute, Dallas (972) 248-1777; Aikido of Dallas (972) 241-3221; North Dallas Martial Arts, Dallas (214) 956-7374; USA Martial Arts and Fitness, Plano (972) 985-7738 and Frisco (214) 387-8727; and Karate for Kids, Richardson (972) 680-1147. Look in the *Yellow Pages* under "Karate and other Martial Arts" for private instruction.

MOTOR SPORTS: CARS, CARTS, AND MODEL PLANES

GO-KARTS, MINI-VIRAGE CARS, SLOT CARS, ATVS

Adventure Landing, 17717 Coit Rd., Dallas (972) 248-4966.

Barnwell Mountain Recreation Area, Gilmer (903) 845-6261; ATV safety course: (800) 887-2887. Trails for ATVs, Jeeps, Motorcycles.

Celebration Station, I-30 and I-635, Mesquite (972) 279-7888.

Lonestar Slot Car, 2540 Avenue K #380, Plano (972) 424-7208.

Mesquite Go Carts, 1630 E. Hwy. 80, Mesquite (972) 288-4888 .

Neil's Wheels Slot Car Speedway, Spring Creek Pkwy. and Alma #290, Plano (972) 517-2277.

North Texas Kartway, I-35 at Exit 474, North of Denton (972) 488-8224.

Precision Karting, 2525 Southwell, Dallas (972) 243-0714.

Speedzone, 11130 Malibu, Dallas (972) 245-RACE.

TBC Indoor Kart Racing, 8625 N. Stemmons, Dallas (214) 634-5278.

Many hobbyists in the area enjoy the remote-controlled (RC) cars and planes, model rockets, and the slot cars. Supplies for all sorts of RC vehicles may be found at Texas RC Modelers, 230 W. Parker Rd., Plano (972) 422-5386, and Mickey's A-1 Hobby Shop at 1425 Gross Rd., Mesquite. Contact the **Metro East Radio Control Club** (www.mercc.org) for places to fly the planes. The club offers classes for beginners. After some instruction, you will be less likely to crash your plane on its maiden flight or watch it fly away into the wild blue yonder.

ORIENTEERING

In orienteering, hikers use a compass and topographical map to go from one point to another. Many children learn this skill through the Boy Scouts or Girl Scouts. Orienteering clubs with members of all skill levels sometimes have theme meets or canoe trips. The **North Texas Orienteering Association** offers a family membership. Call (214) 369-1823 or look online at www.ntoa.com. Their mailing address is P.O. Box 832464, Richardson, Texas 75083-2464.

PAINTBALL

Probably best for families or youth groups with junior high school students, paintball is a team game in which team members eliminate the other team's players while they try to capture the other team's flag and protect their own. They carry air-powered guns that shoot colored paint pellets and wear masks, goggles, and long-sleeved shirts. **Action Paintball Games of Dallas** at (972) 554-1937 and **Official Paintball Games of Texas** at (972) 564-4748 are two local places to play.

RAFTING, CANOEING, TUBING, AND KAYAKING

Although the area around New Braunfels, San Marcos, and Glen Rose has some great tubing and rafting, there are a few popular spots closer to home. Canoes may be rented from High Trails Canoe, 3610 Marquis Dr., Garland at (972) 2-PADDLE or www.hightrailscanoe.com, and North Texas Canoe Rentals, 2316 Daybreak, at (972) 245-7475, which also provides shuttles. One recommended Trinity River trip is on the Elm Fork from TX 121 near the dam at Lake Lewisville to I-35 bridge (5.5 mi) or on to McInnish Park on Sandy Lake Rd. in Carrollton (9.4 mi). For information about the river, call (214) 434-1666.

Single or family memberships are offered at **Dallas Downriver Club** (www.down-river.com). Their address is P.O. Box 820246, Dallas, Texas 75382-0246. They participate in the annual Trinity River Challenge, an eleven-mile paddle-sport race in September, starting and finishing at Carrollton's McInnish Park. Canoes and kayaks may be rented on area lakes. See **Day Trips** for information about Glen Rose and Tyler State Park. Texas River Expeditions plans family rafting, canoeing, and sea kayaking weekends and one-day trips. Call (800) 839-7238 or look online at www.texasriver.com.

Some of the community colleges, such as Eastfield and Richland, offer canoeing trips.

ROCK CLIMBING

The only way is up at local rock-climbing gyms. Kids can scale boulders using safety equipment and also take classes. They may require parents to sign an insurance-liability release form. Some gyms offer classes and after-school climbing for youths.

Exposure, 2389 Midway #B, Carrollton (972) 732-0307 Website: www.exposurerockclimbing.com.

Dyno-Rock, 608 E. Front St., Arlington (817) 461-3966 Website: www.dynorock.com.

Stone Works Indoor Rock Gym, 1003 Fourth Ave., Carrollton (972) 323-1047 Website: www.stoneworkssilos.com.

The **Texas Mountaineers Club** promotes outdoor climbing in Texas and other states. Members must be eighteen or older, but the club website gives information about sites to climb, such as **Mineral Wells State Park**.

ROCKETRY

The **Dallas Area Rocket Society** has a full calendar of events. One site for launches is McLendon-Chisolm Park in Rockwall County, and the general public is welcome. The society also has a science education outreach program, which can be reached online at www.dars.org/rockets. The website www.flyrockets.com offers helpful information for beginners, a discussion of many aspects of rocketry, and a list of local clubs and links.

ROLLER-SKATING

In the Dallas area, both roller-skating and ice rinks are listed in the *Yellow Pages* under "Skating Rinks." Skaters may bring their own skates, but that usually does not affect admission prices. Most rinks will let preschoolers wear their Fisher-Price skates if the skates are in good condition. On Sundays, some rinks let parents skate free with their children, and some have special preschool skating hours during the week. Lessons, group rates, and birthday parties are usually offered.

Thunderbird Roller Rink, 3200 Thunderbird, Plano (972) 422-4447.

Westlake Skate Center, 413 S. Yale, Garland (972) 272-0921.

Westlake Skate Center, 311 Gross Rd., Mesquite (972) 285-9058.

White Rock Skate Center, 10055 Shoreview, Dallas (214) 341-6660.

RUNNING

See Chapter Two about the hiking, biking, and jogging trails in the nature areas of the Metroplex. The Sports section of the *Dallas Morning News* mentions upcoming runs in "Around the Area," and many of these have a children's division and a one-mile fun run/walk. These runs are often part of festivals or fundraisers, such as Artfest Run for the Arts, Zoo Run, Thanksgiving Turkey Trot, the Symphony Fun Run, and the companion/pet SPCA runs. Most area communities have jogging trails and par courses. There are par courses at Richland College, White Rock Lake, and Bachman Lake. Just contact the Parks and Recreation

Department for locations. The **Cross Country Club of Dallas** (www.cccd.org) has races each first Saturday at Winfrey Point, 950 E. Lawther, White Rock Lake. Call (214) 855-1511.

SAILING AND MOTOR BOATING

Many area lakes, including White Rock, have sailing clubs that feature regular sailing events and beautiful regattas. The U.S. Coast Guard Auxiliary offers lessons and certification in boating. Look under "Boat Rental" and "Charter" in the *Yellow Pages* and in the **Lakes, State Parks, and Recreation Areas** section of this chapter about renting boats of all kinds. Some of the marinas with rentals also offer lessons in boating and waterskiing. Some private yacht clubs offer lessons for nonmembers, and students do not have to have their own boats.

Remember, the Coast Guard Auxiliary requires that all children in a boat wear approved life jackets, and a jacket should be in the boat for all adults on board. For information about the nearest certified safety instructor for Texas Parks and Wildlife's boating safety course, call (800) 253-4536.

Chandler's Landing Yacht and Tennis Club, Lake Ray Hubbard, Rockwall (972) 771-2002 Website: www.chandlerslanding.com.

Corinthian Sailing Club Junior Sailing Program, White Rock Lake (214) 826-3998 Website: www.cscsailing.org/junior_pgm.html.

North Texas Sailing School at Rush Creek Yacht Club, Lake Ray Hubbard, Rockwall (972) 771-2002 Website: www.northtexassailing.com.

Texas Sailing Schools, Lake Lewisville and Lake Texoma, 132 Grandpappy Dr., Denison (214) 215-7245 Websites: www.texassailingschools .com and www.saildallas.com.

SCUBA DIVING

For information about learning to scuba dive, look under "Divers Instruction" in the *Yellow Pages*. Some of the businesses that sell equipment also offer PADI lessons, and the first Discover Scuba lessons are free. Scuba lessons may also be offered through recreation centers, YMCAs, some of the community colleges' continuing education departments, and the Tom Landry Sports Medicine and Research Center at (214) 820-7800. Dive West has an indoor heated pool at its Plano location, at 1108 Dobie Dr. (972) 424-6563. A second location is 6336 Greenville Ave., Dallas (214) 750-6900. The **Scuba Ranger** program begins at age eight for pool certification only. At age ten, juniors may achieve Open Water Certification with a depth limit. Aqua Adventures stocks kids' equipment and offers PADI scuba courses. Popular lakes for scuba diving are Possum Kingdom, Squaw Creek, and Lake Travis.

Athens Texas Scuba offers underwater visibility of up to seventy feet, twelve dive platforms, and camping sites. Owners sank Clint Eastwood's houseboat, Ray Price's tour bus, an airplane, and more to interest divers. It operates from May to November, Friday to Sunday. 500 N. Murchison St., Athens (903) 675-5762.

SKATEBOARDING AND ROLLERBLADING

Skateboarders have a good variety of parks to have fun and hone their skills. Some parks ask that you bring your own equipment, and some have equipment to rent. A helmet is always recommended.

Cyclone Indoor Skatepark, 975 S. Central Expwy., McKinney (972) 562-2752.

Eisenbergs Skatepark, 930 E. 15th St., Plano (972) 509-7725 Website: www.eisenbergs.com.

GPX Skatepark, 1000 Lone Star Pkwy., Grand Prairie (972) 237-4370.

SKIING, WATER

Waterskiing is usually great on area lakes from June through September. Listen to news reports for wind advisories. Marinas with boat rentals may offer skiing lessons, and some summer sports camps offer lessons. **Top Gun Water Ski School** at Metro (817) 360-4990 operates on Lake Worth by the former Carswell Field. **Dallas–Ft. Worth Water Ski and Wakeboard School and Camp** operates on a private lake. Call (903) 527-4692 or visit www.dfwski.com.

SOCCER

Millions of youngsters across the nation are enthusiastically playing a game that their parents knew little about as children. Soccer has become incredibly popular as a sport for both boys and girls and will probably become even more popular as a spectator sport as these young players become adults. Soccer teams are fielded by recreation centers, YMCAs, and private athletic associations. For the name of an association near you, call the **North Texas State Soccer Association** (NTSSA), which is the regulating group for area soccer, at (972) 323-1323. Also, look in the *Yellow Pages* under "Soccer Clubs" or online at www.ntxsoccer.org. *The Pitch* is an informative monthly publication of NTSSA.

Soccer usually begins with an under-six league and ends with under nineteen; members play on a team determined by where they live or go to school. Avid players may try out for a select team at the under-eleven age group and sign yearly contracts. Children also play indoor soccer almost year-round. Some indoor facilities have pro shops, concessions, and video games. Below are listed some indoor parks:

American Indoor Soccer Facility, 1400 Hebron Pkwy., Carrollton (972) 939-1100 Website: www.americanindoorsports.com

Inwood Soccer Center, 14801 Inwood Rd., Dallas (972) 239-1166 Website: www.inwoodsoccercenter.com

Mesquite Indoor Soccer Center, 1600 E. Hwy. 80, Mesquite (972) 329-4625 Website: www.miscgoal.com

Soccer Spectrum, 1251 Digital, Richardson (972) 644-8844 Website: www.soccerspectrum.com

The Rockwall Indoor Sports Expo, a new facility at 2922 S. Hwy. 205, Rockwall, offers two soccer fields, two basketball courts, and facilities for roller hockey, volleyball, flag football, lacrosse, roller hockey, tae kwon do, flag guard, and outdoor baseball, as well as a virtual-reality baseball batting cage area and a six-person football field, with outdoor soccer fields to be added later. Website: www .RISE-Rockwall.com.

An exciting annual youth tournament is the **Dallas Cup** held each April at Lake Highlands High School Wildcat-Ram Stadium. Approximately 170 teams from twenty-five countries compete for championships in five boys' divisions and two girls' divisions. What is hoped to be an annual event showcasing international teams is the adult International Challenge Cup held in the Cotton Bowl during the State Fair of Texas.

Other helpful online sites are www.soccer.org, www.usysa.org, and www.soccerjr.com.

Camps and clinics are offered by FC Dallas and Bobby Moffat.

SPECIAL OLYMPICS AND DISABLED SPORTS ASSOCIATION

Each year, more than 3,700 athletes and 1,700 coaches participate in the Special Olympics for athletes who are both mentally and physically disabled. The Olympics begin with an opening ceremony on a Wednesday night and end with a closing ceremony on Friday afternoon in May. Cities bid on the right to host the games. For more information, call (214) 943-9981.

The organization For Relaying Information/Education on the Needs of the Disabled (FRIEND) sponsors wheelchair basketball, rugby, and Special Olympics training at recreation centers. Call (972) 279-6673. Also, the **Bachman Therapeutic Recreation Center** at (214) 670-6266 offers special programs year-round and summer camps for children with disabilities. More activities are part of the fun at the Variety Wheelchair Arts and Sports Association, which offers sports for children six to eighteen. Call (972) 494-3160. See **Playgrounds** and **Horseback Riding, Riding Instruction, and Day Camps** in this chapter for more activities for physically challenged youths.

SWIMMING

Swimming in the Texas summer heat is next to breathing. The Park and Recreation Department offers pools at twenty-two of their recreation centers. Samuell-Grand and Lake Highlands North have a wading pool. Swimming lessons are offered at many of the recreation centers for a low fee. A responsible person sixteen years or older must accompany children ages six or under. Below is a list of Dallas's public pools:

Bachman, 2750 Bachman Blvd. (214) 670-6266 (persons with disabilities only)
Bonnieview, 2124 Huntington Ave. (214) 670-1960
Churchill, 7025 Churchill Way (214) 670-6177
Everglade, 5100 N. Jim Miller (214) 670-0940
Exline, 2430 Eugene St. (214) 670-0350
Fretz, 14739 Hillcrest (214) 670-6464
Glendale, 1534 Five Mile Dr. (214) 670-1951
Grauwyler, 2157 Anson Rd. (214) 670-6444
Harry Stone, 2403 Millmar (214) 670-0950
Hattie R. Moore, 3122 N. Winnetka (214) 670-1391
Jaycee, 3125 Tumalo Trail (214) 670-6465
Juanita Craft, 3125 Lyons St. (214) 670-0343
Kidd Springs, 807 W. Canty (214) 670-6817
Lake Highlands North, 9940 White Rock Trail (214) 670-1346
Martin Weiss, 3440 W. Clarendon (214) 670-1989
McCree, 9016 Plano Rd. (214) 670-0389
Pleasant Oaks, 8701 Greenmound (214) 670-0941
Samuell-Grand, 3201 Samuell Blvd. (214) 670-1379
Thurgood Marshall, 1808 Ariel (214) 670-1917
Tietze, 6115 Llano (214) 670-1380
Tipton, 3607 Magdaline (214) 670-6466
Tommie M. Allen, 6901 Bonnie View (214) 670-0982
Walnut Hill, 4141 Walnut Hill Ln. (214) 670-6433

Members of the YMCA also enjoy swimming and lessons, and some of the community colleges schedule lessons for youths and adults and public swimming hours. Many public and private pools offer a summer swim team. Swimming for ages six and older and diving classes are taught at Southern Methodist University. Call (214) 692-2200. A popular indoor swimming pool is **Don Rodenbaugh Natatorium** located at 110 E. Rivercrest Blvd., Allen, Texas (972) 747-4150.

Wave pools and lazy rivers are popular at **Garland's Surf 'N Swim** and **Hawaiian Falls** as well as Arlington's **Six Flags Hurricane Harbor** mentioned in Chapter One. **Sandy Lake** also has a very large public pool, and the White Rock Yacht Club restaurant has a volleyball pool and playground alongside its sand volleyball courts. **NRH2O** is a wave pool with water slides, endless river, and children's area in North Richland Hills on Grapevine Hwy. across from Tarrant County Junior College N.E. Campus. Call (817) 427-6500. Swimming pools with more are **Rowlett Wet Zone**, 5304 Main St. (214) 607-1434, and Grand Prairie's **Splash Factory**, 601 E. Grand Prairie Rd. (972) 263-8174. **Burger's Lake** is a favorite swimming hole near Ft. Worth.

The YMCA and Sportsridge Athletic Club indoor pools are available for rental for parties.

Call the Parks and Recreation Department or the school district's athletic director in your community to see if they have competitive swim teams for youths. Dallas's Loos Natatorium, 2839 Spring Valley (972) 888-3191, is the site of some exciting swim meets. Their **Dallas Aquatics Club** is a swim team for children ages six to eighteen. Call about tryouts; there is a fee to join. A child may accompany an adult in lap swimming.

The **Pirouettes of Texas**, a synchronized swim team that practices at North Lake Natatorium in Irving, accepts girls ages eight to eighteen (972) 254-4010. To find a swim team or swimming lessons near you, try www.clubswim.com.

See the **Lakes, State Parks, and Recreation Areas** and **Day Trips** sections for more great swimming holes. Other community pools and facilities include the following in case you would like to try new pools every week:

Carrollton. **Rosemeade Aquatic Center**, 1330 Rosemeade Pkwy. (972) 492-1791. Pools: wading pool with fountain, training pool, main pool, diving well with three platforms, water volleyball.

DeSoto. **Mosely Park Pool**, 600 E. Wintergreen Rd. (972) 224-7370. Pools: baby pool, wading pool, main pool. Across from a Leathers-designed playground.

Duncanville. **Armstrong Swimming Pool**, 200 James Collin Blvd. (972) 780-5083. Pools: wading pool, main pool. By Leathers-designed playground **Kidsville**.

Farmers Branch. **Don Showman Pool**, 14302 Heartside (972) 243-9079. Pools: baby pool, main pool with water slides and high dive.

Mesquite. **Evans Pool**, 1200 Hillcrest (972) 289-9151. Pools: wading pool, main pool with water slide.

Plano. **Jack Carter Pool**, 2800 Maumelle (972) 578-7173. Pools: wading pool, main pool with diving board.

Richardson. **Cottonwood Park**, 1321 West Belt Line (972) 680-8209. Pools: wading pool, main pool, and diving pools.

TENNIS

Tennis is a favorite sport year-round in Dallas, especially with some communities and clubs offering indoor courts. **The City of Dallas** operates five tennis centers, which offer lessons, ball machines, tennis merchandise, racket repair, league play, and lighted courts. Court reservations can be made one day in advance. See **Spectator Sports** for popular tournaments.

Fair Oaks, 7501 Merriman Pkwy. (214) 670-1495.

Fretz, 14700 Hillcrest (214) 670-6622.

Kiest, 2324 W. Kiest Blvd. (214) 670-7618.

L. B. Houston, 11223 Luna Rd. (214) 670-6367.

Samuell-Grand, 6200 E. Grand Ave. (214) 670-1374.

Call (214) 670-8745 for reservations at neighborhood courts. The Parks and Recreation Department works in cooperation with the **National Junior Tennis League** to provide year-round tennis programs for children of all ages, including lessons, clinics, and tournaments. Call the **Dallas Tennis Association** at (972) 387-1538 for more information.

The **National Junior Tennis League** is an eight-week summer program in which the Park Department, in conjunction with several sponsors, provides instructors, courts, and equipment for clinics, lessons, and tournaments for youths in more than thirty recreation centers. Call your nearest recreation center for more information. Some of the community colleges and Southern Methodist University offer summer lessons, and some country club tennis programs include nonmembers in lessons.

SUMMER SPORTS DAY CAMPS

With schoolwork out of the way, the summer is a great time to sharpen skills in favorite sports. A good place to check for camp listings is the February issue of *dallas child* or at their annual Kid Camp and Sports Expo, also in February; visit www.dallaschild.com. The American Camping Association (ACA) at (765) 342-8456 or www.acacamps.org provides a database of camps that have ACA approval. Recreation centers and the YMCA offer day camps in most of the popular sports for youths. Look under **Tennis, Swimming**, and **Golf** in this chapter for opportunities with the Dallas Parks and Recreation Department. Some private schools, such as St. Marks, Jesuit, Greenhill, Episcopal School of Dallas, and Hockaday, offer sports camps with instruction in more than one sport in addition to other types of day camps. **Trinity Christian Academy Camps** at (972) 391-8325 include football, basketball, wrestling, baseball, and tennis for boys and volleyball, basketball, and tennis for girls. **Premier Sports Camps** offers camps for basketball, football, and volleyball at various locations. Call (972) 481-9400 or look online at www.allstarcamps.com. Listed below are some programs that provide instruction and fun. Sometimes only websites are listed because the locations of the camps may change each summer.

VARIETY OF SPORTS/FITNESS

Cooper Fitness Center, 12100 Preston Rd., Dallas (972) 233-4832 Website: www.cooperfitnesscenter.com.

PowerKids Sports and Fitness, 7130 Campbell Rd. #206–7, Dallas (972) 818-KIDS Website: www.818kids.com.

Signature Athletic Club—Kid's Zone, 14725 Preston Rd., Dallas (972) 419-6417 Website: www.signatureac.com.

Springpark Sports Camp, 3330 Springpark Way, Richardson (972) 675-1272 Website: www.springpark.org.

YWCA Summer Fun Camps, various branches. Call (214) 584-2335 or visit www.ywcadallas.org.

Prestonwood Country Club Summer Sports Camps, 15909 Preston Rd., Dallas (972) 239-1935 Website: www.prestonwoodcc.org.

T Bar M Racquet Club, 6060 Dilbeck, Dallas (972) 233-4444. All-Star Camp for tennis and swimming; Fit for Life Summer Camp. Visit www.tbarmtennis.com.

Top Achievers Cross-Training Sportsplex, 3115 W. Parker Rd. # 298, Plano (972) 867-7677 Website: www.tacrosstraining.com.

Skyhawks Sports Programs, various locations. Call (800) 804-3509 or visit www.skyhawks.com.

The Zone Sportsplex, 5702 Alpha, Dallas (972) 701-8444 Website: www.thezonesportsplex.com.

HORSEBACK RIDING

Rocking M Stables, 7807 Fair Oaks, Dallas (214) 682-8922, ages eight up.

Capricorn Equestrian Center, 6101 Ben, Sachse (972) 530-1124 Website: www.capricornhorse.com.

Wagon Wheel Ranch Summer Riding Camp, 816 Ruth Wall Rd., Grapevine (972) 462-0894.

The Highland Horses School of Riding, 440 Briar Glen, Rockwall (972) 771-6272.

Rockin' River Ranch, 13100 East Hwy. 121, Frisco (972) 335-8000

North Texas Equestrian Center, 1765 Southview Dr., Wylie (972) 442-7544 Website: www.uswarmblood.com.

VOLLEYBALL

Dallas Summit Volleyball Camp, Summit Sports Complex, 12750 Perimeter, Ste. 144, Dallas (214) 613-7475 Website: www.dallassummit .com.

SKATEBOARDING, IN-LINE SKATING, BMX BIKING

Eisenbergs Summer Camp, 930 E. 5th St., Plano (972) 918-9593 Website: www.eisenbergs.com.

ICE-SKATING AND HOCKEY

The Ice at Stonebriar, Stonebriar Centre, 2601 Preston Rd., Frisco (972) 731-9600 Website: www.stonebriarice.com.

America's Ice Garden Summer Camp, 700 N. Pearl, Dallas (214) 720-8080 Website: www.icesk8aig.com.

Dr Pepper Star Centers, multiple locations. Website: www.drpepper starcenter.com.

SAILING

North Texas Sailing School, Chandler's Landing Yacht & Tennis Club, 501 Yacht Club Dr., Rockwall (972) 771-2002 Website: www .chandlerslanding.com.

GOLF

Sherrill Park Golf Course Junior Golf Clinics, 2001 E. Lookout at Jupiter, Richardson (972) 234-1416 Website: www.sherrilparkgolf.com.

The Golf Institute Junior Golf Camps, 2101 Walnut Hill, Dallas (972) 418-1042 Website: www.golfinstituteschools.com.

U.S. Junior Team Golf, various golf courses. Call (972) 934-2789 or visit www.usjtg.com.

Golden Bear Junior Camps, 2538 Golden Bear Dr., Carrollton (972) 733-4111 Website: www.gbgc.net.

SOCCER

Smudger's Soccer Camps, various locations. Call (972) 233-3146 or visit www.smudgersoccercamps.com.

Bobby Moffat's Summer Soccer Camps, various locations. Call (972) 699-3653 or visit www.soccermoffat.com.

American Indoor Sports Facility Soccer Camps, 1400 W. Hebron Pkwy., Carrollton (972) 939-1100 Website: www.americanindoorsports .com.

MLS Soccer Camps. Various locations. Website: www.mlscamps .com.

BASEBALL/SOFTBALL

Texas Rangers Baseball/Softball Camps, Dr Pepper Youth Ballpark, The Ballpark in Arlington, 1000 Ballpark Way, Arlington (817) 273-5297 Website: www.texasrangers.com.

Dallas Baseball Academy of Texas, 4131 Lindburgh Ln., Addison (972) 387-3228 Website: www.dallasbat.com.

Jesuit Ranger Baseball Camp, 12345 Inwood, Dallas (972) 387-8700 Website: www.jesuitcp.org.

Darrell Richardson Baseball Academy, 13450 Stemmons Fwy., Ste. 400, Farmers Branch 75234 (972) 406-1777.

Home Run Alley, 3221 Skylane, Dallas (972) 447-9066 Website: www.homerunalley.org.

SWIMMING

Aquatots Swim Program, Sportsridge Athletic Club, 1600 Jay Ell, Richardson (972) 890-7946 E-mail: aquatots@swbell.net.

SwimPlus, 2301 No. Central Expwy., #140, Plano (972) 671-7946 Website: www.swimplus.com.

Emler Swim School, Park Blvd. at Ohio, Plano (972) 599-7946 Website: www.emlerswim.com. Also, locations in Colleyville and Arlington.

TENNIS

Brookhaven Country Club All-Star Tennis Camp, 3334 Golfing Green, Dallas (972) 241-5961 Website: www.brookhavenclub.com (also swimming, soccer, basketball).

Fair Oaks Tennis Camp, 7501 Merriman Pkwy., Dallas (214) 670-1495 Website: www.eteamz.com/fairoaks.

Jesuit Junior Tennis Camp, 12345 Inwood, Dallas (972) 248-6833 Website: www.jesuitcp.org.

SMU Summer Tennis Camp, 6024 Airline Rd., Dallas (214) 768-3840 Website: www.smutennis.com.

BASKETBALL

Dallas Mavericks Hoop Camp, various locations. Call (214) 747-6287 or visit www.dallasmavericks.com.

GYMNASTICS

Gymstar Summer Blast, 2432 Preston, Plano (972) 612-4141 Website: www.gymstarplano.com.

Ridgewood Gymnastics Summer Day Camp, 6818 Fisher Rd., Dallas (214) 373-9615 E-mail: ridgewoodgymnastics@sbcglobal.net.

Canyon Creek Gymnastics and Tumbling Camps, 817 Canyon Creek Square, Richardson (972) 907-2248 Website: www.canyoncreek gym.com.

Metroplex Gymnastics Summer Camps, three locations in Dallas, Allen, Arlington. Website: www.metroplexgymnastics.com.

FOOTBALL

Jay Novacek Sports International Football Camps, call (800) 555-0801 or visit www.footballcamps.com.

Jesuit Rangers Football Camp, 12345 Inwood, Dallas (972) 387-8700 ext. 345 Website: www.jesuitcp.org.

Garland Owl Youth Football Camp, Williams Stadium, 710 Stadium Dr., Garland (972) 494-8589 Website: www.garlandowls.com.

RECREATION CENTERS AND YOUTH ORGANIZATIONS

RECREATION CENTERS

The recreation centers in Dallas literally have something for everyone from tots to seniors. The Parks and Recreation Department operates more than forty centers, and half of them have swimming pools. Signing up for classes and teams is usually done quarterly, and those for youths include almost all popular sports, arts and crafts, cooking, music, and performing arts. Gymnastics Mom and Me classes begin as early as age two, and swim lessons are offered at many of the pools. Most of these classes are free or inexpensive.

Summer day camps are annual favorites, with some conducted at the recreation center and some that include many field trips. S.L.Y. (Slow Learner Youth) Camp is held at some recreation centers, such as Lake Highlands North. Performing-arts groups, such as the Junior Players, and sports facilities, such as bowling lanes and skating rinks, combine resources with the centers to provide excellent instruction. Programs for children and adults with disabilities are available at Bachman Recreation Center. For youths ages six to twenty-two with disabilities, an after-school program from 3 PM to 6 PM and once-a-month special activities are offered. Call (214) 670-6266 for program information. Special events, such as Easter egg hunts and Fourth of July parades, are scheduled regularly at the recreation centers. Look online at the City of Dallas Park and Recreation website at www.dallascityhall.com for details.

YOUTH ORGANIZATIONS

BOY SCOUTS OF AMERICA (214) 902-6700 Website: www.circle10.org. The **Circle Ten Council** and national headquarters are located in Irving. In addition to traditional favorite activities such as hiking and camping, the Boy Scouts have included atomic energy and computers into their merit badge activities. In the last ten years, the number of Scouts in the Dallas council has risen from 29,000 to more than 50,000, and more than 6,000 have physical disabilities. Boys may begin at age six as a Tiger Cub and move up. The Boy Scouts sponsor both day camps and resident camps in the summer. *Family Camping* is a guide offered by the Scouts at their stores to encourage families to camp anywhere from the backyard to state parks.

BIG BROTHERS AND SISTERS OF METROPOLITAN DALLAS (214) 871-0876. This organization pairs up disadvantaged youths with individuals or couples for two to four hours per week of one-on-one companionship for a period of at least one year. Often, the children come from single-parent homes where there is no father. After applying, there is a screening process, and a case worker makes the assignment.

BOYS AND GIRLS CLUBS OF GREATER DALLAS, INC. (214) 821-2950. Boys and Girls Clubs have seven branches in the metro area, and two of these locations have swimming pools. Youngsters ages six to eighteen pay for a yearly membership, and there are no other fees so that disadvantaged youths can participate. They meet after school Tuesday to Friday and on Saturday during the school year and on Monday to Friday in the summer. Activities include a variety of sports, tutoring, computers, arts and crafts, woodshops, creative arts, and game-room activities.

CAMP FIRE GIRLS AND BOYS (214) 824-1122 Website: www .campfireusadallas.org. The **Lone Star Council** of Camp Fire now accepts both boys and girls in the program. The club tries to meet the emotional, social, and physical needs of today's kids through camping, community service, and self-care programs. Boys and girls who are five years old may join, and both day camp and resident camp are offered. White Rock Day Camp is a popular summer camp by the lake that plans canoeing, archery, outdoor cooking, and nature crafts for ages six to fifteen. They also learn safety and survival skills. Camp Fire operates **Kidtalk**, which is a telephone line answered by volunteers for children who are home alone or worried about something and need someone to talk to: (214) 522-1144 or TDD (214) 522-1188.

GIRLS INCORPORATED OF METROPOLITAN DALLAS (214) 350-8115. Four centers are operated for girls, ages six to eighteen, by Girls Inc. There is a small membership fee but no fee for activities. The purpose is to provide after-school care and build self-esteem to help prevent pregnancy and substance abuse and help girls learn how to deal with other challenges. Programs include Operation Smart to help girls excel in science and math and Job Shadowing, in which a girl follows a role model who has a job that interests her. In conjunction with the Parks and Recreation Department, summer day camp is offered for both boys and girls, with the weekly fee based on family income.

GIRL SCOUTS OF AMERICA (972) 349-2400 Website: www .tejasgsc.org. The headquarters of the **Tejas Girl Scout Council** are located in Dallas, and this twenty-county council has more than 32,000 members. With an emphasis on community service, the Girl Scouts are actively involved in projects to help the community, in outdoor activities, and in wellness education. Girls may begin the program at age five as Daisies. Troops are available for girls with special needs, and some literature is printed in Spanish.

ADVENTURE GUIDES (formerly Indian Guides and Indian Princesses). A YMCA program originally designed to bring boys and girls and their fathers closer together, this group sometimes involves moms, too. Guides usually meet once a month in members' homes and participate in two or three campouts, which are often held at Camp Grady Spruce at Possum Kingdom Lake. These groups may form in kindergarten, and most continue through the second or third grade. Even fathers who are very reluctant campers look forward to the campouts and enjoy the friendship of the other dads and the time with their children. The general YMCA number is (214) 880-9622.

YMCA (214) 880-9622 Website: www.ymcadallas.org. The YMCA has around fifteen branches in the Metroplex area, and participants in the programs may buy memberships. There are additional fees for classes, camps, and other programs, but the fees are reduced for members. Some of the activities and services include full-day and after-school on-site child care, programs for preschoolers, sports lessons and teams, babysitting while parents participate in classes, summer day and resident camps, Christmas and spring break camps, and Adventure Guides.

YOUNG LIFE (214) 265-1505 Website: www.younglifenorthtexas .org. Young Life is a nondenominational Christian organization for youths in grades seven to twelve. The main group meeting is held by grade level twice each month at a designated location for junior high and high school students. Some groups have Campaigners, which are smaller groups that meets in members' homes during the weeks when there is not a general meeting. The purpose is to strengthen Christian values and provide good, clean fun and fellowship for teenagers. Some groups go on day trips and campouts. Their leadership is usually made up of young adults who are positive role models.

PLAYGROUNDS

One activity of which youngsters never tire is time at the playground, and thankfully, this activity is free. The Metroplex area has seven fantastic playgrounds designed by New York architect Robert Leathers, who consults with children about what they would like in a playground before designing it. His castlelike wooden playgrounds are listed below:

Armstrong Park, 200 James Collins, Duncanville
Friendship Park, 525 Polo, Grand Prairie
Grimes Park, 600 E. Wintergreen, DeSoto
Kidd Springs, 711 E. Canty, Oak Cliff
Prestonwood Elementary, 6625 LaCosa, Dallas
Victoria Park, Northgate and Pleasant Run, Irving
Waggoner Park, 2122 N. Carrier, Irving

Baby swings may be found at Armstrong, Grimes, Victoria, and Waggoner Parks. At Armstrong Park's Kidsville and Safety Town, (972) 780-5074, youngsters can ride their bicycles and tricycles down a miniature street, which has traffic signs and a railroad crossing. A trip to Kidd Springs might include a walk through the oriental gardens nearby.

Toddlers especially enjoy the small, picturesque playground at **Central Square** on Swiss Ave. by the Wilson Block near downtown. A larger preschool playground is at **Lake Highlands North Recreation Center** at Church Rd. and White Rock Trail. Both have sandy floors, so a pail and shovel would be a plus. Playgrounds for both preschoolers and older children are at **Lakewood Park**, 7100 Williamson; **Ridgewood Park**,

Trammel and Fisher; Richardson's **Huffines Park**, 1500 Apollo Rd.; Richardson's **Cottonwood Park**, Cottonwood and Belt Line; Garland's **Audubon Park**, Oates and O'Banion (site of Surf 'n Swim); and Highland Park's **Prather Park**, Lexington and Drexel. Toddlers enjoy **Bob Woodruff Park** at 2601 San Gabriel Park in Plano, while older kids circle the lake and ride on the bike trail.

The following are some more highly rated parks: **Caruth Park**, Hillcrest and Greenbriar; **Cherrywood Park**, Cedar Springs at Hedgerow; **University Park** at Lovers Ln. and Dickens; **City Lake Park**, Lakeside and Parkview, Mesquite (allows catch-and-release fishing in the city lake); **Gussie Waterworth Park** next to City Hall in Farmers Branch; **Martha Pointer Park** on Scott Mill Rd.; and **Kid's Corral** in **Mary Heads Carter Park** on Kelly Blvd. in Carrollton; **Willowdell Park**, 12225 Willowdell, east of Central and north of Forest; and **Kid's Country** across from Coppell City Hall. Another large, wooden castlelike playground is **KidsQuest** at **DeBusk Park**, 1625 Gross Rd. at LBJ in Mesquite.

Special-needs playgrounds include the **Scottish Rite Hospital Playground**, 2222 Welborn, which is primarily for hospital use; Oak Cliff's **Fantasy Landing**, which is wheelchair accessible, in **Kiest Park** at 3080 S. Hampton; Farmer's Branch's **Oran Good All Children's Playground** (Lion's Playground), 2600 Valley View; Grand Prairie's **C. P. Waggoner Park** on North Carrier Pkwy. near N.W. 19th St., **Friendship Park** on Polo Rd., and **Nance James Park** at 2000 Spikes St., which is used by Dalworth Elementary School; and Plano's **Enfield Park** at Legacy Dr. and Alma. **Casey's Clubhouse** at **Dove Park** in Grapevine has ramps and surfaces wide enough for wheelchairs. It is a completely handicapped-accessible play structure. Near Scottish Rite Hospital, at 3505 Maple, is a playground at **Reverchon Park** for kids with special needs. It has wheelchair access and signs in Braille. Call the Parks and Recreation Department of the city in which the park is located for particular information about suitability.

RANCHES AND HORSEBACK RIDING

Head up the family and move 'em out to a dude ranch for a day of Western fun Texas style or maybe just for an hour-long trail ride through beautiful woods with a picnic afterwards. Families who enjoy ranch life and would like to stay a week should contact two towns in the Hill Country, **Wimberley** at (512) 847-2201 or www.wimberley.org and **Bandera** at (800) 364-3833, for a list of their dude ranches. Closer to the Metroplex are some ranches and equestrian centers that offer horseback riding, Western- and English-style riding lessons, stables for boarding horses, and more fun through hayrides, barbecues, camps, and swimming pools. It is important to call first to make reservations. Most have a brochure.

Southfork Ranch, made famous by the television show *Dallas*, is open for tours, shopping, and special events. Call (972) 442-7800.

DUDE RANCHES

Double D Ranch (972) 289-2341. Double D Ranch has a general admission fee, which includes use of a picnic area, paddleboat rides, pony rides, miniature golf, petting zoo, playground, and pond fishing (bring your own bait and gear). Trail rides for ages eight and up and hayrides are extra. Children under three are free. Although the ranch is reserved mainly for groups, sometimes there will be space for families. Group rates include more activities. Double D is located in Mesquite southeast of LBJ and Lake June Rd. on Eastgate.

Coyote Texas is the new name for the former Texas Lil's Diamond A Ranch, opened under new ownership in March 2005. The ranch is a 193-acre facility equipped with many amenities and improvements, including an old western town, outdoor concert area, enclosed pavilion, swimming pool, rodeo arena, plus much more. Coyote Texas is northwest of Dallas in Justin. Check the Internet for contact information, not available at press time.

Rocking L Ranch (903) 560-0246 Website: www.rockinglranch.com. Horseback riding at the Rocking L is great, but for an additional grounds fee, cowpokes may fish, swim, picnic, and play games in the recreation room. Hayrides are also offered. Three rooms and a bunkhouse that sleeps sixty-five to seventy people are available for use, except during the summer when the resident horsemanship camp is held for ages eight to fifteen. Birthday parties are also welcome. This ranch is east of Dallas, near Terrell.

Wagon Wheel Ranch and Stables Metro (817) 481-8284 Website: www.awagonwheelranch.com. At Wagon Wheel Ranch, guided horseback riding over 300 acres is available as are night rides, hayrides, barbecues, picnics, lessons, and ponies for birthday parties. The ponies may be ridden there or taken to another location. Wagon Wheel Ranch is northwest of Dallas in Coppell.

HORSEBACK RIDING, RIDING INSTRUCTION, AND DAY CAMPS

Capricorn Equestrian Center (972) 530-1124. Lessons, horse shows, special events, birthday parties, summer day camps. Located in N. Garland at 1105 E. Blackburn.

Jolabec Riding Stables (972) 562-0658. Horseback riding in wooded area, picnic tables. Located north on Preston at Hwy. 380.

Las Colinas Equestrian Center (972) 869-0600. Horse shows, boarding, lessons. Located at 600 Royal, Las Colinas, Irving.

Merriwood Ranch (972) 235-5177, (972) 495-4646. Lessons, horse shows, summer day camp (instruction in riding and swimming, tennis, volleyball). Located in N. Garland at 2541 Big Springs Rd.

Palmerosa Ranch (972) 222-2732. Hayrides and cookouts, boarding, English- and Western-style lessons, birthday parties for young 'uns with Welsh ponies to ride (may take to another location). Located at 5790 Lumley in Mesquite.

Rocking M Stables (214) 682-8922. Riding programs for ages eight to adult. Show team events. Summer day camps. Located at 7807 Fair Oaks at Walnut Hill, Dallas.

THERAPEUTIC HORSEBACK RIDING

Equest (214) 827-7100. Therapeutic horsemanship. 2909 Swiss Ave., Dallas.

TROT Therapeutic Riding of Texas (972) 296-6334. Rollin' C Ranch, 1916 Westmoreland, DeSoto.

LAKES, STATE PARKS, AND RECREATION AREAS

Texans gravitate to the area lakes and state parks year-round for fishing, camping, and water sports. They provide public boat ramps, fishing piers, picnic areas, campsites, and marinas that rent boats and sell bait. Beautiful wooded areas inspire hikers and other nature lovers, and spotting wildlife is pure delight for all ages.

For information about the facilities at the lakes and state parks, write Texas Parks and Wildlife Department, 4200 Smith School Rd., Austin, Texas 78744, look online at www.tpwd.state.tx.us, or call (800) 792-1112 for their brochure "Information: Texas State Parks." The Texas Parks and Wildlife Department (TPWD) sells a $50 Conservation Passport, which is good for one year and offers unlimited entrance to state parks and a discount on overnight facility fees. It also offers a discount on the *Texas Parks and Wildlife Magazine* rates.

Park entrance fees range from $1 to $7 per person, and children twelve and under are admitted free. Overnight camping ranges from $4 to $36; rates are higher for screened shelters and cabins. Facilities, which range from primitive campsites to rustic cabins, may be reserved eleven months in advance by calling the central reservation number at (512) 389-8900. The central cancellation number is (512) 389-8910. For information about other Texas campsites, call the Texas Association of Campground Owners at (800) 657-6555 for a booklet called "RV and Camping Guide to Texas," or you may contact the Corps of Engineers or Park superintendent at the lake you wish to visit. Be sure to contact the lake during rainy seasons to see if flooding has closed facilities.

Many park areas have a day-use and overnight-camping fee, and campers pay both each day. Some parks operated by the Corps of Engineers and those privately owned also charge an additional fee for use of boat ramps and beaches. Look online at www.swf-wc.usace.army.mil/index.htm for the Ft. Worth District U.S. Army Corps of Engineers under "Recreation and General Information" for Texas reservoirs. Some entrance fees are per carload and some per person. Call (800) 460-9698 for a home boater course or look online at the TPWD site. On public lakes, fishermen seventeen or over must have a fishing license.

Two popular fishing programs for youths are KIDFISH and Get Hooked on Fishing, Not Drugs at (800) 792-1112 ext. 65. National Fishing Week is the first week of June.

At the following local fishing ponds, no license is necessary:

Catfish Corner (972) 222-2823. Catfish are raised here, and fishing is year-round from about 8 AM until dark. Admission is $2, with a fee of $1.85 per pound of fish caught. Bait is available. The pond is located east of Mesquite at 120 Lawson off I-30 East.

Gone Fishin' Metro (972) 427-6694. Channel catfish are caught year-round. A bait-and-tackle shop, drinks and snacks are available. There's not much shade. Located off Hwy. 175, Exit 741, at Crandall (nine miles from LBJ Fwy.).

Texas Freshwater Fisheries Center (903) 676-BASS Website: www.tpwd.state.tx/fish. A super fish hatchery and aquatic nature complex with 300,000 gallons of aquaria and home of the ShareLunker Program. Fish are stocked in a two-acre casting pond, and here children can learn the fundamentals of fishing. Rods, reels, and bait are included in the entrance fee. Special programs for junior anglers are scheduled regularly. No license is required for catch-and-release fishing. The center is open Tuesday to Saturday.

Bonham State Recreation Area Rt. 1, Box 337, Bonham, Texas 75418 (903) 583-5022. 300-acre park with 65-acre lake. Picnic sites and campsites, an overnight group facility and day-use group facility, playgrounds, a boat ramp, a boat dock, a fishing pier, and swimming. Take Texas Hwy. 78 South one mile to FM 271. Then go east about two miles.

Cedar Creek Reservoir Chamber of Commerce website: www.cedarcreeklakechamber.com. 33,750-acre reservoir. Commercial campsites, public boat ramps, marinas with boat rental, fishing, skiing, sailing, golf courses, and swimming. **Chamber Isle** is a small, public park with boat ramps, picnic tables, and swimming located between Seven Points and Gun Barrel City on the south side of 334 (small fee). **R. H. Lee Park** is located on FM 3062 (fee). **Sunny Glenn Marina Fishing Pier** is on Hwy.

198 (903) 489-0715. To reach Cedar Creek, take 175 South. Exit at SH 274 South. Go nine miles to Seven Points. Take 334 East toward Gun Barrel City. The lake is about seventy miles southeast of Dallas.

Cooper Lake and State Park Corps of Engineers at (903) 945-2108. 22,740 acres. This is a new lake with a state park being developed. It features the most facilities for handicapped visitors. Call about **Doctor's Creek Unit** (903) 395-3100 and the **South Sulphur Unit**. South Sulphur has campsites, screened shelters, and fifteen cabins for rent. Equestrian area and hiking trail. Located seventy-five miles east of Dallas between Commerce and Cooper, Texas.

Daingerfield Lake and Daingerfield State Park Rt. 1, Box 286-B, Daingerfield, Texas 75638 (903) 645-2921. Eighty-acre lake surrounded by 581 pine-covered acres. A lighted pier, a swimming area, a boat ramp (5 mph), canoe/paddleboat/rowboat rentals, three cabins, fifty-two campsites, and a group facility for twenty people. Take I-30 to Mt. Pleasant, exit at Ferguson Rd., and take Hwy. 49 East for about eighteen miles.

Grapevine Lake Rt. 1, Box 10, Grapevine, Texas 76051 (817) 481-4541. 7,380-acre reservoir. Seven public parks with boat ramps and camping facilities, fishing, swimming, and picnicking. **Silverlake Park** offers a visitor center, boat rentals, fishing supplies, and swimming. Call Silverlake Marina, Metro (817) 481-1918. Just for Fun at Silverlake Marina rents ski boats and pontoon boats. Call (817) 310-3000 or visit www .jff.net. **Oak Grove Park** has Scott's Landing Marina. Call (817) 481-4549. Take I-635 to Hwy. 121 and go west to 121 and Fairway Dr. Get a lake map for park sites. Ask about summer boating lessons for children by the U.S. Coast Guard Auxiliary.

Joe Pool Lake P.O. Box 941, Cedar Hill, Texas 75104 (972) 291-3900. 7,470-acre reservoir with a 1,800-acre state park (354 campsites) and 1,700 acres of other parkland (over 200 campsites) maintained by the Trinity River Authority. **Loyd Park** has 221 campsites, group campsites, showers, fishing piers, two playgrounds, a four-lane boat ramp with a dock, softball field, hiking trails, and the October Forest of Fear hayride and haunted trail. **Lynn Creek Park** has two four-lane boat ramps, a beach, eighty-one picnic sites, three group sites, a playground, restrooms, and an amphitheater on shore with lawn seating for more than 1,000. Lynn Creek Marina at Metro (817)640-4200 rents ski boats, fishing boats, pontoon boats, and party barges at 5700 Lake Ridge Pkwy. Take I-10 West to the Great Southwest exit. Go south. Southwest becomes Lake Ridge. The **Oasis** is a floating restaurant located at Lynn Creek. **Cedar Hill State Park**: $5 per person; children age twelve and under are free. Eight boat-launching lanes and two fishing jetties, 355 wooded campsites, two group pavilions, four playgrounds, a swimming beach, picnic sites, twelve comfort stations, a perch pond for kids, a bike trail, and **Penn Farm Historic Site**: gift shop (FM 1382). Joe Pool Marina and Park Store offers ski-boat rentals, wave runners, paddleboats, pontoon boats, and a houseboat with a slide. Call (972) 299-9010. Located ten miles southwest of Dallas, FM 1382.

Lake Arlington Green Oaks Blvd., south off Loop 303, Arlington, Texas. .2,275-acre lake. Boating, fishing, and picnics. **Arkansas Lane Park**, 6300 W. Arkansas. **Bowman Springs Park**, 7001 Poly Webb Rd.

Lake Bonham Recreation Area P.O. Box 305, Bonham, Texas 75418 (903) 583-8001. 1,200-acre city lake. Eighty-seven campsites, boating, fishing, skiing, swimming, miniature golf, and nine-hole golf. From 75 North, take the 121 exit to Bonham. In Bonham take 82 East (go to the right off 121), turn left on 78 North, turn right on FM 898, turn right on FM 3 to the welcome sign, and turn left into the park.

Lake Lavon P.O. Box 429, Wylie, Texas 75098 (972) 442-5711, (972) 442-3141. 21,000-acre reservoir northeast of Dallas. Twenty public parks. **Collin Park** offers swimming, boat ramps, camping. Lavon Boat Rental, (972) 429-7500, at Collin Park Marina, (972) 442-5755, rents ski boats, fishing boats, sailboats, jet skis, and pontoon boats and offers lessons in skiing and wakeboarding. To reach **Collin Park Marina and Campgrounds**, take US 75 to Parker Rd. (2514) and turn right. Turn right onto 1378 South and then take County Rd. 727 to Collin Park.

Lake Ray Hubbard Rockwall and Garland, Texas (972) 205-2750 ext. 2761. 22,745-acre lake. Fishing, sailing, and skiing (no swimming beaches). **Harbor Bay Marina** (exit Ridge Rd. from I-30): fishing barge, $6 per person (972) 771-0095. **Marina Del Ray** (2413 Rowlett, exit Belt Line off I-30): rents small fishing boats, jet skis, pontoon barge; fishing on the bank; fishing dock, adults, $4.50, children 12 and under, $2.50. Call (972) 240-2020. **North Texas Sailing School** at **Chandler's Landing Yacht Club** (Hwy. 740, 501 A Yacht Club Dr.): Twenty-foot boats, skipper available, lessons, renter must pass check-out. Call (972) 771-2002. **Captain's Cove Marina** (5965 Marina Dr.): rents a pontoon boat and ski boats. Call (972) 226-7100. Exit Ridge Rd. from I-30 for public boat ramps next to the highway. **Texas Queen riverboat** offers excursions and dinner cruises. Call (972) 771-0039. City of Rockwall Lakefest, mid-June. Fireworks, July 4.

Lake Ray Roberts Denton (940) 686-2148. New 29,350-acre reservoir. **Isle Du Bois State Park** at (817) 686-2148. 1,397 acres off FM 455 east of the dam. 115 multiuse campsites with water and electricity, fourteen equestrian campsites, a lighted boat ramp, a beach area, picnic sites, group picnic pavilions, a lighted fishing pier, 12 miles of dirt trail, 4.5 miles of paved trail (part is handicapped accessible), and playgrounds. **Johnson Park** at (940) 637-2294, north shore. 1,514 acres. When completed, there will be more than 4,000 acres in parklands and large wildlife management area.

Lake Texoma Project Manager, Denison Dam, Rt. 4, Box 493, Denison, Texas 75020 (903) 465-4990 Website: www.laketexoma.com. 89,000-acre lake in Texas and Oklahoma. Fifty parks, 100 picnic areas, marinas, fishing, boating, skiing, the **Cross Timbers Hiking Trail** (14 miles), tours of the powerhouse dam (1 PM), and the **Hagerman Wildlife Refuge** at (903) 786-2826. **Eisenhower State Park**, Rt. 2, Box 50K, Denison, Texas 75020 (903) 465-1956. 457 acres. Fishing piers, the Eisenhower Yacht Club Marina, a 4.2-mile hiking trail, thirty-five screened shelters, forty-eight campsites with water, fifty trailer campsites, forty-five campsites with water and electricity, a sandy beach, picnic areas, a group recreation hall, and a pavilion. Take US 75 to 1310. Go west to Park Road 20 and the park entrance.

Texoma marinas and resorts include the following:

Grandpappy Point Marina: Sailboat charters and lessons, cabins, RV hookups, rental ski boats, wave runners, pontoon boats, located just outside Denison; call (888) 855-1972.

Highport: yachts, volleyball and basketball courts, beach, located on Highport Rd. in Pottsboro; call (903) 786-7000.

Cedar Bayou: boat ramp and rental, store, located in Gordonville; call (903) 523-4248.

Cedar Mills: campground, boat charters, cabins, RV and trailer hookups, sailing school, store, and restaurant (open Wednesday to Sunday), located in Gordonville; call (903) 523-4222.

Tanglewood Resort Hotel and **Conference Center** located in Pottsboro; call (800) 833-6569. Denison Chamber of Commerce at (903) 465-1551.

Lake Texoma Resort Park (800) 654-8240. Located ten miles west of US 69 on SH 70 between Durant and Kingston, Oklahoma. Lodge, ninety-two guest rooms; sixty-seven cottages; 500 campsites; group camp for 160 people; eighteen-hole golf course; indoor recreation and fitness center; stables; full-service marina; Funland with bumper boats, go-carts, and miniature golf; park naturalist and planned activities. See **Day Trips** for more things to do around Denison.

Lake Whitney P.O. Box 5038, Laguna Park Station, Clifton, Texas 76634-5038 (817) 694-3189 Website: www.lakewhitney.com. 23,560-acre reservoir with fourteen federal parks and **Lake Whitney State Park**. Marinas, a tour of the dam, fishing, swimming, boating, and scuba diving. Lake Whitney State Park, P.O. Box 1175, Whitney, Texas 76692 (817) 694-3793. 1,315-acre park, two-hour drive southwest. Seventy-eight campsites, a recreation hall, boat ramps, a lighted airstrip, hiking and mini-bike trails. Ask about a swimming beach and screened shelters (problems with flooding). **Lake Whitney Marina at Juniper Cove**, (254) 694-3129 or (866) 600-1206, air-conditioned cabins, campgrounds, boat rentals, and a fishing barge. From I-35, exit Hillsboro and take Hwy. 22 West to Whitney. Follow signs west three miles on FM 1244.

Lewisville Lake 1801 N. Mill St., Lewisville, Texas 75057 (972) 434-1666. 23,280-acre lake and fourteen parks. Fishing, skiing, swimming, sailing, and camping. **Lake Park**, operated by the City of Lewisville at (972) 219-3550: swimming, boat ramps, camping, and a fishing barge to the northwest; call (972) 436-9341. Take I-35 North. Exit at Justin Rd. (407) and take a right to Lake Park Rd. Fee. **East Hill Park**, operated by the Corps of Engineers at (972) 434-1666: swimming, fishing, ramps, and the Pier 121 Marina; call (972) 625-2233. Just for Fun rents a variety of boats; call (972) 370-7700. **Hidden Cove Park** (formerly Lewisville State Park), Rt. 2, Box 353H, Frisco, Texas 75034 Website: www.gorp.away.com, operated by The Colony: 721 acres. Fifty campsites, thirty-eight screened shelters, three pavilions, an enclosed dining hall that seats 100 at water's edge, a playground, picnicking, ramps, and swimming in the day-use area. Daily entrance fee. Take Hwy. 423 to Hackberry Rd. The park is at the end of the road.

Possum Kingdom Lake (888) 779-8330 Website: www.possum kingdomlake.com. 17,700-acre lake. Campsites, marinas, scuba diving to 150 feet, swimming, and boating. **Possum Kingdom State Park**: Forty miles west of Dallas, 1,724 acres, official state longhorn herd, 116 campsites, six air-conditioned and heated cabins, a lighted fishing pier, a boat ramp, playgrounds, a swimming area, a park store, restrooms, showers, and wildlife; call (940) 549-1803. In peak season, tent and popup camper rentals are available. Ask about the kids' fishing rodeo in late March or April. Take US Hwy. 180 to Caddo. Drive seventeen miles north on Park Road 33. **Camp Grady Spruce** (866) 656-2267 Website: www.campgradyspruce.org, YMCA camp.

Purtis Creek State Park Rt. 1, Box 506, Eustace, Texas 75124 (903) 425-2332. 355-acre lake. Fifty-nine campsites with water and electricity, twelve primitive campsites with water nearby, a two-lane boat ramp, two docks, a fifty-boat limit with wake-speed restriction, picnic sites, a playground, a hiking trail, fishing for bass on a catch-and-release basis, but you may keep catfish and crappie, two lighted fishing piers, two rearing/trout ponds, a swimming area, and a park store with canoe and paddleboat rentals. No waterskiing or sailing. Near Cedar Creek Lake. From Dallas, go east on Hwy 175 to Eustace. Turn left (north) on FM 316 for 2.5 miles to park.

5. FESTIVALS AND SPECIAL EVENTS

Around Dallas there is always something to celebrate. The theme for the festival might be related to cultural heritage, history, physical fitness, the arts, nature, sports, or technology and products. Whatever the reason for the gathering, appreciative crowds show up for the fun, and very often, worthy service and health organizations benefit from the proceeds. Call or watch for newspaper announcements about the festivals because all may not be held annually, or they may change months or locations. Keeping current telephone numbers for information is also difficult. If the number listed is out of date, try calling the visitor center of the city in which the event takes place, and its personnel can probably give you some information. Please look in Chapter Three for **performing-arts festivals** and in Chapter Four for **sporting events**. The Dallas Convention and Visitors Bureau maintains a calendar of major events on its website at www.visitdallas.com. Also try www.2chambers .com to locate suburban cities.

JANUARY

SBC Cotton Bowl Classic. Fair Park. This annual college football game is a clash between two of the nation's best teams. Call (214) 634-7525.

Kidfilm. Angelica Theater. Kidfilm, an international children's film festival sponsored by the USA Film Festival, takes place on a Saturday and a Sunday afternoon. Call (214) 821-6300.

Martin Luther King, Jr., Birthday Events. Look for special events and parades announced in the newspaper at places such as Southern Methodist University, Martin Luther King Jr. Recreation Center, South Dallas Cultural Center, and other area colleges and community centers, as well as the African American Museum.

Dallas Winter Boat Show. Dallas Market Hall, 2200 Stemmons. Motorboats and sailboats, exhibits, water-sports products and services, and the trout fishing tank fill Market Hall during this show. It's family fun even if a boat is not in your budget. Call (469) 549-0673.

Texas Fishing and Outdoor Show. Big Town Exposition Center, Big Town Blvd. and Hwy. 80, Mesquite. Exhibits of rods, reels, lures, and boats turn the heads of avid fishermen at this exhibition. Call (972) 673-8304 or visit www.texasfishingshow.com.

Chinese New Year Events. Celebration of the new year usually takes place at the Crow Collection of Asian Art and Chinese restaurants in the area. Call (214) 979-6430 or visit www.crowcollection.com.

Dino Dash and Discovery Fest. This annual race to benefit the Science Place at Fair Park also features activities for children. Call (214) 428-5555 or visit www.scienceplace.org.

Second Saturday on the Square. Old Downtown Lancaster. Crafts and unique items are for sale, and there's music and entertainment each second Saturday of the month. Call (972) 227-2579.

Canton First Monday Trade Days. Canton, Hwy. 19. Thursday to Sunday before the first Monday of each month. Call (903) 567-6556.

Third Monday Trade Days. 4550 University, McKinney. Friday to Sunday preceding the third Monday of each month. Call (972) 562-5466.

FEBRUARY

Harlem Globetrotters. American Airlines Center. Basketball at its best and funniest is the forte of this traveling troupe. Call (214) 373-8000.

African American History Month Activities. Check the newspapers throughout February for special activities at museums, bookstores, galleries, recreation centers, colleges, and performing-arts centers.

Texas Rangers Mid-Winter Banquet and Carnival. Arlington Convention Center, 1200 Stadium Dr., Arlington. Outstanding players are honored at this annual banquet and carnival.

Valentine's Day Events. Many of the public libraries plan special activities for Valentines, and the arboretum sometimes offers free admission for sweethearts. Look for the special Hearts and Flowers market at the Farmers Market downtown.

Dallas Spring Home and Garden Show. Dallas Market Hall. This large show features must-have items for the home and garden and includes demonstrations and entertainment. Call (800) 654-1480.

Golden Gloves Tournament. Fair Park Coliseum. For more than sixty-seven years, this annual boxing tournament has been in Dallas. Call (214) 670-8400.

Trout Fish Out. Armstrong Pool, Duncanville. Two days of fishing for all age groups. Call (972) 780-5090.

MARCH

North Texas Irish Festival. Fair Park. Forty musical groups on eight stages, Irish food and drink, performance workshops, jugglers, magicians, and the Urchin Street Children's Faire highlight this celebration of the Irish held on an early March weekend. Call (214) 823-4370.

Dallas Blooms. Dallas Arboretum and Botanical Garden, 8617 Garland Rd. The opening of Dallas Blooms signals that springtime has arrived in Dallas. The event lasts about one month, and the beautiful flowers are breathtaking every year. Call (214) 327-4901.

Arts and Letters Live Jr. Dallas Museum of Art. A pint-size version of the adult series that includes lectures, readings, discussion groups, and maybe even food and movies. Call (214) 922-1219 or visit www.dm-art.org.

Downtown Dallas St. Patrick's Day Parade. Intersection of Commerce and Griffin to Ervay, west on Pacific to West End. This midafternoon celebration features marching bands, floats, clowns, and more. At about 4 PM, the West End Festival on the Plaza begins with more family entertainment, live music, and food. Call (214) 234-2040.

Hoop-It-Up Spring Warmup. Lone Star Park, Grand Prairie. Three-on-three outdoor basketball tournament on a weekend. Call (972) 392-5750.

Big 12 Women's and Big 12 Men's Basketball Games. These college basketball games are played by the best of the season. Men: call (214) 221-8326, American Airlines Center. Women: call (214) 939-2770, Reunion Arena.

Greenville Avenue St. Patrick's Day Parade. On Greenville from Blackwell to Yale. A very informal, enthusiastic parade of inventive floats and bands is planned annually for Greenville Ave. from 11 AM to 1 PM. Call (214) 368-6722.

Texas Storytelling Festival. Denton, Texas. Civic Center Park on the weekend. Call (940) 387-8336.

Dallas New Car Auto Show. Dallas Convention Center. Call (214) 939-2700.

Very Special Arts Festival. Plano Centre, 2000 E. Spring Creek. Held on a Sunday afternoon, this free arts festival is tailored for children with special needs and includes hands-on artwork, various performing-arts groups, free refreshments, and a goody bag to take home. Call (972) 941-7272.

Dino Day. Museum of Natural History, Fair Park. In celebration of dinosaurs, a parade and costume contest, films, scavenger hunt, and art work are featured each year. Call (214) 421-DINO.

Spring Breakout. Six Flags. Look for special events in addition to regular Six Flags fare. Call (817) 530-6000.

Shrine Circus. Resistol Arena, Mesquite Rodeo Grounds. Call (972) 285-8777.

Annual Dallas Video Festival. Angelica Theater and Dallas Museum of Art. A film festival that is primarily for adults features screenings of local, regional, and internationally produced programs. Call (214) 428-8700.

Special Olympics Uptown Run and Trolley Walk. Annette Strauss Artist Square. This event has been held for more than seventeen years and includes a Kids K and a special Olympian run. Call (214) 528-1290.

Disney on Ice. American Airlines Center. Skaters portray favorite Disney characters. Call (214) 222-3687.

Out of the Loop Festival. Water Tower Theatre, Addison Theatre Centre. Family performances and entertainment highlight this festival. Call (972) 450-6232.

Kite Weekend Celebration. Heard Museum, McKinney. This high-flying event includes stunt kite demonstrations, kite-making workshops, nature walks, and more festivities. Call (972) 562-5566.

Texas . . . History Alive! Farmers Branch Historical Park. 2540 Farmers Branch Ln. The Texana Living History Association promotes this annual fest with historical costumes, prairie campsites, crafts, and Wild West–era games. Call (214) 426-2121.

APRIL

Ennis Bluebonnet Trails. Pierce Park, 112 N.W. Main, Ennis. Follow a map guiding you to brilliant fields of bluebonnets during mid to late April. Arts and crafts, food, an antique show, and more add to the festival. Call the Texas Department of Transportation hotline at (800) 452-9292 for information on where to spot beautiful wildflowers. Call (888) 366-4748.

Dallas Cup Youth Soccer. Young people from around the world compete at this annual event held at various fields and stadiums. Call (214) 221-3636.

Hot Dogs and Hoops Fest. American Airlines Center, Dallas. A basketball hotdogging competition for kids fourteen and under and family entertainment highlight this festival. Six winners get to compete at a Mavericks home game. Free admission and parking. Call (972) 393-8453 or visit www.americanairlinescenter.com.

USA Film Festival. Various theaters. For more than thirty years, films, filmmakers, and fans have gathered for films and discussions. Call (214) 821-6300.

Scarborough Faire. FM 66 and I-35E, Waxahachie. At Scarborough Faire, an English Renaissance village, families watch knights in armor competing, feast on hearty foods, marvel at the falconer and his birds of prey, watch jugglers and sorcerers, enjoy a variety of performing artists, and browse in village shops. The festival takes place on weekends and on Memorial Day from later April to mid-June. Call (972) 938-3247.

North Texas Jazz Festival. Hotel Intercontinental, Dallas. For more than four years, this festival has brought both nationally and locally recognized jazz musicians to perform incredible music. Call (972) 450-6221.

Folklorico Festival. Annette Strauss Artist Square. Multiethnic artists share their music, food, customs, and dance at this two-day festival. Call (972) 788-0604.

The Learning Fair. Northpark Center. Sponsored by the Brain/Behavior Center, the fair brings together both public and private agencies to provide services for the learning disabled. Counselors, educators, and parents are at thirty-five booths, and entertainment is scheduled. Free.

Galleria Primavera. Galleria, LBJ and Dallas Pkwy. Garden exhibits, music, and ice-skating events are scheduled in the shopping mall during one week in April. Call (972) 702-7100.

Metroplex Annual Doll Show. Plano Centre, Plano. This large annual doll show sometimes changes locations. Call (972) 263-4577.

Easter Egg Hunts: Farmers Branch Historical Park, Garland Easter Eggstravaganza, Las Colinas, recreation centers, West End Marketplace, selected Grand Prairie parks, Grapevine parks, Plano parks, Rockwall parks. **Easter Bunny**: Valley View Center, downtown Carrollton, Highland Park Village. **Parties**: Recreation centers and libraries. Zoo parade and scavenger hunt. **Sunrise service**: Check with the Biblical Arts Center and local churches.

Easter Brunches with Special Celebration: Check with Antares, The Adolphus, Blue Mesa, Harvey Hotel–Plano, Lawry's The Prime Rib, Maggiano's Little Italy, Embassy Suites Park Central Area, The Old Warsaw, Westin Stonebriar Resort, Arboretum, Fairmont Hotel, Gaylord Texan Resort.

Easter Concert. Lee Park. The Dallas Symphony celebrates Easter with a free performance. Call (214) 692-0203.

Arbor Day/Earth Day Celebrations: Dallas Museum of Natural History, Grapevine Treefest, Heard Museum, state parks, White Rock Lake, Dallas Arboretum, Farmers Branch Mallon Park, downtown festivals in Annette Strauss Artist Square and Pegasus Plaza.

KSCS Country Fair. Texas Stadium. Concerts and rodeo.

Art Fiesta. Old Downtown Carrollton. Arts and crafts, food, children's activities, and music entertain visitors at this annual festival. Call (972) 416-6600.

Prairie Dog Chili Cook-off and World Championship of Pickled Quail Egg Eating. Traders Village, Grand Prairie. In addition to the chili cook-off, enjoy music, more food, and the flea market. Call (972) 647-2331.

Mesquite Rodeo Parade and Celebration. Mesquite. This annual parade kicks off rodeo season, which runs from April through September. The parade features horses, floats, bands, stagecoaches, and drill teams on a Saturday afternoon. Call (972) 285-8777.

Cardboard Boat Regatta. Hurricane Harbor, Arlington. Call (817) 860-6752, (800) 342-4305.

Sports: Seasons begin for the Mesquite Rodeo, Lone Star Park Thoroughbred Horse Racing, and the Texas Rangers.

Kennedy Center Imagination Celebration. Old City Park. A free celebration of visual and performing arts for children. More than thirty arts-related organizations take part. The site and month sometimes changes. Call (214) 421-5141.

MAY

Richardson Wildflower and Music Festival. Galatyn Park, US 75 at Campbell, Richardson. On a weekend, visitors get a taste of Richardson, music, food, and spring wildflowers to admire. Call (972) 744-4581.

Memorial Day Concert. Flag Pole Hill. The Dallas Symphony performs outdoors for families. Bring a blanket or lawn chair. Call (214) 692-0203.

Cinco de Mayo Celebrations: Greenville Ave., Fair Park (midway, music, food), Texas Stadium, Latino Cultural Center, Traders Village, Samuell-Grand Recreation Center, Pike Park. **Riofest**: Sponsored by radio stations and held at Trinity River Bottom, at Commerce and Industrial.

Artfest. Fair Park. Artfest is a lively, colorful, weekend celebration of the arts that includes the work of 300 jury-selected artists, Artfest for Kids, outdoor concert stages with a variety of musical entertainment, and food. Artfest Week includes a variety of activities around town. Call (214) 565-8400 or visit www.dallasartfest.com.

Boy Scouts Annual Scout Show. Dallas Market Center. The largest Scout event in Texas, the Circle Ten Council Show is highlighted by more than 400 booths with demonstrations, games, and exhibits. Other activities include outdoor cooking, a climbing tower, music, and crafts. Call (214) 902-6700 or visit www.circle10.org.

PetPallooza. River Legacy Parks West, 701 N.W. Green Oaks Blvd., Arlington. Pets and their people enjoy exhibits, a one-mile pet and people walk, entertainment from pet associations, an adoption center, and more. Call (817) 860-6752.

KidFish. City Lake Park, S. Galloway and Parkview, Mesquite. There is fishing for sixteen and under at a stocked lake. Equipment is provided if the child does not have his or her own. Free. Call (972) 290-2108 or visit www.mainstreetmesquite.com.

Main Street Days. Main St., Grapevine. Main Street Days celebrates Grapevine's railroad and agricultural heritage with musical entertainment, food, reenactments, and children's activities. Call (817) 410-3185 or visit www.grapevinetexasusa.com.

McKinney Art and Jazz Festival. Downtown McKinney, one mile east of US 75, on Louisiana. Jazz and blues, art, food, a car show, and art for children liven up this annual festival. Call (972) 562-6880.

Safari Days. Dallas Zoo. The annual family day includes zoo animals, live music, a bounce house, and crafts. Call (214) 670-5656.

Texas Black Invitational Rodeo. Fair Park Coliseum. The best of America's black cowboys and cowgirls participate in rodeo events.

Taste of Addison. Addison Conference Center and Theatre Center. Food, music, entertainment, and activities for kids spell fun at this festival. Call (800) 233-4766.

Mother's Day Weekend and Brunch. Dallas Arboretum and Botanical Garden. The arboretum plans a special weekend for Mom and the family each year. Reservations are required for brunch. Call (214) 327-8263.

Spring Flower Festival. Farmers Market, 1010 S. Pearl, downtown. Farmers Market celebrates spring with flowers, music, arts and crafts, games, and more. Call (214) 939-2808.

Main Street Days. Main Street Historic District, Grapevine. Plans for this celebration include arts and crafts, music, food, carnival rides, and a street dance. Call (817) 481-0454.

Cottonwood Art Festival. Cottonwood Park, Belt Line at Cottonwood Dr. in Richardson. Visitors may browse and purchase artwork by local artists. The festival includes food, entertainment, and ArtStop for Kids. Call (972) 638-9116 or visit www.cottonwoodartfestival.com.

Asian Festival. Artists Square. This festival includes music, dance, food, arts and crafts, martial arts, and activities for children. Call (972) 241-8592.

Chestnut Square Art Festival. McDonald and Anthony St., McKinney. Art work is displayed on the porches and lawns of historic homes in this two-day event. Call (214) 724-8461 or visit www.chestnut square.org.

White Rock Prairie Fest. Bath House Cultural Center, 521 E. Lawther, White Rock Lake. This annual festival celebrates the prairie on which we live with prairie-related demonstrations, Indian dances, wildflower walks, and more. Call (214) 670-8885.

JUNE

Pepsi Kid Around. Annette Strauss Artist Square. For more than eleven years, this event has provided a variety of activities to promote creativity, safety, and education. Sometimes the location changes. Call (214) 443-7764 or (214) 559-2170.

Saturday in Fair Park. A special day is planned in Fair Park so that families can enjoy its museums and entertainment. Call (214) 670-8400.

Juneteenth Festivals: City Hall Plaza, Fair Park, and South Dallas Cultural Center are usually sites of celebration. Texas Scottish Festival and Highland Games. Maverick Stadium, UTA. The weekend festival includes bagpipe and drumming competitions, Scottish food, Scottish and Celtic athletic events, children's games, and a dog show. Call (817) 654-2293 or visit www.texasscottishfestival.com.

Hoop-It-Up. West End, downtown. This three-on-three basketball tournament is for children and adults, and wheelchair teams are included. Each team plays at least three games. Call (972) 392-5750.

Toad Holler Creekfest. DeSoto Towne Center. Games, arts and crafts, food, children's activities, and music add to the fun in DeSoto on the first Saturday in June. Call (972) 224-3565.

Irving Heritage Festival. Heritage Park, 2nd and Main, Irving. Demonstrations of historic crafts, food, arts and crafts, and music take place on a Saturday. Call (972) 259-1249.

Fritz Park Petting Farm Parade and Carnival, Fritz Park, 312 E. Vilbig, Irving. The parade in honor of the opening of the Petting Farm usually forms at Senter Park (900 S. Senter) on a Saturday morning in early June and proceeds to Fritz Park for the carnival. The Petting Farm is open in June and July. Call (972) 721-2716.

Garden of Music Evenings. Dallas Arboretum. Thursdays at 7 PM during June and July. Relax and listen to live music outdoors. Call (214) 327-4901.

July Fourth Celebrations: Dallas and almost all surrounding cities plan festivities and fireworks to celebrate America's independence. Contact your chamber of commerce for its celebration plans if they are not listed here. Fireworks are illegal within the city limits without a permit because they are a fire hazard. Please check Chapter Three for performing-arts festivals on the Fourth.

Trinity Fest. Downtown Reunion Arena grounds. Trinity Fest includes food, entertainment, kids' activities, arts and crafts, and fireworks. Call (214) 571-1000.

Old-Fashioned Fourth at Old City Park. 1717 Gano. This old-fashioned celebration includes an all-join-in parade, contests, dance, music, games, and tours. Call (214) 421-5141.

Park Cities Fourth of July Parade. Highland Park Town Hall, 4700 Drexel, to University Park Town Hall, 3800 University. For more than thirty years, this Fourth of July Parade has delighted residents because they join in the parade. They ride on floats, bicycles, antique cars, and go-carts and march in bands. Snow cones and hot dogs are awaiting them at the end of the line at Goar Park.

Star Spangled Fourth of July. Downtown Garland. This colorful celebration includes food, crafts, C & W entertainment, children's activities, and fireworks. Call (972) 205-2749.

Star Spangled Spectacular. Clark Recreation Center, Plano. Patriotic festivities, food, music, and fireworks finish the day. Call (972) 422-0296.

Kaboom Town. Addison. An incredible display of fireworks at the corner of Arapaho and Quorum is simulcast with patriotic music on KVIL radio station on July 3. It's a good idea to get to the area by 8 PM to find a good spot. Call (800) 233-4766.

Arlington Fourth of July Parade. Downtown Arlington. More than thirty-eight parades have celebrated Independence Day in Arlington. The parade, which has more than 150 entries, begins at 9 AM. Call (817) 303-5700 or visit www.arlington4th.com.

Las Colinas. Williams Square, Irving. There are concerts and fireworks and a parade at Rock Island and O'Connor. Call (972) 831-8818.

Richardson Fourth of July. Breckinridge Park, Richardson. Richardson's celebration usually begins in the early evening with demonstrations by groups, such as kite flyers and remote-controlled car clubs. Adding to the fun are performing-arts entertainment, clowns, and face painters. Fireworks end the evening with a bang. Call (972) 680-7943.

Recreation Centers' July 4th Celebrations: Check with local recreation centers for special events. Lake Highlands North Recreation Center holds an annual neighborhood parade for all family members.

Ringling Brothers and Barnum & Bailey Circus. American Airlines Center. This favorite three-ring extravaganza is anticipated each July. There is usually a designated family night when the admission is less expensive. Call (214) 222-3687.

Taste of Dallas. West End Historical District. During this delicious event, restaurants present samples of their best fare. Outdoor entertainment and a children's area are included in the well-attended festivities. Call (214) 741-7185.

Dallas Zoo Dollar Day. Dallas Zoo. The zoo says thanks through a $1 admission price all day. Call (214) 670-5656.

AUGUST

Dallas Cowboys Preseason Games. Texas Stadium. For those who miss the Cowboys and can endure the summer heat, the preseason games begin in August. Call (972) 785-5000.

Dallas Morning News Dance Festival. Annette Strauss Artist Square. This festival showcases new and seasoned professional dance companies. Sometimes it is held around the first of September. Call (214) 953-1977.

Young Audiences of North Texas: Showcase. Booker T. Washington High School for the Performing Arts. The yearly showcase features nonstop performances on eight stages, workshops, booths about children's programs, and more. Call (214) 520-0023.

SEPTEMBER

Labor Day Parade and Jaycee Jubilee. Central Park, Garland. In honor of Labor Day, the Jaycees plan a downtown parade, a festival with crafts, a carnival, and the Junior Miss Garland Program over a four-day period. Call (972) 463-1971.

Grapefest. Main St., Grapevine. Grapevine honors its namesake in this festival, which includes wine tasting and judging, vintage cars, GrapeFair, and children's GrapeGames. Call (800) 547-6338.

TACA Family Festival. Meyerson Symphony Center. This festival features hands-on art for ages two to ten, as well as special guests and entertainment. Call (214) 692-0203.

Japanese Fall Festival. Fujitsu Bldg., 2811 Telecom Pkwy., Richardson. Japanese food, dancers, demonstrations, and music are featured. Call (972) 458-0478 or visit www.godja.org.

National Championship Indian Powwow. Traders Village, Grand Prairie. Tribes and spectators gather annually for the weekend powwow, which features Indian dancing and competition, food, arts and crafts, exhibits of teepees, and more entertainment. Call (972) 647-2331.

International Air Show. Alliance Airport. A variety of aircraft perform for families. Call (817) 491-9381 or visit www.allianceairshow.com.

Oktoberfest. Arapaho and Quorum, Addison. German food, a carnival, and children's entertainment are featured in this fall celebration. Call (800) 233-4766.

Greek Food Festival. Holy Trinity Greek Orthodox Church. This weekend festival offering Greek food, cookbooks, music, and crafts draws appreciative crowds annually. Call (972) 991-1166.

Family Fun Festival. Heard Museum and Wildlife Sanctuary, McKinney. Nature activities, crafts, games, wagon rides, nature trails, animals, and food entertain families at the annual Fun Festival. Call (972) 562-5566.

Great Fountain Plaza Festival. Richardson Civic Center, Central and Arapaho. Family games and entertainment are featured. Call (972) 234-4141.

Oak Cliff's Tour of Homes and Arts Festival. Kidd Springs Park, 711 W. Canty. A tour of six homes and a family festival that usually includes a parade, an arts-and-crafts show, entertainment, and children's events is fun for all on a September weekend.

Plano Hot-Air Balloon Festival. Oak Point Park, Plano. Hot-air balloon races, arts and crafts, and music are featured during this colorful weekend event. Call (972) 867-7566 or visit www.planoballoonfest.org.

Texas Heritage Crafts Festival, Six Flags Over Texas, Arlington, Metro (817) 640-8900. More than 200 crafts folk set up shop at Six Flags on two weekends in September. Live music and food as well as demonstrations of almost-forgotten pioneer crafts add to the entertainment. Call (817) 530-6000.

OCTOBER

State Fair of Texas. Fair Park. See Chapter One for highlights of Texas's three-week fair, including concerts, midway, exhibits, food, contests, game booths, parades, the Pan American Livestock Exposition, rodeo competition, and much more. The state fair is Dallas's second most popular attraction.

Smith's Pumpkin Patch. This three-acre pumpkin patch, located in Aubrey near Denton, is open for pick-your-own pumpkins right out of the patch. This field trip is great fun for groups such as Scouts. Call (940) 365-2201 or visit www.the-pumpkinpatch.com.

American Indian Art Festival and Market. Annette Strauss Artist Square. More than 150 documented American Indian visual and performing artists from the Southwest shine at this downtown fest. Sometimes held in November. Call (214) 891-9640.

West End Cattle Drive. West End Historic District. An Old West–style cattle drive is held through the streets of the West End. Call (214) 891-9640.

Women's Swimming and Diving Classic. Southern Methodist University's Perkins Natatorium. The competition is among the best women's NCAA swimming programs. Call (214) 768-2883.

Dallas Blooms Autumn. Dallas Arboretum and Botanical Garden. The arboretum, coated in many brilliantly colored flowers, lures native Dallasites and visitors alike to the month-long celebration of plants and gardening. Demonstrations, plant sales, special exhibits, and entertainment are scheduled for the entire family. Call (214) 327-4901.

Texas–OU Cotton Bowl Football Game. Fair Park. This annual football clash is held on Saturday afternoon during the state fair. Fans gather for all sorts of celebrations on Friday night, and the winners continue to celebrate throughout the weekend. Call (214) 670-8400.

Harvest Fest. Armstrong Park, Duncanville. This shindig is held on the third Saturday in October with more than 120 art-and-crafts vendors, exhibits and demonstrations, an auto show, and a children's area. Call (972) 780-5090.

Country Day on the Hill. Cedar Hill. Food, games, entertainment, and the Children's Corner add up to a down-home good time. Call (972) 291-7817.

Vineyard Fair. Howell St. between McKinney and the Crescent on Cedar Springs. A benefit for the Creative Learning Center, the Vineyard Fair draws thousands of shoppers, who browse at booths stocked by artisans, sample food and wine, and listen to live musical entertainment.

Oktoberfest, Traders Village. 2602 Mayfield, Grand Prairie. Oktoberfest is a European-style festival featuring oompah music, German food, a beer garden, and dancing. Call (972) 647-2331.

Fall Harvest Festival. Dallas Farmers Market, 1010 S. Pearl, downtown. This celebration of fall's bounty includes music, Pumpkin Junction, fresh produce, and exhibits on Saturday and Sunday. Call (214) 670-5880.

Harambee Festival. Martin Luther King Community Center, 2922 MLK Blvd. This all-day festival showcases African American culture. Call (214) 670-8355.

Fright Nights. Six Flags Over Texas, Arlington. A variety of creepy creatures gather for a Halloween celebration at Six Flags. Call (817) 530-6000.

Haunted House at the Palace of Wax. Ripley's Believe It or Not! and the Palace of Wax, 601 E. Safari, Grand Prairie. What is alive and what is not is difficult to ascertain in this annual walk of terror. Call (972) 263-2391.

Boo at the Zoo. Dallas Zoo. Games, prizes, music and costumed characters are planned for Halloween fun. Call (214) 670-5656.

Halloween in the Park. Farmers Branch Historical Park, Farmers Branch Ln. at Ford Rd. A haunted house, hayrides, carnival, and more treats are presented for the entertainment of spooks of all ages.

Batty at the Ballpark. South side of the Ballpark in Arlington. Legends of the Game Museum sponsors this annual event with pumpkin decorating, face painting, games, and stories. Call (817) 273-5097.

Haunted Houses: Begin checking the Friday "Guide" section in the *Dallas Morning News* from mid-October through Halloween for listings of organizations that offer haunted houses, carnivals, and other Halloween events. *Dallas Family* and *dallas child* magazines also list Halloween activities that are appropriate for children in their October issues. The March of Dimes presents haunted houses at multiple locations. Some events are too frightening for young children. Call first if you have questions about suitability.

NOVEMBER

Dallas YMCA Turkey Trot. Dallas City Hall Plaza. This annual 3.5-mile run showcases the downtown area and benefits a shelter for homeless and abused teenagers. A family tent has activities for children. Call (214) 954-0500.

Texas Stampede. American Airlines Center. This is an exciting combination of country music and championship rodeo. Call (214) 520-8874 or visit www.texasstampede.org.

Annual Dallas Cowboys NFL four-on-four flag football. This is a competition with 100 different divisions and special youth teams.

Senior Citizens Craft Fair. Automobile Building, Fair Park. Family members of all ages will appreciate the talents behind the handmade items at this benefit craft fair sponsored by the Junior League of Dallas.

Chi Omega Christmas Market. Dallas Convention Center. This is a favorite annual bazaar featuring over 130 merchants. Call (214) 890-8131.

Dallas Video Festival. Dallas Museum of Art. Presented by the Video Association and the Dallas Museum of Art, this video festival is an exhibition of more than 250 screenings produced by independent media artists for adults and children, and it is scheduled from Thursday to Sunday in either the first or second weekend in November. Parents and children enjoy the kid-video programs and hands-on workshops offered on Saturday and Sunday. Some of the videos are made for children, and some are made by children.

Christmas Activities: Check the newspapers toward the end of November because some tree lightings and special events begin the last weekend of November. Galleria: (972) 702-7100. Highland Park Village: (214) 559-2740.

DECEMBER

Tree Lightings, Parades, and Carriage Rides: Most of the city halls and some of the shopping, entertainment, and community centers, such as the Galleria, Crescent, and West End, have breathtaking tree lightings to celebrate the Christmas season. Some, like Dallas, Carrollton, Allen, Richardson, and Grapevine, include parades. Call your chamber of commerce for specific dates and times. The **Dallas Holiday Tree Lighting and Parade** takes place at City Hall Plaza and includes a visit from Santa, Santa's Village, choirs, dancers, Christmas critters, and refreshments. Carriage tours of lights are usually offered at Highland Park Village, Old City Park, Old Downtown Plano, and the West End.

Although Dallas rarely has a white Christmas, it truly is a wintery wonderland of holiday entertainment for families, as the following festivities will attest. Also, look for special musical and theatrical events in Chapter Three's Performing Arts festivals.

Adolphus/Children's Christmas Parade. Commerce and Griffith, Downtown Dallas. More than 160,000 people come out to cheer on the annual parade featuring floats, bands, antique cars, horses and riders, clowns, favorite characters, and celebrities. Check the newspapers or call for the route. Call (214) 456-8383. For reserved bleacher seating, call (214) 456-8630.

Holiday at Shops of West End Marketplace. West End Historical District. Be there for the tree lighting, entertainment, kids' activities, and food. Call (214) 741-7185.

Holiday at the Arboretum. Dallas Arboretum. The December celebration at the arboretum offers a tour of the DeGolyer mansion decorated for Christmas, workshops for children, an outdoor market, and entertainment provided by handbell choirs, chorale singers, and more. It may have Family Fun Sundays, which include Santa, reindeer, and carolers. Call (214) 327-4901.

Christmas in the Branch. Farmers Branch Historical Park, Ford Rd. at Farmers Branch Ln. Christmas in the Branch begins early in December with Dickens in the Park, which features horse-drawn carriage rides, tours of historical buildings, bells, and choirs. The Christmas Lighting Display Driving Route leads visitors from City Hall into the park. Authentic English teas and demonstrations of Christmas past are also part of the celebration. Call (800) BRANCH9 for a calendar.

Kwanzaa. This celebration of African culture includes the principles of unity, creativity, faith, collective work, responsibility, cooperative economics, and self-determination. The Kwanzaa seasonal events are usually held at many locations around town, including the following: Fair Park, Paul Quinn College, St. Phillip's School and Community Center, Martin Luther King Jr. Recreation Center, Lincoln High School, and the South Dallas Cultural Center.

Trains at Northpark. Northpark Center. Take a trip through a magical collection of twelve O-gauge trains with 350 cars and 2,500 feet of track traveling through miniature scenes created realistically in minute detail. Call (214) 361-6345. **Candlelight Tour** at Old City Park. 1717 Gano. The beauty of this annual event never dims. Special activities include tours of decorated historic buildings, musical entertainment, a children's tent, surrey rides, refreshments, and holiday shopping on a weekend in mid-December. Call (214) 421-5141.

Jingle Bell Run. Meyerson, 2301 Flora. Festive costumes of all descriptions for individuals, groups, and their pets are in vogue for the annual Jingle Bell Run benefiting the Blood Care Center. A 5K run, a one-mile fun run, a pooch parade and costume contest, and treats at Santa Land are planned for all ages. Call (817) 412-5500.

Holiday in the Park. Six Flags Over Texas, Arlington. Held mainly on weekends from November through January, Holiday in the Park offers exciting holiday shows, an exhibition of beautifully decorated trees, carolers and other musical groups, rides, and sledding on a hill of snow. Call (817) 530-6000.

Deck the Hall Holiday Concert. Meyerson Symphony Center. The Greater Dallas Youth Orchestra, dancers from Booker T. Washington Arts Magnet School, and choristers combine for a yuletide celebration. Call (214) 692-0203.

Christmas in Heritage Park. 4th and Austin, Garland. The Junior League of Garland presents an annual craft bazaar, Santa Claus, music, food, and children's entertainment. Call (972) 272-9160.

A Christmas Carol. The Dallas Theater. This play is a much anticipated holiday favorite. Call (214) 522-8499.

Lantern Light Tours. Heritage Farmstead Museum, Plano. Special holiday foods, music, crafts, and a decorated two-story Victorian farmhouse capture the holiday spirit for visitors at the Lantern Light Tour. Call (972) 424-7874.

Dickens Downtown Christmas. Historic Downtown Plano, E. 15th St. Held in conjunction with the Christmas Tree Lighting in Haggard Park, this holiday celebration includes live music, strolling jugglers and costumed characters, refreshments, caroling, and a visit from the jolly old elf. Call (972) 941-7250.

Christmas Boat Parade and Bonfire. Lynn Creek Park, Grand Prairie. Decorated boats, Santa, carolers, and fireworks celebrate the season. Call (972) 264-1558.

Star of Bethlehem Planetarium Shows: The re-creation of the Star of Bethlehem and the Christmas story are presented at area planetariums, such as Richland College, St. Mark's, and The Science Place.

Santa's Appearances: Confusing as it may be to little children, Santa seems to be everywhere they go. Most shopping malls, larger shopping centers, Christmas festivals, recreation-center holiday parties, and parades keep Santa very busy in Dallas. Some malls and large department stores offer **Breakfast with Santa** and other special decorations and activities, such as the model trains, puppet shows, and chorale singers at Northpark, and the spectacular holiday tree in the center of the ice rink at the Galleria. Website: www.oldcitypark.org.

6. DAY TRIPS

Sometimes the best way for a family to get to know one another better is to leave home in the family car to a new or favorite destination for the day where they can play and learn new things together away from the hectic routine at home. Most destinations outlined in this chapter are within a one- to two-hour driving time. If you have time to plan ahead, writing the town's chamber of commerce for tourist information or looking it up on the Web and talking with friends who have been there for ideas about what to do and what to take will add to the enjoyment of the trip. When using this guide, remember to call ahead because attractions open and close regularly.

When traveling with children, it is helpful to stop by the bookstore or public library for some favorite books and books-on-CD or -tape. Some older kids like to take along a battery-powered book light, in case some of the travel time is at night, as well as their own personal CD or cassette player with headphones. Sing-along CDs, snacks, drawing kits, and travel-sized games also help to pass the time peacefully. Some moms pack a surprise bag with play items that the children have never seen before. Including an S&S (stop-and-stretch) time about midway through travel helps to work out the wiggles. Always take a first aid kit that has bandages and something for insect bites. If you will be outdoors, insect repellent and sunscreen are good ideas. Also, remember the camera because there will very likely be some moments to capture.

BONHAM

Bonham was settled by a former Arkansas sheriff, Bailey Inglish, in 1837, and was named for James Butler Bonham, a defender of the Alamo. A statue of James Bonham by Dallas sculptor Allie Tennant is on the courthouse square of this Texas Main Street City. Tourist information is available at the Bonham Area Chamber of Commerce, 110 E. First, Bonham, Texas 75418 (903) 583-4811 Website: www.bonhamchamber.com. Ask about a "Walkabout on the Square" brochure for an interesting trip around town. Be sure to call to verify hours and days.

FANNIN COUNTY MUSEUM OF HISTORY

One Main St. (903) 583-8042

This museum houses eleven rooms of historical artifacts of Bonham and Fannin County in the restored 1900 Texas and Pacific Railway Depot. New exhibits highlight Bonham in World War II with the Jones Field Room, a display of antique firefighting equipment, which includes a 1918 American LaFrance fire truck, and an extensive collection of Sulphur River fossils and Native American artifacts.

Hours: April 1 to September 1: Tuesday to Saturday, 10 AM to 4 PM; September 2 to March 31: Tuesday to Saturday, 12 PM to 4 PM. Groups of ten or more must give forty-eight hours advance notice.

Admission: Free.

FORT INGLISH MUSEUM AND PARK

US Hwy. 56 at 121 (903) 583-8042

Located adjacent to the Sam Rayburn Library, Fort Inglish is a replica of the fort built by Bailey Inglish to protect the ten pioneer families that he brought with him from Indian raids. Displays are featured in three authentic 1830s log structures and three carefully designed replicas. In the various buildings are the re-creation of a trading post, residential cabins, a school/church, and a blacksmith shop containing tools, historic documents, clothing, and other elements of Texas frontier life.

Hours: April 1 to September 1: Tuesday to Saturday, 10 AM to 12 PM and 1 PM to 3 PM.

Admission: Free, but donations are appreciated.

SAM RAYBURN LIBRARY AND MUSEUM

P.O. Box 309, Bonham, Texas 75418; US Hwy. 56, half a mile west of the courthouse square (903) 583-2455

Housed here are books, records, gifts, a collection of gavels, a replica of the speaker's office in Washington, a complete collection of the Congressional Record, and other memorabilia of Rayburn and his more than forty-eight years in office and seventeen years as Speaker of the House.

Hours: Monday to Friday, 9 AM to 5 PM; Saturday, 1 PM to 5 PM.

Admission: Free.

SAM RAYBURN HOUSE

US Hwy. 56, 1.5 miles west of Bonham (Mailing address: P.O. Box 308, Bonham, Texas 75418) (903) 583-5558

Originally built by Rayburn for his parents in 1916, the two-story, fourteen-room white house was primarily occupied by Sam and his sister and contains their furnishings and clothes. Changing displays of gifts given to the Rayburn family, such as silver and china, represent the esteem in which Rayburn was held. He died in 1961 and is buried at Willow Wild Cemetery, W. 7th and TX Hwy. 121.

Hours: Closed Sunday and Monday. Tuesday to Saturday, 10 AM to 4 PM. Winter hours may change. Groups should make reservations.

Admission: Free.

BONHAM STATE PARK AND LAKE BONHAM RECREATIONAL AREA

These sites feature lakes and outdoor activities. See Chapter Four under **Lakes, State Parks, and Recreation Areas.**

Events: January: Rayburn Birthday Celebration; **July:** Kueckelhan Ranch Rodeo on Wednesday to Saturday during the last week of the month; **September:** Greater Dallas Bicyclist Association Bicycle Rally during the second week; **October:** Autumn in Bonham on the first Saturday; Fannin County Fair held Thursday to Saturday during the third weekend; **December:** Christmas parade on the first Saturday. **Trades Day** is the first weekend following the first Monday of each month, Thursday to Sunday.

Directions: US Hwy. 75 North, sixty miles to TX Hwy. 121 East. Approximately seventy-five miles northeast of Dallas. It is about a thirty-minute drive from Bonham to downtown Denison, which is the next entry.

DENISON

The MK&T Railroad gave birth to Denison in 1872 as land was purchased and a town was mapped out, and the new town was named after Katy vice president George Denison. Former president Dwight D. Eisenhower's father was a Katy Railroad employee, and Ike was born here on October 14, 1890. Another important event in Denison's history occurred when Denison Dam was constructed across the Red River, creating Lake Texoma, which covers 89,000 acres in Texas and Oklahoma. Brochures for historical driving and walking tours of Denison, an official Texas Main Street City, are available from the Denison Convention and Visitors Bureau, P.O. Box 325, Denison, Texas 75021. Call (903) 465-1551 or visit http://denisontx.com.

EISENHOWER'S BIRTHPLACE STATE PARK

609 S. Lamar Ave., Denison, Texas (903) 465-8908
Website: www.eisenhowerbirthplace.org

Dwight David Eisenhower, a five-star general of the army and two-term U.S. president, was born in this house and lived here for two years until his family moved to Abilene, Kansas. The furnishings represent the 1890s. Guided tours: Tuesday to Saturday from 10 AM to 4 PM and Sunday 1 PM to 5 PM. Closed Christmas and New Year's Day. A pavilion with picnic tables and handicapped-accessible restrooms, as well as a headquarters which houses the visitor center, gift shop, and office, are across the street. Guided tours of the ten-acre park may be scheduled by calling (903) 465-8908. Park admission: adults, $2; students, $1.

GRAYSON COUNTY FRONTIER VILLAGE

Loy Lake Park, Rt. 1, P.O. Box 273C, Denison, Texas 75020
(903) 463-2487 Website: http://community.texomalink.com

Located in a wooded area that has a lake, pier, and picnic areas, the Frontier Village includes homes and other structures dating back to the 1840s, as well as a crafts and gift shop. The village is the site of arts-and-crafts shows in April and November and a Frontier Festival in September.

Hours: Open daily 1 PM to 4 PM. Closed major holidays.

Directions: Loy Lake Park is located southwest of Denison. From south of Denison on US 75, exit at Loy Lake Exit. Go left (west). Park is on the right.

KATY DEPOT

101 E. Main (903) 465-1551

Built in 1914, the MK&T Depot was an active part of life in Denison for many years. The restored depot now houses businesses, shops, a restaurant, which is open for lunch, and the small Red River Railroad Museum. The park in front looks much like it did in 1914. The museum hours are Monday to Saturday, 10 AM to 1 PM and 2 PM to 4 PM. Call (903) 463-6238.

HAGERMAN WILDLIFE REFUGE

6465 Refuge Rd., Sherman, Texas 75092-5817 (903) 786-2826
Website: http://southwest.fws/refuges/texas/hagerman

The refuge includes 11,319 acres of habitat for 280 species of migratory birds. Visitors bird-watch, picnic, take pictures, hike, and look over interpretive panels at the Visitors Center. The peak time to see migrating waterfowl is from October through March in early morning or at dusk. Shore birds are often most prevalent in midsummer. Boat fishing is allowed from April through September within the refuge, which surrounds the Big Mineral arm of Lake Texoma, but camping, skiing, and swimming are prohibited within refuge boundaries. Remember your binoculars and camera. A leaflet for a self-guided auto tour is in the headquarters.

Refuge hours: Sunrise to sunset, daily. **Office hours:** Call ahead.
Admission: Free.

Directions: From US 75 at Sherman, go west on FM 1417 and turn right into the refuge. Call first during periods of heavy rain.

EISENHOWER STATE PARK AND LAKE TEXOMA

50 Park Road 20, Denison, Texas 75020 (903) 465-1956
Website: www.tpwd.state.tx.us.

Events: March: Art and Wine Renaissance; **April:** Texoma Lakefest Regatta; **May:** Memorial Day Parade; **July 4:** Fireworks; **September:** U.S. National Aerobatic Competition; **October:** Main Street Fall Festival; **December:** Tour of Homes and Christmas Parade.

Hours: 8 AM to 5 PM. For information about this 457-acre park on Texas's third largest reservoir, please look in Chapter Four under **Lakes, State Parks, and Recreation Areas.**

Directions: Denison is approximately seventy-five miles north of Dallas on US 75.

FORT WORTH

Will Rogers said that Ft. Worth is where the West begins, and Dallas is where the East peters out. Ft. Worth's Western heritage is very much alive in Sundance Square, the Stockyards, Western art museums, Log Cabin Village, Will Rogers Memorial Center, and annual celebrations. Ft. Worth began as a frontier outpost in 1849 to help protect incoming settlers from renegade Indian raids. Cattle drives ran through Ft. Worth on the Chisholm Trail after the Civil War. Cowboys stopped here to load up on provisions on the way to Abilene and Kansas, and they stopped to spend their money and have a good time on the way home, which produced a very rowdy area of town called Hell's Half Acre. Townspeople worked hard, including their own physical labor, to get the railroad tracks to Ft. Worth and succeeded, and their town became known as Cowtown. Cattle were shipped to Ft. Worth, and the business of meatpacking thrived at the Stockyards. The arrival of the military bases, the discovery of oil, and the use of trucking to replace railroads all had their impact on the development of Ft. Worth, as did an increase in interest in the arts influenced by philanthropists Amon Carter and Kay Kimbell.

To receive information about Ft. Worth, write or call the **Convention and Visitors Bureau**, 415 Throckmorton, Ft. Worth, 76102, Downtown/

Sundance Square (800) 433-5747 and (817) 336-8791; Historic Stock-yards, 130 E. Exchange (817) 642-4741; Cultural District/Zoo, 3401 W. Lancaster Ave (817) 882-8588; or look online at www.fortworth.com. If you are just driving in, stop at the Visitor Center at the Stockyards and select brochures of places that interest you as well as a map of the Stock-yards. You might stay there and enjoy what the Stockyards have to offer or go downtown to the Historic Sundance Square to begin your tour at **Fire Station No. 1**. Ft. Worth Transportation Authority, the T, offers a Premium Pass that is good for three types of transportation. For about $4.50, visitors have unlimited day-pass travel on the regular city bus and trolley service as well as the Trinity Railway Express that links Dallas and Ft. Worth. Call (817) 215-8600 for information or check online at www.the-T.com and www.trinityrailwayexpress.org. The Events Hotline number is (817) 332-2000. Call for details of special events.

SUNDANCE SQUARE

The old and new blend in the historic Sundance Square in Ft. Worth's central business district. The square is defined by W. 2nd St., Houston, W. 4th, and Commerce. Brick streets and restored, turn-of-the-century buildings add to the charm of this area named for the out-law Sundance Kid who, along with Butch Cassidy, often entertained himself at the disreputable Hell's Half Acre. Shops, the Bass Perfor-mance Hall, restaurants, AMC movie theaters, the Sid Richardson Collection of Western Art, Fire Station No. 1, and other points of his-torical interest make Sundance Square a great place to begin your tour of Ft. Worth. As you walk around the square, be sure to notice the clock, which was made in 1893 outside Haltom's Diamonds at Main and E. 3rd, the *trompe l'oeil* ("fool the eye") artwork of Richard Haas in the Chisholm Trail mural on the southwest side of Main and 3rd, and the suit of armor high above the Knights of Pythias Hall at Main and 3rd. Historical markers around the square explain important buildings and events. For information, call (817) 255-5700 or visit www .sundancesquare.com.

FIRE STATION NO. 1

Second and Commerce (817) 255-9300

Built in 1873, Fire Station No. 1 now houses a free walk-through exhi-bition called 150 Years of Fort Worth, which chronicles the history of the land and people who lived in Texas and the Ft. Worth area. It's a satel-lite of the Ft. Worth Museum of Science and History.

Hours: Daily, 9 AM to 7 PM.
Admission: Free.

SID RICHARDSON COLLECTION OF WESTERN ART

309 Main St. (817) 332-6554 Website: www.sidrmuseum.org

This museum houses the private collection of oilman Sid Richardson (1891–1959). Many paintings by Frederic Remington, such as *The Buffalo Runners*, *Ambush*, and *Bear Hunting*, are displayed. Paintings of buffalo hunters and Native Americans, as well as bronzes by Charles M. Russell, are also showcased. Saddles, vests, and chaps with beautiful leather and silver artistry are on exhibit. The museum has a gallery brochure for children that contains a visual scavenger hunt. Housed in a replica of an 1895 building, the museum also has a bookstore.

Hours: Tuesday and Wednesday, 10 AM to 5 PM; Thursday and Friday, 10 AM to 8 PM; Saturday, 11 AM to 8 PM; Sunday, 1 PM to 5 PM. Closed Monday and major holidays.

Admission: Free.

BASS PERFORMANCE HALL

525 Commerce St. (817) 212-4200 Website: www.basshall.com

Designed to look like a classic European Opera House, Bass Hall has a great dome eighty feet in diameter atop the Founders Concert Theater, and two forty-eight-foot angels made from Texas limestone watch over the Grand Facade. It's the permanent home of the Ft. Worth Symphony, the Ft. Worth Opera, the Texas Ballet Theater, and the Van Cliburn International Piano Competition and Cliburn Concerts. Bass Hall hosts musicals, concerts, and a variety of other performances.

FORT WORTH RAIL MARKET

1401 Jones St. (817) 335-6758 Website: www.fortworthrailmarket.com

The Rail Market is located two blocks east of the Convention Center in the southeastern part of downtown and one long block east of the Intermodal Transportation Center, where the Trinity Railway Express arrives. Housed in the former Santa Fe Freight House, merchants offer a unique shopping and dining experience. Casual, independently owned restaurants and stores are open Monday to Saturday, 10 AM to 6 PM. The spring and summer Farmers Market offers fresh, locally grown produce and craft items. Parking is available in the front and rear.

MUSEUMS AND EXHIBITIONS

In Ft. Worth's **Cultural District**, within walking distance of one another are the Amon Carter Museum, the Fort Worth Modern Art Museum, the Kimbell Art Museum, the Fort Worth Museum of Science and

History, and the National Cowgirl Hall of Fame. The Visitor Information Center for the Cultural District is located in a building by the Will Rogers Memorial Center; it has the tower. Admission is free at some of these museums, and groups must schedule their visits to the museums in advance. Handicapped access is available at all of the above listed museums.

AMON CARTER MUSEUM

3501 Camp Bowie at Montgomery (817) 738-1933
Website: www.cartermuseum.org

The collection of works by artists such as Sanford Robinson Gifford, Thomas Cole, Georgia O'Keefe, Winslow Homer, Frederic Remington, and Charles M. Russell within this museum was assembled by the late publisher and philanthropist Amon G. Carter Sr. and represents 150 years of American art. Tours are held daily at 2 PM. There is a museum store featuring books of the art collections.

Gallery maps and adult and children's audio tours are available. The museum website provides links to art collections that both students and teachers will find useful.

Hours: Tuesday to Saturday, 10 AM to 5 PM; Sunday, 12 PM to 5 PM. Weekend hours subject to change.

Admission: Free.

THE CATTLE RAISER'S MUSEUM

1301 W. 7th St. between Summit and Henderson (817) 332-7064
Website: www.cattleraisersmuseum.org

The spirit of longhorns, cattle drives, and cowboys is relived through interactive monitors located in the West Texas town setting, the talking longhorn entrance diorama, a wall explaining cattle breeds, a branding-iron room, and other exhibits that tell the story of the cattle and ranching industry.

Hours: Monday to Saturday, 10 AM to 5 PM.

Admission: Adults, $3; seniors and young adults ages 13–18, $2; ages 4–12, $1.

FORT WORTH MUSEUM OF SCIENCE AND HISTORY

1501 Montgomery St., one mile north of I-30 (817) 255-9300, (888) 255-9300 Website: www.fwmsh.org

This museum presents such permanent exhibits as Lone Star Dinosaurs, Comin' Through Cowtown, and Hands on Science, plus interactive traveling exhibits. **KIDSPACE** is a children's area that features interactive exhibits, such as a fishing dock, kid's market, and build-a-house display.

Amateur paleontologists can dig for dinosaur bones and fossils in Dino-Dig, an outdoor discovery area.

The **Noble Planetarium** presents thirty-minute star shows throughout the day. The **Omni Theater** uses an eighty-foot domed screen and seventy-two speakers to present forty-five-minute IMAX films, which change every three to four months. Some shows may be too intense for those with motion sickness or for very small children. Call about suitability.

Hours: Monday to Thursday, 9 AM to 5:30 PM; Friday and Saturday, 9 AM to 8 PM; Sunday, 11:30 AM to 5:30 PM. Open daily except Thanksgiving and December 24–25. Omni shows are presented daily. Times and films vary, so phone ahead or access the website. Planetarium shows are updated quarterly and offered daily.

Admission: General admission (including exhibits, and Omni show, and a planetarium show) is adults, $13; children (3–12) and seniors, $10. Individual tickets for Omni are adults, $7; children/seniors, $5. Exhibits only are adults, $7; children/seniors, $5. Planetarium shows are $3.50.

KIMBELL ART MUSEUM

3333 Camp Bowie, west of University (817) 332-8451, Metro (817) 654-1034 Website: www.kimbellart.org

The Kimbell Art Foundation was established in the 1930s by Kay Kimbell, who left his art collection and fortune to the foundation in 1964 to build an art museum. Outstanding collections in the museum span 3,000 years. There are works of Egyptian, Asian, Mesoamerican, and African origin and others from Western Europe. The collection of Asian arts is particularly remarkable, featuring Japanese screens, hanging scrolls, Chinese paintings, and sculptures of various origins. Free tours, the Buffet restaurant, and a bookstore are available as is a noncirculating library by appointment.

Hours: Tuesday to Thursday, 10 AM to 5 PM; Friday, 12 PM to 8 PM; Saturday, 10 AM to 5 PM; Sunday, 12 PM to 5 PM.

Admission: Free. Free parking is available off Arch Adams St.

MODERN ART MUSEUM OF FORT WORTH

3200 Darnell St. (817) 738-9215, Toll free (866) 824-5566 Website: www.themodern.org

Covering more than 53,000 square feet on two floors, the new Modern Art Museum is located in the Cultural District, opposite the Kimbell Art Museum. Designed by Japanese architect Tadao Ando, the museum houses a permanent collection that consists of approximately 150 works by 125 artists. Various movements, themes, and styles are represented, including abstract expressionism, color field painting, pop art, and minimalism, as well as new image painting from the 1970s and beyond. Also represented are recent developments in abstraction and figurative sculpture and contemporary movements in photography, video, and digital imagery. Sculpture is both indoors and outdoors, and children will especially like the reflecting pools. The Modern offers lunch at a cafe (www.themodern.org/cafemodern.html) and a gift shop.

Hours: Tuesday to Thursday, 10 AM to 5 PM; Friday, 10 AM to 8 PM; Saturday, 10 AM to 5 PM; Sunday, 11 AM to 5 PM.

Admission: General (ages 13 to adult), $6; students with ID and seniors, $4; children (12 and under), free.

NATIONAL COWGIRL MUSEUM AND HALL OF FAME

1720 Gendy St., Ft. Worth, Texas 76107 (817) 336-4475
Website: www.cowgirl.net

The National Cowgirl Museum and Hall of Fame is the only museum in the world dedicated to honoring and documenting the distinguished women of the American West. Located in Ft. Worth's Cultural District, it houses artifacts and memorabilia of the Western woman, including the honorees in its Hall of Fame, and it also seeks out those women who continue to blaze trails with the true grit of the American cowgirl, not only as ranchers and rodeo riders but in today's world as writers, artists, teachers, and entertainers.

As visitors approach the museum, they should take a look at the Richard Hall **mural** on the east side of the museum. The mural features three-dimensional imagery of riding cowgirls. Inside, visitors usually begin with an eight-minute presentation that introduces them to the many faces of the cowgirl and then explore the interactive exhibits depicting a cowgirl's life on the ranch and her influence on our culture. Two exhibits of note include Dale Evans's silver-and-black leather saddle and Annie Oakley's .12-gauge, double-barrel shotgun. The gift shop invites browsers, and the Cowgirl Café lures them in for a snack. Special summer programs and birthday parties are offered for the young 'uns. A free docent-led tour is held on Sundays at 2:30 PM.

Hours: Tuesday to Saturday, 10 AM to 5 PM; Sunday, 12 PM to 5 PM. Closed Monday.

Admission: Adults, $6; seniors, $5; children (6–18), $4; ages 5 and under, free.

NATIONAL COWBOYS OF COLOR MUSEUM AND HALL OF FAME

3400 Mt. Vernon St., Ft. Worth, Texas 76104 (817) 534-8801
Website: www.cowboysofcolor.org

This cowboy museum honors blacks, Hispanics, and American Indians and their role in developing the American West through art, artifacts, historical records, and current events. Located in the **Renaissance Cultural**

Center, the museum includes a gift shop that sells the Cowboys of Color Calendar to benefit the museum. The **Cowboys of Color Rodeo** is held in September at Will Rogers Coliseum.

Museum hours: Wednesday to Saturday, 11 AM to 6 PM.

PATE MUSEUM OF TRANSPORTATION

18501 Hwy. 377 South, Cresson, Texas (Mailing address: P.O. Box 711, Ft. Worth, Texas 76101) (817) 396-4305

Just outside Ft. Worth on the highway that leads to Granbury is the Pate Museum, where the history of transportation is visualized through a collection of classic, antique, and special-interest automobiles such as the Pierce Arrow and Packard, as well as a collection of aircraft that ranges from helicopters to transports to jet fighters. An unusual item on exhibit is a Minesweeper Boat 5 because few museums display a sea-going vessel inland. The museum also has a mock-up of the nose cone of a space capsule. Picnic tables are available, but groups of more than six must make reservations. The museum is about a twenty-minute drive south of Ft. Worth, and from the museum it is only about a fifteen-minute drive on to Granbury.

Hours: Tuesday to Sunday, 9 AM to 5 PM. Closed Monday.
Admission: Free.

HISTORICAL SITES

LOG CABIN VILLAGE

2100 Log Cabin Village Ln. and University (817) 926-5881
Website: www.logcabinvillage.org

Located across from the zoo in a pretty, wooded area, Log Cabin Village consists of seven authentic log homes and a one-room schoolhouse originally built in the mid-1800s. Staff and volunteers who dress in period costumes are on the grounds and demonstrate pioneer crafts, such as spinning, weaving, and candle dipping.

Hours: Tuesday to Friday, 9 AM to 4 PM; Saturday and Sunday, 1 PM to 5 PM.
Admission: Adults, $2.50; seniors and children (4–17), $2.

STOCKYARDS HISTORIC DISTRICT

N. Main and 130 E. Exchange
Visitor Center: (817) 625-9715
Website: www.stockyardsstation.com

Anyone who wishes to recapture the spirit that was the West, if only for a few hours, must visit the 125-acre Stockyards, especially during a festival, such as the Red Steagall Gathering in September and the Texas Frontier Forts Muster in May.

A stop at the **Visitor Center**, located toward the end of E. Exchange (east of Main St.), will help you get your bearings in this ten-block historic district. A map of the Stockyards and brochures covering most major attractions in the Ft. Worth area are available there. The Visitor Center also offers walking tours of the Stockyards and Billy Bob's Texas for a fee.

Hours: Monday to Friday, 8:30 AM to 6 PM; Saturday, 9 AM to 10 PM, and Sunday, 11 AM to 5 PM.

With the arrival of the railroad in 1876, Ft. Worth became the shipping destination for cattle, and the Union Stockyards Company was built. The Fort Worth Stockyards Company bought the company out in 1893 and held the first livestock show three years later. Meatpackers Armour & Company and Swift & Company moved in around 1902, and construction of the present Livestock Exchange Building began. Today, the meatpackers are gone, and the 100 acres of stock pens have been reduced to fifteen acres. Visitors enjoy the major livestock buildings, shops, museum, sculptures, horse-drawn carriage rides, and restaurants.

The **Fort Worth Mounted Patrol** has its barns at 131 E. Exchange. Risckys' restaurants offer steak, barbecue, Mexican food, and seafood. Covered picnic tables are located in a little park west of Main at 26th and Ellis, and some family spots for meals are the Old Spaghetti Warehouse, Booger Red's, and the Star Cafe. Nearby are Cattleman's Steakhouse and Joe T. Garcia's. **Directions:** From Dallas, take I-30 or I-20 to Ft. Worth and go north on I-35 to the Historic Stockyard District exits.

Stockyards Station, 130 E. Exchange, is a Western destination near the end of Exchange St. offering more than twenty-five unique shops, restaurants, entertainment venues, indoor and outdoor event facilities, historic walking tours, horseback rides, and the **Texas Cowboy Hall of Fame**. It's the depot for the historic **Tarantula** train. Call (817) 625-9715 or visit www.stockyardsstation.com. For horseback riding, wagon rides, riding lessons, boarding horses, and birthday parties, call **Stockyards Livery and Stables** at (817) 626-3446.

At Stockyards Station begin the **Texas Trail of Fame**, a virtual chronological history of U.S. Western heritage and of the Ft. Worth Stockyards. Bronze stars, which resemble an old-fashioned marshal's badge, are placed in the walkways. Inductees include John Wayne, Will Rogers, Zane Grey, Charles Goodnight, and Roy Rogers.

The **Livestock Exchange Building** houses businesses and a **museum** that contains memorabilia from the 1986 Sesquicentennial Wagon Train Collection and artifacts related to the development of the Stockyards. It's toward the back of the main hall on the left. Call (817) 625-5087. Satellite cattle auctions are held every other Friday on the first floor.

Hours: Monday to Saturday, 10 AM to 5 PM.

Admission: Free.

The **Ft. Worth Herd's Cattle Drive** takes place daily, weather permitting. Longhorn cattle usually depart from the Livestock Exchange Building twice daily at 11:30 AM and 4 PM, head down Exchange Ave. and back to their holding pens behind the Exchange Building. If the trail boss doesn't think the critters are feeling sociable enough for a walk, he can cancel. Two of the best places to see the drive are in front of the Visitors Center and the lawn in front of the Exchange Building. If you miss their grand tour, you can still see them behind the Exchange Building to the east. Call (817) 336-HERD (4373) or visit www.fortworthherd.com.

Cowtown Coliseum was the site of the world's first indoor rodeo in 1918. It is open Monday to Saturday from 8 AM to 4:30 PM, and Sunday afternoons just to look through. The **Ft. Worth Championship Rodeo** is held every Friday and Saturday night at 8 PM and lasts about two hours. For information about the rodeo or special events, call (817) 654-1148, toll free (888) COWTOWN, or look online at www.cowtowncoliseum .com. Call Ticketmaster at Metro (214) 647-5700 or (214) 373-8000.

Texas Cowboy Hall of Fame honors the best cowboys and cowgirls who achieved greatness in the sports of rodeo and cutting through displays that contain photographs, memorabilia, and video. Inductees include Neal Gay, Larry Mahan, and George Strait. The **Sterquell Wagon Collection** includes more than sixty horse-drawn vehicles, and the **John Justin Trail of Fame** pays tribute to the owner of the Justin Boot Company and civic leader in Ft. Worth with a variety of boots. New inductees into the Hall of Fame are selected by committee each year. The hall is located at 128 E. Exchange Ave. in Stockyards Station in what were once horse and mule barns. Call (817) 626-7131 or visit www.texascowboy-halloffame.com.

Hours: Monday to Thursday, 10 AM to 6 PM; Friday and Saturday, 10 AM to 7 PM; Sunday, 12 PM to 6 PM.

Admission: Adults, $4; seniors, $3; children (3–12), $2; family package, $10.

The **Stockyards Hotel**, 109 E. Exchange, was built in 1907 and restored in 1984, and it offers fifty-two rooms. You might peek in or stay for lunch at the **Booger Red's Saloon and Restaurant** next door to see the saddle bar stools, the five ceiling fans that are turned by one belt, and the mounted buffalo head and horns of the longhorn. The story of Booger Red is framed on the wall. A children's menu is offered, but service is not fast. Call (817) 625-6427 or (800) 423-8471 or visit www .stockyardshotel.com.

Billy Bob's Texas, 2520 Rodeo Plaza, claims to be the world's largest honky-tonk. Under a 100,000-square-foot roof are top-name entertainment, a dance floor, pro bull riding every Friday and Saturday, a gift shop, an arcade, and restaurants. Tours are available during the day. Call (817) 624-7117 for information or tickets or visit www.billybobs texas.com.

Cowtown Cattlepen Maze, Inc., 145 E. Exchange Ave., covers 5,400 square feet of wooden pathways that look like the cattle pens of the Old West. Visitors can compete against themselves or each other. A second-story observation deck allows the player to see the maze before he or she begins or watch others as they wind through it. Call (817) 624-6666 or visit www.cowtowncattlepenmaze.com.

Hours: Monday to Thursday, 10 AM to 5 PM; Friday and Saturday, 10 AM to 8 PM; Sunday, 12 PM to 6 PM.

Admission: Adults, $4.25; ages 5–12, $3.25; ages 4 and under, free with a paid adult.

PARKS, GARDENS, AND WILDLIFE

BOTANIC GARDEN

3220 Botanic Garden Blvd., Ft. Worth, Texas 76107
(817) 871-7686, (817) 871-7673 **Website:** www.fwbg.com

Located in Trinity Park, the Botanic Garden consists of several different gardens on 114 acres. **Rose Gardens** contain more than 3,400 roses, which peak in late April and October. Lush tropical plants fill the 10,000-square-foot **Conservatory**. Exotic orchids are housed in the **Exhibition Greenhouse**; flowering plants such as colorful azaleas are the highlights of the **Perennial Garden**; and seasonal flowering plants bloom in the **Trial Garden**. Leaves release their scents in the **Fragrance Garden**.

The beauty and tranquility of the **Japanese Gardens** will be a delight to all family members. This 7.5-acre, hilly garden features beautiful pools and waterfalls, a tea garden, a pagoda, and other structures emphasizing simplicity and harmony. Children enjoy feeding the large koi, imperial carp. A gift shop is available. No tripods for cameras are allowed.

Lunch is a treat at the **Gardens Restaurant**, 3220 Rock Springs Rd. (817) 731-2547. Closed Monday.

Hours: Grounds open daily, 8 AM to 11 PM. **Japanese Gardens:** April to October, daily, 9 AM to 7 PM; November to March, Tuesday to Sunday, 10 AM to 5 PM. Closed Monday. **Conservatory:** April to October, Monday to Friday, 10 AM to 9 PM; Saturday, 10 AM to 6 PM; Sunday, 1 PM to 6 PM; November to March, Monday to Friday, 10 AM to 9 PM; Saturday, 10 AM to 4 PM; Sunday, 1 PM to 4 PM. Gift shop is open 10 AM to 4 PM in the Japanese Gardens.

Admission: Admission to the grounds is free. **Japanese Gardens**: Adults, weekdays, $3, weekends, $3.50; children, 4–12, $2; children under 4, free. **Conservatory**: Adults, $1; children, 50 cents.

HERITAGE PARK

E. Belknap at Houston, behind the Tarrant County Courthouse

Heritage Park, a small park on a bluff, has refreshing waterfalls and water walls. It is safest to visit this park in the daytime. At the bottom of the bluff is an eight-mile asphalt trail for bicycling, walking, jogging, or skating alongside the Trinity River.

FORT WORTH NATURE CENTER AND REFUGE

Rt. 10, Box 53 or 9601 Fossil Ridge, Ft. Worth, Texas 76135 (817) 237-1111

Classes, workshops, story hours, and festivals are held at this 3,600-acre protected habitat for buffalo, deer, many varieties of birds, and more wildlife. It's the largest city-owned nature center in the United States. Visitors may stop by the visitor center for information about hiking on twenty-five miles of trails, and guided trail walks are offered by appointment. A boardwalk over a marshy area allows a closer look at waterfowl. Ask about naturalist-guided hikes on Saturdays and a guided canoe tour along the West Fork of the Trinity. Picnic tables are available for families but not groups. There is a gift shop.

Hours: Tuesday to Saturday, 9 AM to 5 PM; Sunday, 12 PM to 5 PM. Closed Monday.

Interpretive Center hours: Tuesday to Saturday, 9 AM to 4:30 PM; Sunday, 12 PM to 4:30 PM.

Admission: Free.

Directions: Take TX Hwy. 199 (Jacksboro Hwy.) two miles past the Lake Worth Bridge.

FORT WORTH WATER GARDEN

1502 Commerce and 15th St. (817) 871-5757

This 4.3-acre water garden designed by Phillip Johnson has five water pools called Cascade, Wet Wall, Quiet Water, Aerated Pool, and Active Pool, and children love the steps leading down to the pools. Many pretty trees shade the area, which is across the street from Tarrant County Junior College and near the Convention Center. This is certainly worth a visit, and it is free. Water displays are between 10 AM and 10 PM daily.

FORT WORTH ZOO

1989 Colonial Pkwy. at University, south of I-30 (817) 759-7555
Website: www.fortworthzoo.org

The sixty-eight-acre Fort Worth Zoo, which opened in 1909, features more than 3,500 animals, including jaguars, lions, and Asian elephants. Two popular habitats are the World of Primates, a 2.5-acre indoor exhibit that simulates a tropical rain forest, and Asian Falls, which features waterfalls, hills, trees, and an elevated boardwalk. Below the boardwalk are Indochinese tigers, sun bears, and white Bengal tigers. The zoo's latest addition is Texas Wild!, an eight-acre re-creation of the Lone Star State, featuring nearly 300 native Texas animals and interactive displays.

Visitors may wish to browse in the Safari Shop and General Store and dine at the zoo's Burger King, Grandy's, or Bluebonnet Cafe. Other concessions are available throughout the zoo. Strollers are available for rent. Ask about overnight camping for a group of fifteen or more.

Although not part of the zoo, just by it is the **Forest Park Train**, a miniature steam train that carries visitors into Trinity Park on a ride that lasts about forty-five minutes. **Fare:** Adults (13 up), $3; children (1–12), $2.50; seniors (65+), $2.50. **Summer hours:** 11 AM to 6 PM, Tuesday to Sunday. Closed Monday. Call (817) 336-3328. **Winter hours:** Saturday and Sunday, 12 PM to 4 PM. All train rides are subject to weather conditions. The zoo is across the street from **Log Cabin Village** and not far from the **Botanic Gardens**.

Hours: Subject to change. Approximately early April to mid-October, Monday to Friday, 10 AM to 5 PM, and Saturday to Sunday, 10 AM to 6 PM; mid-October to mid-February, daily, 10 AM to 4 PM; mid-February to early April, daily, 10 AM to 5 PM.

Admission: Adults, $9; children, ages 3–12, $6.50; and seniors, $5.50. Wednesday is half-price day. Parking, $5.

Directions: From I-30, exit at University and turn left on Colonial. Continue about 1/2 mile.

MORE ENTERTAINMENT

BURGER'S LAKE

1200 Meandering Rd. (817) 737-3414 Website:
www.burgerslake.com

Near the former Carswell Air Force Base, this spring-fed lake provides great summer entertainment for families on the two sandy beaches. Kids can slide into the lake on a water slide, dive from the diving board, or swing in from a trapeze. There is plenty of shallow water for little ones. Twenty acres are available for picnicking, and there are picnic tables, a concession, and a volleyball court. Recommended items to bring are lawn chairs and floats. A discount is available for groups, and no alcohol or pets are allowed.

Summer to Labor Day hours: 9 AM to 7:30 PM daily.

Admission: Adults, $8; children 6 and under, free.

CASA MANANA

3101 W. Lancaster at University, directly across from Farrington Field (817) 332-2272 Website: www.casamanana.org

Casa Manana is a theater-in-the-round with 1,800 seats that is covered by a geodesic dome. Families enjoy musicals, concerts, and plays. Children's theater and summer camp are very active as is a theater school for all ages.

TARANTULA TRAIN

140 E. Exchange, Stockyards Station, Ft. Worth, Texas
(817) 625-RAIL, (800) 457-6338

Cotton Belt Depot, 709 S. Main, Grapevine, Texas

Websites: www.stockyardsstation.com,
www.grapevinesteamrailroad.com

Once aboard the *Tarantula* train, you can easily imagine what passenger train travel was like not that many years ago when great iron horses, like the 1896 Steam Engine #2248, called Puffy, that now pulls four beautifully restored passenger cars, crossed the country carrying passengers who had not even dreamed of air travel. The seats in each railcar have backs that swivel so you can face others in your party or always be facing forward. Rich mahogany wood, shining brass, and ten ceiling fans in each car add to the beauty. The cars are heated in winter, and the fans and open windows cool them in summer. When the whistle blows, passengers at Stockyards Station may begin a nine-mile, one-hour round-trip, called the **Trinity River Run**, which crosses the Trinity and follows the old Chisholm Trail to 8th St. and then turns back to the Stockyards. The scenery is not terrific along much of the trip, but the atmosphere is not to be missed. Dusk is a beautiful time to ride because the lights come on downtown and are reflected in the Trinity River. The train also runs from **Grapevine** to Stockyards Station in the morning and returns to Grapevine in the late afternoon. The round-trip is forty-two miles. Special-event trains run on special days and holidays.

A small restroom is located in each car, but no food, drink, or gum is allowed. Picking up your tickets early is a good idea. The depots open one hour before departure. If you love the ride, write or call the Ft. Worth mayor to let her or him know. Birthday parties may be arranged.

Hours: Wednesday to Sunday. Call or check the website for departure and arrival times.

Admission: Trinity River Run: Ranges from $6–$15. Grapevine to Stockyards Run: Ranges from $10 to $20.

MORE SITES OF INTEREST

Ft. Worth Brahmas Hockey, 1111 Houston St. (817) 336-4423.

Ft. Worth Cats Baseball, LaGrave Field, 301 N.E. 6th St. (817) 226-2287.

Ft. Worth Convention Center, 1111 Houston St. (817) 570-2222.

TCU (NCAA) Sports, (817) 257-7967.

Will Rogers Memorial Center, 3401 W. Lancaster (817) 871-8150.

SPECIAL EVENTS

Southwestern Exposition and Livestock Show and Rodeo: January and
  February, seventeen days
The Last Great Gunfight: February 8
Cowtown Marathon: Last Saturday in February
Main St. Arts Festival: Early April
Texas Frontier Forts Muster: April/May
Mayfest: First weekend in May
Colonial Golf Tournament: Mid-May
Chisholm Trail Roundup: Second full weekend in June
Juneteenth: Mid-June
Symphony Concerts in the Garden: June/July
Fort Worth 4th!: July 4
Cowboys of Color Rodeo: August/September
Gran Fiesta de Fort Worth: July
Fort Worth Air Show: October
Red Steagall Cowboy Gathering and Western Swing Festival: Late
  October
Parade of Lights: Late November, after Thanksgiving
Christmas in the Stockyards: December

GLEN ROSE

To study the relevant history of Glen Rose, you would literally have to return to the age of the dinosaurs. They have fascinated scientists and three-year-olds alike with the large three-toed footprints they left behind in the bed of the lazy Paluxy River, which flows through the town.

Settlers moved into the area known for its wild roses in the 1870s, and the county seat was established here. Glen Rose citizens were also known for their use of petrified wood as a building material, and some examples of its use are still around. Another claim to fame for a while in the 1920s and 1930s was the use of sulphur water for medicinal purposes in the bathhouses.

Today, the town is still built around the rock courthouse, and no one seems in much of a hurry, which is one of its many great appeals. From Hwy. 67, exiting on Hwy. 205 will take you past **Oakdale Park**, which is the site of many wonderful festivals and a large public swimming pool, past a great swimming area on the Paluxy called the Big Rocks, which you will easily recognize, and into the heart of the square. While in town, stop by the **Somervell County Museum**, located at Elm and Vernon, and soak up local history through the varied collections of fossils and pioneer memorabilia. Call (254) 898-0640. When we were there, for a small fee visitors could purchase an authentic dinosaur hunting license (just in case).

The Glen Rose Inn and Suites at (254) 897-2940 and the Best Western Inn and Suites by the Expo Center at (800) 280-2055 offer rooms and a swimming pool, and Oakdale Park at (254) 897-2321 or online at www.oakdalepark.com rents cabins. Campgrounds are at Oakdale Park, along the Brazos, and in Dinosaur Valley State Park if your family is having too much fun to go home at the end of the day. Oakdale Park also rents canoes and tubes. Hideaway Country Log Cabins rents five cabins located on a 150-acre property, which also has a swimming pool. They are located sixteen miles west of Glen Rose. Call (254) 823-6606. Low Water Canoe Rental, located about three miles east on FM 200, also has rentals. Call (254) 897-3666. Just as you approach the city limits on Hwy. 67 is the Expo Center, which includes facilities for conventions and reunions as well as a rodeo arena and equestrian center. Contact the Glen Rose Convention and Visitors Bureau, P.O. Box 2037, Glen Rose, Texas 76043 (254) 897-3081 Website: www.glenrosetexas.net. The drive takes about two hours.

COMANCHE PEAK NUCLEAR PLANT

Visitor Information Center, Texas Utilities Generating Co., P.O. Box 1002, Glen Rose, Texas 76043 (254) 897-2976

As you pass Cleburne and get closer to Glen Rose, the terrain becomes hilly, and you can see for miles. Look to your right for the two white domes, which are Comanche Peak's nuclear reactors. Please read under **Science** in Chapter Two for more details about the plant. Squaw Creek Lake at (254) 897-0500, which is around four miles north of Glen Rose off Hwy. 144, is a 3,300-acre lake that services the power plant but is also used for recreation, including scuba diving. Since September 11, it has been closed to the public for security reasons, but that could change.

Hours: Monday to Saturday, 9 AM to 4 PM

Admission: Free.

Directions: To reach the plant from Hwy. 67, exit on FM 201 and go north. The **visitor center** is about 1/2 mile inside the front gate.

DINOSAUR VALLEY STATE PARK

P.O. Box 396, Glen Rose, Texas 76043 (254) 897-4588

Reservations only: (512) 389-8900

Website: www.tpwd.state.tx.us/park/dinosaur

The Paluxy River, which is a tributary of the Brazos River, runs through this heavily wooded state park, which is best known for the tracks left in the river bed by dinosaurs about 113 million years ago. The visitor center is located just inside the park, and friendly rangers will accept the admission fee and answer questions. They often will be down at the river explaining the history of the region to interested groups. A little further down the road on the right are the two life-sized replicas of the Brontosaurus and the Tyrannosaurus rex, which were donated to the park after the New York World's Fair Dinosaur Exhibit in 1964–1965. Very young children who are not too sure that the dinosaurs are really extinct might look at this on the way out instead of in. On the left is a shaded picnic area with some playground equipment. The best tracks are on the road to the left, and park signs guide you. Steps lead down to the river, and they are somewhat steep.

Wearing beach shoes (not flip-flops) or old tennis shoes with some tread on the bottom is best. You can walk across the river bottom on large, exposed rocks, but they can be slippery. The river is usually shallow enough to see the tracks, but in times of heavy rainfall, calling ahead would be a good idea. Two necessary tools for youngsters from two to seventy-two are a small plastic bucket with a handle and a small aquarium fish net. The guppies and tadpoles flourish in the nooks and crannies among the rocks, and trying to catch them is great fun. If you're not already in a swimsuit, remember a change of clothes because a slip into the water is very likely. Sunscreen is a must. Shaded campgrounds are available here as are restrooms with showers. A small amphitheatre provides some interesting summer entertainment, and there are both nature and hiking trails.

Hours: Open daily from 8 AM to 10 PM for day use and overnight for campers.

Admission: State park admission is adults, $5; 12 and under, free. Camping is additional.

Directions: From US Hwy. 67, south of Glen Rose, take FM 205 to Park Road 59.

FOSSIL RIM

2155 County Rd. 2008, Glen Rose, Texas 76043
(254) 897-2960 Website: www.fossilrim.org

Endangered species are always the focus at this 2,700-acre private wildlife reserve. Excited kids can already spot ostriches as parents pay to enter the park. They will get an audio cassette tape that will narrate the safari, and they will probably want to buy cups of food to feed the exotic animals while you are driving through. More food may be purchased at the Nature Store, which is about midway through the ten-mile drive. Parents might want to keep the windows rolled up until they are past the ostriches because the large birds will stick their heads and long necks into the car as they check for food. The terrain is hilly, and there is lots of dense cedar and small shrubbery, so a pair of binoculars and sharp eyes will help in spotting more recalcitrant species. Taking snapshots or videos is also fun.

An interesting nature store, a restaurant, restrooms, a short hiking trail, picnic tables, and a petting-zoo area that all will enjoy are located at the midpoint. The overlook view of the countryside is spectacular here, and spring and fall are particularly beautiful times to visit. For those with a real spirit of adventure, Fossil Rim offers the Foothills Safari Camp, but children eighteen and under must attend preplanned family safaris. All proceeds go toward wildlife conservation efforts. A guided tour, a behind-the-scenes tour, and a conservation tour are offered. Lodging is available at Safari Camp or the Lodge at Fossil Rim.

Hours: Admitting visitors to the park: March through October, 8:30 AM to 5:30 PM; November through February, 8:30 AM to 3:30 PM.

Admission: Adults, $16.95; children, ages 3–11, $10.95; under age 3, free; seniors (62+), $12.95. Wildlife feed is available for purchase at the entrance and the park store. Group rates are available with reservations.

Directions: On Hwy. 67 South of Glen Rose, drive about three miles. Signs will direct you to the preserve.

TRES RIOS

2322 CR 312, Glen Rose, Texas 76043 (254) 897-4253

Once a YWCA camp, Tres Rios is now privately owned and offers air-conditioned, rustic cabins and motel-type rooms of various sizes in a wooded area. At the entrance is a store with groceries and fishing supplies. The camp was named for the three rivers, Brazos, Squaw Creek, and Paluxy, that meet beside it. Tres Rios offers canoe and tube rentals, a swimming pool, a volleyball area, a 9,000-square-foot pavilion, and camping areas. There is no beach on the Tres Rios side of the river. Call or look online for a calendar of events.

Directions: From Hwy. 67 East of Glen Rose, exit south on County Hwy. 312 (old Hwy. 67). Signs will direct you. Fees vary depending on type of accommodations.

TEXAS AMPHITHEATER

P.O. Box 8, Glen Rose, Texas 76043 (254) 897-4509
Website: www.glenroseexpo.org

The Promise (800) 687-2661
Website: www.thepromiseglenrose.com

On Saturday evenings from June through October, the life story of Jesus unfolds in an outdoor, contemporary musical drama, *The Promise*, which is produced on a 65 × 100–square foot, trilevel stage that has a six-story archway towering above it. Parts of *The Promise* may be a little intense for very young children. Texas Amphitheatre also hosts concerts and special events. Just in case some Texas-size mosquitoes decide to attend the festivities, bringing some insect repellent and not wearing perfume or lotions are good ideas. Concessions are available. Ask about backstage tours, preshows, and barbecue dinners.

Hours: Friday and Saturday, arrive at 7 PM for the 8 PM performance.

Admission: Adults, $24, $22, $19; children, $13. Call for reservations.

Directions: Driving in on Hwy. 67, pass Hwy. 144. Turn right onto Bo Gibbs Dr. and go 1/4 mile. At the Texas Amphitheater/Promise sign, turn right onto Texas Drive, and go 1.5 miles to the amphitheater.

SPECIAL EVENTS

April: Oakdale Bluegrass Jamboree, Sunrise Services; **May:** Oakdale Splash Weekend, Oakdale Bluegrass Picnic and Crafts Fair, Art on the Square; **July:** Fourth Celebration, Oakdale Bluegrass Pickin' under the Stars/Fiddlers' Carousel; **September:** Oakdale Camper's Jamboree, Labor Day Concert, Tres Rios Fall Bluegrass Festival; **October:** Oakdale Bluegrass Reunion, Tres Rios Southwestern Bluegrass Festival, Halloween on the Square; **December:** Christmas on the Square.

TEXAS STATE RAILROAD/PALESTINE AND RUSK

TEXAS STATE RAILROAD STATE HISTORICAL PARK

P.O. Box 39, Rusk, Texas 75785 (800) 442-8951 in Texas or (903) 683-2561 Website: www.texasstaterailroad.com

Steam rises and the whistle blows as the 1896 iron horse pulls out from the Palestine Depot carrying its passengers on a fifty-mile round-trip excursion through the East Texas Piney Woods. Aboard the train, passengers visit unhurriedly, tour the different cars, and visit the concession for soft drinks and ice cream. If small children will be aboard, bringing some small games and toys would be a good idea. Older children might enjoy a game or deck of cards. Bring a camera to take pictures at the depot as children talk to the engineer and fireman and tour the engine cab. At the midpoint, the two trains pass each other as one heads toward Rusk and the other toward Palestine.

Flowers and blooming dogwoods are beautiful in the spring, and fall is breathtaking as the leaves change colors. Picnicking at the Rusk Depot is lots of fun, and families may bring their own food or buy fast food at the concession, which also has souvenirs. You might bring a little extra to feed the ducks on the lake at the Rusk Depot. Passengers then board for the return trip. The Palestine park offers water-only campsites, picnic tables, pavilions, and a playground. At Rusk there are full hookups for campers.

Hours: Spring schedule is Saturday and Sunday from mid-March to late May. **Summer** schedule is Thursday to Sunday from June through July. **Fall** schedule is Saturday and Sunday from August to early November. The train leaves the Palestine Depot at 11 AM and returns at 3:30 PM, and the gates for boarding trains are opened forty-five minutes before train departure. Seating is on a first-come, first-served basis, so families need to arrive at least by 10 AM. Reservations are recommended.

Admission: Regular round-trip prices: Adults, $16; children, ages 3–12, $10. One-way tickets: adults, $11; children, $7. Prices are higher for the air-conditioned cars.

Directions: Take I-45 South to Corsicana. Go southeast on US Hwy. 287 to Palestine, and then take US Hwy. 84 East about four miles. Palestine is about 120 miles from Dallas, which is approximately a three-hour drive.

MUSEUM FOR EAST TEXAS CULTURE

400 Micheaux Ave., Palestine, Texas 75801 (903) 723-1914
Website: http://museumpalestine.org/exhibits.htm

Located in a former high school built in 1915, this historical museum houses a replica of a classroom in a country school as well as railroad memorabilia. The latest renovation is an 1856 log dogtrot cabin, which is in the gym area. The museum is in John H. Reagan Park, which has picnic tables and a playground.

Hours: Tuesday to Saturday, 10 AM to 5 PM; Sunday, 1 PM to 4 PM.

Admission: Adults, $1; children ages 3–12, 50 cents; under 3, free.

Directions: The museum is located about three miles from the Texas State Railroad. Take Hwy. 84 through the downtown business district and past the railroad underpass. Go one block.

TEXAS DOGWOOD TRAILS AND DAVEY DOGWOOD PARK

Just north of Palestine on N. Link St. off US Hwy. 155

Palestine Convention and Visitors Bureau, P.O. Box 2828, Palestine, Texas 75802 (903) 729-6066 Website: www.visitpalestine.com

Each year for three weekends in March and April, the dogwood blossoms and Palestine itself open for visitors to enjoy. In the 400-acre **Davey Dogwood Park**, visitors may drive or walk through the beautiful, white-blossomed trees. Additional festivities include a parade, arts and crafts, trade days, tours of Victorian homes, trolley rides, fishing tournaments, and more. Special events include the Hot Pepper Festival in October and a Christmas Parade and Pilgrimage in early December. The Convention and Visitors Bureau offers information about walking and driving tours of Palestine. A stop by **Eilenberger Bakery** at 512 N. John is a treat. Call (903) 729-2253. Also, the **National Scientific Balloon Facility** is located five miles west on Hwy. 287N to FM 3224. Call (903) 729-0271. Look under **Science** in Chapter Two for more information.

OTHER PLACES OF INTEREST

Engeling Wildlife Refuge, located twenty miles west of Palestine on Hwy. 287, is home for a great variety of animals, including deer, wild hogs, birds, fox, squirrel, and rabbits. Fishing is free in Catfish Creek, and camping is allowed. Call (903) 928-2251. **Lake Palestine**, a 22,500-acre lake located twenty miles north of Palestine, offers boating, swimming, and other water sports. Camping areas and motels are around the lake.

TYLER

Called **The Rose Capital of America**, Tyler's Municipal Rose Garden and annual Texas Rose Festival in mid-October draw thousands of visitors each year. The sandy soil is particularly adapted to growing azaleas, pine trees, peaches, and blueberries, also. See the **Farmers Markets and Pick Your Own** section of Chapter Two for those in the Tyler area.

Tyler was named in the mid-1800s for U.S. President John Tyler, who penned his name on the joint resolution that enabled Texas to be admitted as a state. Once the center of the booming oil business in East Texas, Tyler now focuses more on gardening and other types of agriculture and forestry as major industries since the oil business has declined. One-third of the commercially grown rose bushes in the world originate in Smith County. Besides the beautiful gardens, this Piney Woods city offers a variety of activities for visitors in lakes, museums, and a zoo. Tyler is about a two-hour drive east on I-20. For more information, contact the Tyler Convention and Visitors Bureau, 314 N. Broadway, P.O. Box 390, Tyler, Texas 75710. Call (903) 592-1661 or (800) 235-5712 or visit www.tylertexas.com or www.easttexasguide.com.

BROOKSHIRE'S WORLD OF WILDLIFE MUSEUM AND COUNTRY STORE

1600 W.S.W. Loop 323, P.O. Box 1411, Tyler, Texas 75710-1411
(903) 534-2169 Website: www.brookshires.com/company/museum.asp

In honor of Brookshire Grocery Company's founders, Wood and Louise Brookshire, the museum highlights more than 250 mammals, fowl, reptiles, and aquatic species from North America and Africa. The African exhibit also includes artifacts like handmade jewelry and wood-carvings. A life-size replica of a 1920s grocery store, the Country Store, is stocked with old-time goods, antique toys, and antique merchandising equipment. A 1926 Model T Ford and a 1952 big red fire truck are outside on the grounds as are a picnic area, covered pavilion, and playground. Groups of fifteen or more should call two weeks in advance for reservations for guided tours.

Hours: Tuesday to Saturday, 9 AM to 12 PM and 1 PM to 5 PM, with the picnic area and playground open through lunchtime. Closed on major holidays.

Admission: Free.

Directions: Take I-20 East and turn south on Hwy. 69. Go southwest on Loop 323 to the Old Jacksonville Hwy. and turn right. It is located just past the Distribution Center.

CALDWELL ZOO

2203 Martin Luther King Blvd., P.O. Box 4785, Tyler, Texas 75712
(903) 593-0121 Website: www.caldwellzoo.org

The openness of the natural habitats with different species of animals grazing on the lush grasses together is most impressive to visitors at the Caldwell Zoo. More than 2,000 animals from around the world, as well as native Texas critters and fowl, are offered for viewing on eighty-five beautiful acres. A favorite spot is on the veranda of the snack shop where visitors can still see much of the zoo. A picnic area is available. Be sure to visit the hands-on displays in the education center and stop by the petting corral area.

Hours: October 1 to March 31, 9:30 AM to 4:30 PM; April 1 to September 30, 9:30 AM to 6 PM; open daily except some major holidays.

Admission: Ages 13 and older, $6; seniors (55+), $5; ages 3–12, $3.50; ages 2 and under, free. All facilities are wheelchair accessible. No radios or pets allowed.

Directions: Take I-20 East to Tyler and go southeast on US Hwy. 69. Turn left (east) on MLK Blvd., and the zoo is on the left.

CARNEGIE HISTORY CENTER

125 S. College at Elm, Tyler, Texas (903) 593-7989

Housed in the former Carnegie Public Library building, the History Center features exhibits of artifacts of Tyler and Smith counties, as well as Civil War artifacts that were uncovered from the large prisoner-of-war camp that was located in Tyler.

Hours: Tuesday to Sunday, 1 PM to 5 PM.

Admission: Free.

THE DISCOVERY PLACE

308 N. Broadway, Tyler, Texas 75702 (903) 533-8011
Website: http://discovery.tyler.com

The Discovery Place is a hands-on science museum for children. In the tunnels of Discovery Mountain, kids learn about bats, earthquakes, volcanoes, and more. On the ship *Awakening*, they discover the qualities of wind, solar power, magnetism, and navigation. Other fun, hands-on exhibits will be worth the trip.

Hours: Monday to Saturday, 9 AM to 5 PM; Sunday, 1 PM to 5 PM.

Admission: $5 per person; ages 2 and under, free. Educational group rates available.

MUNICIPAL ROSE GARDEN

420 Rose Park Dr., Tyler, Texas (903) 531-1212
Website: www.texasrosefestival.com

The beauty of 30,000 plants exhibiting more than 500 varieties of roses on fourteen acres from May to November is indescribable. In the one-acre **Heritage Rose and Sensory Garden** located in the southwest corner, varieties that date back to 1867 are showcased. Another garden features approximately 168 camellias. The **Rose Museum Complex**, which covers 30,000 square feet and includes a visitor center, is located at Rose Park Dr. and W. Front. The fourteen-acre Rose Garden is the site of part of the **Texas Rose Festival**, including the Queen's Tea, where the public can meet the Texas Rose Festival Queen and enjoy refreshments. Also included in the four-day festival are a parade, coronation, dance, art show, arts-and-crafts fair, rose show, and tours of rose fields.

The **Whistle Stop Ranch Railroad Museum** is open Saturday and Sunday during the Rose Festival and Azalea Trail and other times by appointment. Call (903) 894-6561.

Hours: Monday to Friday, 9 AM to 4:30 PM; Saturday, 10 AM to 4:30 PM; Sunday, 1:30 PM to 4:30 PM. Closed Mondays from November through February.

Admission: The Municipal Rose Garden is free, and it is open all day every day. The museum admission is adults, $3.50; ages 3–11, $3.

TYLER MUSEUM OF ART

1300 S. Mahon, Tyler, Texas 75706 (903) 595-1001

Located on the east side of Tyler Junior College on Mahon at 5th St., the Tyler Museum of Art features changing exhibits of 19th- and 20th-century contemporary art focusing on regional artists. Another highlight is a permanent exhibition of photographs of the East Texas region.

Hours: Tuesday to Saturday, 10 AM to 5 PM; Sunday, 1 PM to 5 PM.

Admission: Voluntary: adults, $3.50; seniors, $1.50; children, $1.50.

TYLER STATE PARK

789 Park Road 16, Tyler, Texas 75706 (903) 597-5338
Website: www.tpwd.state.tx.us/park/tyler

Playing on a 400-foot beach, swimming and fishing for channel catfish and black bass in the sixty-four-acre spring-fed lake, and hiking are some of the outdoor entertainment offered at this 994-acre state park in the Piney Woods. A nature trail, concession, restrooms with showers, and rentals of boats, canoes, and paddleboats during the summer season are also available. Boats are limited to 5 mph. Picnic tables and camping areas that have some screened shelters are accessible from the main road.

Hours: Day use, 8 AM to 10 PM; overnight for camping.

Admission: Adults, $3; 12 and under, free. Camping is additional.

Directions: From I-20, go two miles north on FM 14 to Park Road 16.

SPECIAL EVENTS

Azalea and Spring Flower Trail, **late March to mid-April;** Tyler Heritage on Tour, **early April;** East Texas Fair, **late September;** Texas Rose Festival, **mid-October.**

On the way: Two colorful and energetic towns very much worth a visit are just a little past midpoint between Dallas and Tyler. The town of **Canton** on the south side of I-20 is well-known for its First Monday Trade Days. See the **Shopping** section of Chapter Two for details. A historical park has opened in **Edgewood,** which is just north of I-20. Exit onto Hwy. 859, and drive about eight miles to the park at 106 North. Main. The two-block area called **Heritage Park** contains fifteen log cabins and a cafe, general store, bandstand, blacksmith shop, farm-implement museum, log barn, one-room schoolhouse, barbershop and public bath, early-Americana museum, caboose, depot and water tower, church house, and gift shop. Call the Edgewood Historical Society for hours, admission, and tour group information at (903) 896-1940 or (903) 896-4326.

Just about thirty minutes east on US 80 before it joins I-20 is **Terrell**, which also has some sites of historical interest. Please see **Historic Terrell** in Chapter Two.

WACO

Native Americans, outlaws, and Texas Rangers were early inhabitants of Waco, Texas. The Rangers built an outpost called Fort Fisher where the Texas Ranger Museum is located today. A Spanish explorer first mapped Waco Village in 1542, and a trading post was established in 1844. The Chisholm Trail came through Waco at the Suspension Bridge, which is now only open to foot travel. Dedicated in 1870, the 475-foot bridge across the Brazos River is located at University Parks Dr. near the Convention Center with Indian Spring Park on the west bank and Martin Luther King Park on the east bank. A river walk runs from there at Washington Ave. to the Texas Ranger Museum and beyond, and it is an enjoyable walk unless heavy rains have caused water to close part of it. The railroad came to town in 1871, and Waco has continued to thrive. For more information about Waco, call the **Tourist Information Center**, which is located in Fort Fisher, I-35 and University Parks Dr., Exit 335B. Call (800) WACO-FUN or (254) 750-8696. A twenty-four-hour tourist information recording, which cites special events for the month, is (254) 752-WACO, or visitors may look online at www.wacocvb.com. From Dallas, go left (east) on University Parks. The Visitor Center can be seen from I-35.

BAYLOR UNIVERSITY
Exit 335B off I-35 to University Parks Dr.

The **Wiethorn Information Center** to the right of the main entrance has visitor parking and permits. A map of Baylor may also be obtained at the Visitor Information Center at Fort Fisher, which is a short distance north of the campus. Call (254) 710-1921. Chartered in 1845, Baylor has become the world's largest Baptist university. One of the first stops should be Bear Plaza for a look at the **Baylor Bear** in his fancy lair. Hopefully, he will be awake and know that he has visitors. Bear Plaza is across

Waco Creek from the Baylor Bookstore between 1200 S. 5th and 7th streets.

The **Armstrong Browning Library** contains the world's largest collection of material related to Robert Browning, one of the greatest British poets of the Victorian era. The library also contains major manuscript collections of the work of his wife, Elizabeth Barrett Browning, John Ruskin, Charles Dickens, and Ralph Waldo Emerson. What children will appreciate are the fifty-six stained-glass windows, which illustrate the poems and themes of the Brownings, and the Pied Piper window in the Sturdivant Alcove. The museum is located on 701 Speight Ave. between 7th and 8th streets. Call (254) 710-3566.

Hours: Weekdays, 9 AM to 5 PM; Saturday, 9 AM to 12 AM. Closed Sunday. Closed in August two weeks prior to the fall semester and major holidays.

Admission: Free. Donations appreciated.

Mayborn Natural Science and Cultural History Museum Complex. The Mayborn Museum Complex includes a new 144,000-square-foot museum building and the Daniel Historic Village. Exhibits include both traditional and walk-in dioramas with exploration stations for interactive learning. The walk-ins include a Texas limestone cave, a central Texas forest, and an exhibit on the twenty-three Columbian Mammoths whose skeletal remains were discovered just outside Waco. Other exhibits include a Waco Indian grass hut, a Comanche tipi made of hide, a log cabin, and a Norwegian rock house, all of which existed in the area in the 1850s. Visitors will learn about the cretaceous sea that once covered Texas, complete with sea inhabitants. Exhibits feature plants and animals that have become extinct, as well as specific archeological sites, including the original Waco Native American village.

Children of all ages are encouraged to participate in the Discovery Rooms. Subjects include vertebrates, communication, energy, and recycling, and much more. Young children will enjoy Mrs. Moen's Neighborhood, complete with cars, a house, grocery store, gas station, post office, and more.

Daniel Historic Village focuses on the time period of the 1880s to 1910. It's located on thirteen acres just east of Ft. Fisher Park on the Brazos River. More than twenty wood-framed buildings re-create a farming community in Texas, as well as the life of a river town that had no electricity, water that came from wells and creeks, and wood-burning stoves. Mailing address: P.O. Box 97154, Waco, Texas, 76798-7154. Call (254) 710-1110 or visit www.baylor.edu.

Hours: Open daily. Monday to Saturday, 10 AM to 5 PM, with extended hours until 8 PM on Thursday; Sunday, 12 PM to 5 PM. Closed major holidays.

Admission: Fee for the museum and village.

CAMERON PARK

4th and Herring Streets (254) 750-5980

Cameron Park features 416 acres with wooded picnic sites and various forms of wildlife. Miss Nellie's Pretty Place is a wildflower preserve, and across the street is a children's playground with access for handicapped children. At Cameron Park visitors enjoy sand volleyball, hiking and bridle paths, mountain-biking trails, disc golf, and pavilions for picnicking. The park fronts on the Bosque and Brazos rivers and is the location of the zoo. It's open daily and there is no admission charge.

CAMERON PARK ZOO

Herring and 1701 N. Fourth St. (254) 750-8400

The zoo features both exotic and native wildlife. Highlights include Gibbon Island, Treetop Village and African Savanna, bald eagles, reptile house, educational facilities, and the Texas Heritage area, which includes longhorns, buffalo, and javelina. For more information, contact the Cameron Park Zoological and Botanical Society, Inc. at P.O. Box 7344, Waco, Texas 76714-9931 or visit www.cameronparkzoo.com.

Summer hours: Monday to Saturday, 9 AM to 5 PM; Sunday, 11 AM to 5 PM.

Admission: Adults, $5, children 4–12, $3.

DR PEPPER MUSEUM

300 S. 5th St., Waco, Texas 76701 (254) 757-1025
Website: www.drpeppermuseum.com

Dr Pepper, the oldest major soft drink in America, was first mixed in Morrison's Old Corner Drug Store by Dr. Charles C. Alderton and was served in 1885. The present museum, a tribute to the "Pepper Upper," houses memorabilia in the former Artesian Manufacturing and Bottling Company established in 1906, which manufactured and distributed Dr Pepper as well as several other soft drinks. The museum also features a gift shop and an old-fashioned soda fountain, which sells Dr Pepper and Blue Bell Ice Cream.

Bottling equipment, containers, and an interior artisan well, along with film of twenty-five years of Dr Pepper commercials complete the first floor. The second-floor exhibits concentrate on marketing and advertising campaigns as well as a re-creation of a 1930s corner store. The third floor houses the W. W. "Foots" Clements Free Enterprise Institute, which offers educational programs to scheduled groups, and the Bottlers Hall of Fame.

Hours: Monday to Saturday, 10 AM to 4 PM; Sunday, 12 PM to 4 PM with extended hours during peak periods.

Admission: Adults, $4; students 3–18, $2; preschoolers, free. Advance reservations are required for groups of ten or more.

LAKE BRAZOS AND LAKE WACO

Lake Brazos is a town lake at the confluence of the Brazos and Bosque rivers that is the site of festivals, boat racing, and rowing regattas. Lake Brazos offers unsupervised swimming, boating, camping, fishing, skiing, and other recreational activities. Call (254) 756-5359. Lake Waco's Airport Park off Airport Rd. has drinking water and restrooms, camping (fee), a boat ramp, and a marina with bait and a fishing barge. The swimming beach and shower house are before you get to the camping area, and there is no fee. **Day-use hours:** 6 AM to 11 PM.

LION'S PARK

1716 N. 42nd (254) 772-4340

Lion's Park offers a variety of family entertainment in its facilities, which include a swimming pool, picnics, tennis, miniature golf, bumper boats, go-carts, a playground, a small amusement park with eight rides for children, and a miniature train. Call for current hours as they change with the season.

TEXAS RANGER MUSEUM AND FORT FISHER PARK

100 Texas Rangers Trail, Waco, Texas 76706 (Mailing address: P.O. Box 2570, Waco, Texas 76702-2570) (254) 750-8631
Website: www.texasrangers.org

A visit to Waco might begin by exiting 335B off I-35 to visit the Texas Ranger Hall of Fame, which is on the left of the highway. This is also the location of the Visitor Information Center and **Fort Fisher Park**. Baylor University is just across the street to the south. The collection of firearms and other weapons is most impressive. There are also life-size dioramas of scenes in the lives of the Rangers as well as collections of Indian, Mexican, and pioneer artifacts. One room features an exhibit of items used by James A. Michener in his research and writing about Texas. New exhibits include modern investigation methods and a kid mystery wall. Picnic tables are by the scenic Brazos River, and Fort Fisher Park offers camping and screened shelters. Call (254) 750-8630.

Hours: Daily, 9 AM to 5 PM, except Thanksgiving, Christmas, and New Year's Day.

Admission: Adults, $5; children, $2.50.

Directions: Taking the road along the south side of the Visitor Center leads to the Daniel Historic Village and the Sports Hall of Fame.

TEXAS SPORTS HALL OF FAME

1108 S. University Parks Dr. at I-35, Exit 335B (254) 756-1633
Website: www.tshof.org

Located just east of Fort Fisher Park, the Texas Sports Hall of Fame honors more than 400 favorite sports heroes through a collection of memorabilia and interactive exhibits. Also included in the museum are the Texas High School Football Hall of Fame, the Texas Basketball Hall of Fame, the Texas Tennis Museum, and the Tom Landry Theater.

Hours: Monday to Saturday, 9 AM to 5 PM; Sunday, 12 PM to 5 PM.

Admission: Adults, $5; seniors, $4; students, $2; ages 5 and under, free.

WACO WATER PARK

900 Lake Shore Dr. (254) 750-7900
Website: www.wacocvb.com/waco-water-park.html

Located in Waco Riverbend Park, Waco Water Park offers cool summer fun with two pools, water-shooting playscapes, a twenty-two-foot slide, a zero-depth pool and more. Special features include umbrellas and trees for shade, locker rooms, and a concession stand.

Seasonal hours: Monday to Thursday, 1 PM to 9 PM; Friday, 1 PM to 7 PM; Saturday and Sunday, 12 PM to 7 PM.

Admission: Adults, $7.50; ages 13–17, $6.25; ages 4–12, $5; under 4, free.

DOC AND LADDY'S

3700 I-35, Exit 331 (254) 662-5557
Website: www.docandladdys.com

Entertainment at Doc and Laddy's Family Fun Center includes an arcade, laser tag, and miniature golf.

Hours: Friday, 4 PM to 12 AM; Saturday, 12 PM to 12 AM; Sunday, 12 PM to 10 PM (holiday hours from December 23 to January 3).

EVENTS

April: Brazos River Festival; **Summer:** Summer Sounds Concerts and Brazos Nights Concerts at Indian Spring Park; **June:** Car Show at Fort Fisher; **July:** Brazos Boat Races; **September:** Labor Day Great Texas Raft Race; **October:** Heart O' Texas Fair and Rodeo; **December:** Christmas on the Brazos.

OTHER PLACES OF INTEREST NEARBY

SummerFun USA Water Park, 1410 Waco Rd., Belton, Texas (254) 939-0366 Website: www.summerfunusa.com.

Prime Outlet Center, 104 N.E. Interstate Hwy. 35, Exit 368A or B, Hillsboro, Texas (254) 582-9205 Website: www.primeoutlets.com.

Homestead Heritage: Traditional Crafts Village, P.O. Box 869, Elm Mott, Texas 76640 (254) 829-0417 Website: www.homesteadheritage .com. Visitors may take a walking tour of the Crafts Village of Homestead Heritage's 510-acre working farm, which is operated by a church group. The tour includes the barn, which showcases the work of their craftsmen, blacksmith shop, herb garden, deli and bakery (homemade bread and pies, oh my!), heritage furniture, restored 1750 gristmill, and potter's house. See the craftsmen at work and beautiful wildflowers in the spring. Picnic tables are available. **Special events** include the Labor Day Sorghum Harvest and Thanksgiving Fair, Friday to Sunday following Thanksgiving. Hayrides are on Saturdays. The village is located five miles west of I-35, northwest of Waco.

Hours: Monday to Saturday, 10 AM to 6 PM.

Admission: Free, except for parking at special events.

7. RESOURCES

SPECIAL EVENTS AND
TICKET/RESERVATION HOTLINES

American Airlines Center (214) 665-4200
Dallas Events Hotline (214) 571-1301
Fair Park Info Line (214) 421-9600
Irving Art Centre's Artsline (972) 252-ARTS
MovieFone/movie information (972) 444-FILM
Park and Recreation Special Events (214) 670-7070
SPCA Events Line (214) 651-9611 ext. 160
Tennis reservations/neighborhood courts (214) 670-8745
Ticketmaster (214) 373-8000 (Foley's and Tower Records)
Ticketmaster Arts Line (214) 631-ARTS
Star Tickets (888) 597-STAR

CONVENTION AND VISITORS BUREAUS

DALLAS CONVENTION AND VISITORS BUREAU
Old Red Courthouse, Downtown Historic District, 100 S. Houston
St., Dallas, Texas 75202 (214) 571-1000 Website:
www.dallascvb.com

The Visitor Center would like to say a friendly "Hi, y'all!" to visitors to
the Dallas area as well as to natives who keep up with the latest entertainment. The most current *Dallas! Official Visitors Guide*, a publication of the
Dallas Convention and Visitors Bureau, as well as countless brochures of
great places to visit, are there. The hotline at (214) 571-1301 and the
website at www.visitdallas.com list special events and business and relo-
cation information, and you may request a visitor's packet. The Old Red
Courthouse is the site of the Visitors Bureau, which offers Dallas information kiosks as well as internet and e-mail access. The City of Dallas
website is www.ci.dallas.tx.us.

Hours: Monday to Sunday, 9 AM to 6 PM.

DALLAS/FORT WORTH–AREA TOURISM COUNCIL

This council publishes a free, informative guide to Dallas, Ft. Worth, and surrounding cities called the *Official Visitors Guide to the Dallas/Fort Worth Area*, which is available at the Dallas Visitors Bureau location or by contacting the council at 701 S. Main St., Grapevine, Texas 76051 or by calling (817) 329-2438 or (800) C-Dallas. Some coupons are located in the back of the magazine. You may wish to look up the council online at www.visitdallas-fortworth.com.

STATE DEPARTMENT OF HIGHWAYS AND PUBLIC TRANSPORTATION

Travel and Information Division, P.O. Box 149249, Austin, Texas 78714-9249 (800) 452-9292 Website: www.traveltex.com

This Texas State agency publishes a free, helpful guidebook to Texas cities called *Texas State Travel Guide*, which gives general information as well as information about attractions in the area. Toward the end of the book are descriptions of Texas lakes, parks, forests, rocks, flowers, birds, and tourist bureaus.

Other helpful state websites include the following:

Texas Commission on the Arts: www.dot.state.tx.us
Texas Department of Public Safety: www.txdps.state.tx.us
Texas Fun: www.texasfun.com
Texas Historical Commission: www.thc.tx.us
Texas Outside: www.texasoutside.com
Texas Parks and Wildlife Department: www.tpwd.state.tx.us
Texas Tourism: www.tourtexas.com
Texas Travel: www.traveltex.com

METROPLEX AND NEIGHBORING CONVENTION AND VISITORS BUREAUS

Addison CVB, P.O. Box 9010, Addison 75001 (800) ADDISON Website: www.addisontexas.net.

Arlington CVB, 1905 E. Randol Rd., Arlington 76011 (800) 433-5374 Website: www.arlington.org/cvb.

Canton Chamber of Commerce, 390 W. Dallas (Hwy. 64 West), Canton (903) 567-2991 Website: www.cantontx.com.

Cedar Creek Lake Area Chamber of Commerce, 1907 W. Main, Gun Barrel City 75156 (903) 887-3152 Website: www.cedarcreeklake chamber.com.

Cedar Hill CVB, 300 W. Houston St., Cedar Hill 75104 (972) 291-7817 Website: www.cedarhillchamber.org.

Denton CVB, 414 Pkwy., Denton 76201 (888) 381-1818 Website: www.discoverdenton.com.

Duncanville CVB, 203 E. Wheatland, Duncanville 75116 (972) 780-5000 Website: www.ci.duncanville.tx.us.

Ennis CVB, 002 E. Ennis Ave., Ennis 75119 (888) 366-4748 Website: www.visitennis.org.

Farmers Branch Office of Economic Development and Tourism, 13000 William Dodson Pkwy., Farmers Branch 75234 (800) BRANCH-9 Website: www.farmersbranch.info.

Ft. Worth CVB, 415 Throckmorton, Ft. Worth 76102 (800) 433-5747 Website: www.fortworth.com.

Garland CVB, 200 N. 5th St., Garland 75040 (972) 205-2749 Website: www.ci.garland.tx.us.

Glen Rose/Somervell CVB, P.O. Box 2037, Glen Rose 76043 (888) 346-6282 Website: www.glenrosetexas.net.

Granbury CVB, 116 W. Bridge St., Granbury 76048 (800) 950-2212 Website: www.granburytx.com.

Grand Prairie CVB, 2170 N. Belt Line Rd., Grand Prairie 75050 (800) 288–8FUN Website: www.gptexas.com.

Grapevine CVB, One Liberty Park Plaza, Grapevine 76051 (800) 457-6338 Website: www.grapevinetexasusa.

Irving CVB, 222 W. Las Colinas Blvd. # 1550, Irving 75039 (800) 247-8464 Website: www.irvingtexas.com.

Lancaster Chamber of Commerce, 100 N. Dallas, Lancaster 5146 (972) 227-2579 Website: www.lancastertx.org.

Lewisville Chamber of Commerce/Visitors Bureau, 551 N. Valley Pkwy., Lewisville 75067 (972) 436-9571 Website: www.visitlewisville .com.

McKinney CVB, 1650 W. Virginia, McKinney 75069 (888) 649-8499 Website: www.mckinneycvb.org.

Mesquite Chamber of Commerce and Visitors Bureau, 617 N. Ebrite, Mesquite 75149 (972) 285-0211 Website: www.mesquitechamber.com.

Palestine CVB, N. Loop 256, P.O. Box 2828, Palestine 75802 (800) 659-3484 Website: www.visitpalestine.com.

Plano CVB, 2000 E. Spring Creek Pkwy., Plano 75074 (972) 422-0296 Website: www.planocvb.com.

Richardson CVB, 411 Belle Grove Dr., Richardson 75080 (972) 234-4100 Website: www.ci.richardson.tx.us.

Terrell CVB, 1314 W. Moore Ave., Terrell 75160, Metro (972) 524-5703 Website: www.terrelltexas.com.
Waco CVB, P.O. Box 2570, Waco 76702 (800) WACO-FUN Website: www.wacocvb.com.

PUBLICATIONS

DALLAS NEWSPAPERS

Dallas Business Journal 12801 N. Central Expwy., Dallas, Texas 75243 (214) 696-5959.

Dallas Examiner 1516 Corinth, Dallas, Texas 75215 (214) 428-3446.

Dallas Morning News P.O. Box 655237, Dallas, Texas 75265 (214) 977-8222.

Oak Cliff Tribune 1005 W. Jefferson, Dallas, Texas 75208 (214) 943-7755.

Park Cities News 8115 Preston, Dallas, Texas 75225 (214) 369-7570.

Park Cities People 6116 N. Central Expwy., Dallas, Texas 75206 (214) 739-2244.

The White Rocker News 10809 Garland Rd., Dallas, Texas 75218 (214) 327-9335.

COMMUNITY NEWSPAPERS SERVING NEARBY CITIES

Arlington Star Telegram (817) 261-1191.
Coppell Gazette (972) 393-7424.
Fort Worth Star-Telegram Metro (817) 429-2655.
The Garland News (972) 272-6591.
Irving Journal Metro (817) 259-9500.
The Mesquite News (972) 285-6301.
Plano Star Courier (972) 424-9504.
Richardson News (972) 234-3198.

NEIGHBORHOOD NEWSPAPERS AND NEWSLETTERS (DISTRIBUTED FREE IN RESTAURANTS, LIBRARIES, NEWSSTANDS, ETC.)

Advocate/Lake Highlands-East Dallas-Lakewood (214) 560-4203.
ARTimes in Irving (972) 252-7558.
Richardson Today (972) 238-4270.

FOREIGN LANGUAGE NEWSPAPERS

Dallas Chinese Times (972) 907-1919.
El Hispano Newspaper (214) 357-2186.
Korea Times in Dallas (972) 243-0005.
Novedades (214) 943-2932.

BOOKS

A Guide for Seeing Dallas County History, by the Dallas County Historical Commission, 1987 (trail booklet available at the Hall of State).

A Guide to Dallas Private Schools, by Lynn Magid, Private in Print, 1993.

Hiking and Backpacking Trails of Texas, by Mickey Little, 5th ed., Gulf Publishing, 2002.

City Smart: Dallas/Fort Worth, by Sharry Buckner, Avalon Travel Publishing, 2000.

Dallas: A History of Big D, by Michael V. Hazel, Texas State Historical Association, 1997.

Dallas/Fort Worth Alive! by Kimberly Young, Hunter Publishing, 2001.

Dallas/Fort Worth Metroplex, by Robert Rafferty, Gulf Publishing, 1999.

Exploring Texas with Children, by Sharry Buckner, Republic of Texas Press, 1998.

Dallas Reconsidered: Essays in Local History, by Michael V. Hazel, 3 Forks Press, 2000.

52 Texas Weekends: Great Getaways and Adventures for Every Season, by Patricia Scott, McGraw Hill, 1999.

Fodor's Cityguide: Dallas/Fort Worth, Fodor's, 2001.

Marmac Guide to Dallas, by Yves Gerem, Pelican Publishing, 2004.

Official Guide to Texas State Parks, by Laurence Parent, University of Texas Press, 1997.

133 Fun Things to Do in Dallas/Fort Worth, by Karen Foulk, Into Fun Company Publications, 2000.

Quick Escapes: Dallas/Fort Worth, by June Naylor, 5th ed., Globe Pequot Press, 2004.

Roadside Geology of Texas, by Darwin Spearing, Mountain Press, 2003.

Texas off the Beaten Path, by June Naylor Rodriquez, 5th ed., Globe Pequot Press, 2003.

Texas Outdoor Adventure Guide for Kids, by Melissa Maupin, University of Texas Press, 1999.

Texas Parks and Campgrounds, Revised Edition, by George Oxford Miller, Lone Star Books, 2003.

Texas Wildscapes: Gardening for Wildlife, by Noreen Damude and Kelly Conrad Bender, University of Texas Press, 1999.

Zagat Survey: Dallas/Fort Worth Restaurants, ed. Benjamin Schmerler, Zagat, 2001.

MAGAZINES

D Magazine (214) 939-3636 Website: www.dmagazine.com. *D* is a monthly magazine with information about Dallas personalities, events, and restaurants.

dallas child and *Baby Dallas*, Lauren Publications (972) 447-9188 Website: www.dallaschild.com. This monthly parenting magazine offers helpful articles about child raising, kid-friendly restaurants, and exciting places to go, and it is offered for free at libraries, children's stores, and day cares or by subscription.

Dallas Cowboys Official Weekly, Southwest Professional Sports Publications, Inc. (972) 556-9972 Website: www.dallascowboys.com. Each week this football news magazine highlights games, coaches, plays, and players.

Dallas Family, Family Publications, Inc. (972) 488-3555 Website: www.dallasfamily.com. This monthly parenting magazine has articles about raising healthy children, creating good relationships, entertaining children, educating them, being a good consumer, and selecting child care. There is a very informative events calendar for the month.

Dallas Observer, New Times, Inc. (214) 757-9000 Website: www.dallasobserver.com. Offered free in newsstands or by subscription, this weekly news magazine includes features about controversial personalities, political and other news, a community calendar of events, and live music and concert information. The calendar does include events for children, but it also contains romance ads that are not for children.

The Dallas Weekly, Admast Publishing (214) 428-8958 Online magazine: www.dallasweekly.com. This weekly magazine serving the African American community offers news articles, features, sports, a community calendar, and more information about health, education, and youth. It is offered free at some locations, or readers may subscribe.

Texas Highways, State Department of Highways and Public Transportation (512) 465-7408 Website: www.texashighways.com. Wonderful things about Texas landscape, wildlife, history, and communities are photographed and featured in this colorful monthly magazine.

Texas Monthly, Texas Monthly, Inc., Dallas, Texas (214) 871-7717, (800) 759-2000 Website: www.texasmonthly.com. *Texas Monthly* features interesting people, places, restaurants, and news statewide.

Texas Parks & Wildlife, Texas Parks and Wildlife Department (512) 912-7000 Website: www.tpwmagazine.com. The nature photography is beautiful in this monthly magazine featuring fascinating information about wildlife and endangered or threatened species and activities, such as where to fish, swim, and hike in the state parks. Online are subscriptions, books and other publications, accommodations, reservations for camping, and Texas getaways.

TELEPHONE SERVICES

SOUTHWESTERN BELL GREATER DALLAS YELLOW PAGES (A–K)

The introductory pages of the *Yellow Pages* are a very helpful guide to the Dallas area. They provide telephone numbers of attractions, service organizations, events, and hospitals, as well as maps of seating inside major arenas, maps of Dallas, maps of the DART Rail System, and a map of Fair Park. A zip code directory is also included.

Emergency 911; nonemergency 311
Kid Med, Presbyterian Hospital, day care for ill children (214) 345-7155
Poison Center (800) 222-1222
Road conditions/closings/wildflowers (214) 374-4100
Telephone: to order or change (800) 464-7928; repairs (800) 246-8464
Time-of-day service (214) 844-6611
Weather (214) 787-1111

TOP TWENTY PLACES TO GO FOR FAMILIES

African American Museum
Ballpark/Ameriquest Field, Legends of the Game Museum and Learning Center
Children's Museum at Valley View Center
Children's Theater at Rosewood Center for Family Arts
Dallas Aquarium
Dallas Arboretum and Botanical Garden
Dallas Museum of Art
Dallas Museum of Natural History
Dallas Public Library–Downtown
Dallas World Aquarium
Dallas Zoo
Fair Park, Texas State Fair

Mesquite Championship Rodeo
Nasher Sculpture Garden
Old City Park on Festival Days
Science Place and Planetarium/IMAX Theater
Six Flags Hurricane Harbor, Hawaiian Falls, and NRH2O
Six Flags Over Texas/Music Mill Amphitheatre
Studios at Las Colinas
Texas Discovery Gardens
West End: Tilt, Dallas World Aquarium, Marketplace, JFK Sixth Floor
    Museum

FREE ACTIVITIES FOR FAMILIES

African American Museum at Fair Park
American Museum of Miniature Arts at Hall of State
Animal shelters
Arlington Museum of Art
Art galleries
Arts-and-crafts malls
Bachman Lake
Bath House Cultural Center Gallery
Biblical Arts Center, permanent exhibit
Bike trails
Bolin Wildlife Exhibit in McKinney
Bookstores, story time
C. R. Smith Aviation Museum
Children's Medical Center, miniature trains
Christmas tree lightings
City Hall and Plaza activities
Club activities: Watch R/C Fliers, Dallas-Area Rocket Society, Dallas-
    Area Kite Flying
College campuses: Many have ponds with ducks, fountains, tennis
    courts and walking trails
College theater performances
Collin Co. Youth Park and Museum
Comanche Peak Nuclear Plant
Connemara Conservatory
Convention Center's Pioneer Plaza with trail-ride sculpture
Crow Collection of Asian Art

*During limited hours, these attractions are free to the public, or admission is
free with fees for special exhibits or designated activities.

Dallas Arboretum: designated days/hours
Dallas Center for Contemporary Art
Dallas County Open Spaces, nature preserves
Dallas Farmers Market
Dallas Museum for Holocaust Studies
Dallas Museum of Art, Thursday, 5 PM to 9 PM, and first Tuesday of the
   month
Dallas/Ft. Worth Airport: Founder's Plaza Observation Park
Disc golf
Downtown Dallas historical plazas
Downtown Dallas Underground
Downtown historical squares
Farmers Branch Historical Park
Farmers markets
Festivals and art fairs
Fishing
Flag Pole Hill
Flea markets and trade days
Fritz Park Petting Farm in Irving
Grand Prairie historic homes
Hall of State
Heard Museum and Wildlife Sanctuary
Historic self-guided trails
International Museum of Culture
Interurban Railway Depot in Plano
Kite flying and Frisbee tossing at the park
Lakes
Landmark Museum of Garland
Libraries
Magic shops
McKinney Avenue Trolley
Meadows Museum at Southern Methodist University
Mustang exhibit and Canal Walk at Las Colinas
Nature preserves, parks, greenbelt areas
Nature stores
Nature trails
Nurseries for plants
Outdoor concerts in the park
Owens Spring Creek Farm
Parades

*During limited hours, these attractions are free to the public, or admission is
free with fees for special exhibits or designated activities.

Pate Museum of Transportation
Perry Homestead Museum in Carrollton
Pet stores
Planetariums
Playgrounds
Recreation centers
Shakespeare in the Park, donation
Shopping malls
Skating, outdoors, on trails
South Dallas Cultural Center
Spectator sports: youth and amateur games
Sports for family play: tennis, basketball, softball, badminton, ping
    pong, volleyball
Symphony and community bands, outdoor concerts in parks
Telephone Pioneer Museum of Texas
Tennis on neighborhood courts
Texas Sculpture Garden
Thanks-Giving Square
Tours of the Working World
Trammel Crow Pavilions and Sculpture Garden
Union Station
West End Historical District
White Rock Lake

BIRTHDAY PARTY IDEAS

Adventure Landing
Age of Steam Railroad Museum
Air Combat School, older children
Ameriquest Field, Tour and Museum
Arcade: West End Tilt
Art-a-Rama
Artzy Smartzy
Backyard carnival
Barney birthdays
Barnyard at Park Lane Ranch (214) 349-2002
Batting cages, outdoor and indoor
Bike and skate trails
Bowling lanes

*During limited hours, these attractions are free to the public, or admission is
free with fees for special exhibits or designated activities.

Braum's
Broomball at ice rink
Burger King
Camping at state park
Capricorn Riding Academy
Cedar Hill State Park
Chandler's Landing
Cheerleading school
Children's theater
Chuck E. Cheese's Pizza
Cinemark's IMAX Theater
Concert: Smirnoff, Nokia Live!, Music Mill Theater at Six Flags, American Airlines Center, Reunion Arena
Cooking school
Crystal's Pizza
Dallas Children's Theater
Dallas Fun and Fitness Center
Dallas Summer Musicals
Dallas World Aquarium
DART Rail Line to a destination
Disc Golf
Dress up party/rental trunk
Eisenberg's Skatepark
Festivals
Fire station
Fishing: Catfish Corner, Gone Fishin', Samuell Farm
Fritz Park Petting Farm in Irving, June and July
Frontiers of Flight Museum
FunFest
GameWorks at Grapevine Mills
Go-cart rides, outdoor and indoor
GPX Skatepark
Gymboree, gymnastic centers
Hank Haney Golf Park
Hard Rock Cafe
Hawaiian Falls
Heard Museum and Wildlife Sanctuary
Home Run Alley
Horseback riding, ranch
Ice-skating
Indoor soccer centers
Joe Willy's Restaurant
Joe's Crab Shack

Lake parks
Lakewood Arts Academy
Lone Star Park Tour
Magic show
Magic Time Machine Restaurant
Main Event
McDonald's Friendly Red Caboose in Irving
McKinney Avenue Trolley
Medieval Times Dinner and Tournament
Mesquite Rodeo
Metroplex Gymnastics
Michael's craft party
Miniature golf
Movies
Museum of Miniature Arts, dollhouse museum
Mustang Sculpture in Las Colinas
NRH2O Water Park
Old Tige's Dallas Firefighter's Museum
Paint Yer Pottery
Paintball, junior high or older
Palace of Wax and Ripley's Believe It or Not!
Palmerosa Ranch in Mesquite
Park Lane Ranch Events (214) 349-2002
Petting zoo
Planet Pizza
Planetarium show/IMAX Theater
Playground/picnic
Pocket Sandwich Theater
Pony rides
Puppet show
Purple Cow Restaurant
Purple Crayon
Purple Glaze
Putt Putt
Recreation center
Restaurant
Rock climbing gym: Exposure, Stone Works
Rodeo
Samuell Farm, fishing
Sandy Lake Amusement Park
Scavenger hunt
Science Place/Kids Place
Seventeen Spa

Six Flags Hurricane Harbor water park
Six Flags Over Texas
Skating rinks, ice and roller
Slider and Blue's
Soccer centers
Space Walk of Dallas rentals
Speedzone race cars, miniature golf, arcade
Sports event: Cowboys, Mavericks, Rangers, Stars, Fury, Desperados,
    Burn
Sports Spectrum indoor soccer
Sportsridge Athletic Club
Storytellers
Studios of Las Colinas
Surf 'N Swim
Swimming pool, outdoor and indoor
Tarantula train in Ft. Worth, Grapevine
TBC Indoor Kart Racing
Texas Motor Speedway
Texas Queen riverboat
Texas Stadium tours/games
The Little Gym
Theater, children's play
Theater, early morning rental for private showing and breakfast
Tours of the Working World
Trail Dust Restaurant
Wagon Wheel Ranch
West End: Tilt
Wet Zone, Rowlett
Whirlyball, Laserwhirld
Wild About Harry's
YMCA: indoor pool
Zoo

RAINY WEATHER IDEAS

African American Museum at Fair Park
Airport/aviation museums
Animal shelter
Arcade: Celebration Station, Speedzone, GameWorks, Tilt, Cyber
    Zone
Arena sports

Art galleries
Biblical Arts Center
Bolin Wildlife Museum
Bookstore, story time
Bowling
Burger King's or McDonald's indoor parks
Cavanaugh Flight Museum in Addison
Children's Medical Center, miniature trains
Children's Museum at Valley View Mall
Children's theater
Cinemark IMAX Theater
Dallas Aquarium
Dallas Firefighter's Museum
Dallas Museum for Holocaust Studies
Dallas Museum of Art
Dallas Museum of Natural History
Dallas World Aquarium
Dave and Buster's
Fun Fest
Grapevine Mills Outlet Mall
Hall of State
Hardware store
Heard Museum
High Tech Kids at Northpark
Hobby and craft stores: Michaels, Hobby Lobby
Home Run Alley
Hotel-elevators, restaurants, indoor pools
Ice cream and yogurt parlor
Ice-skating, roller-skating
Indoor archery
Indoor play parks: Planet Pizza
Indoor skate parks
Indoor soccer center
Indoor tennis
International Museum of Culture
Interurban Railroad Museum, Saturday
Legends of the Game Museum
Library
Lone Star Slot Car
Main Event
Meadows Museum at Southern Methodist University
Museum of Miniature Arts
National Scouting Museum

Nature store
Neil's Wheels Slot Car Speedway
Nickel Mania
Nickelrama
Palace of Wax and Ripley's Believe It or Not!
Perry Homestead Museum
Pet store
Planet Pizza
Planetarium show
Puppet show
Recreation center
Rock-climbing gym
Science Place, IMAX Theater
Shopping mall
Sixth Floor Museum
Studios at Las Colinas
Tours of the Working World
Toy store, Lakeshore Learning Store
Underground Downtown Dallas
Valley View Center's Kid's Club
West End Marketplace
Whirlyball, Laserwhirld
Women's Museum at Fair Park

INDEX

D

rainy weather ideas, 250–52
ranches, 177
Rangers Baseball, 149
Rayburn, Sam, 205
recreation centers and youth
    organizations, 173
recycling and conservation, 58
religion, 75, 103, 201
Repertory Theater Company, 140
resorts, 117, 183
resources, 238
restaurants, 118
Reunion Tower, 117
Richardson, 82; Dallas Fury at UTD,
    149; Eisemann Center for
    Performing Arts, 126; Owens
    Spring Creek Farm, 32; Practice
    Tee, The, 158; Repertory
    Company Theatre, 140;
    Richardson Square Mall, 111;
    Symphony Orchestra, 132
Richland College and Planetarium,
    122
Ripley's Believe It or Not! and Palace
    of Wax, 32
Riverboat, 96, 182
rock climbing, 162
Rock Tenn Mill, 58
rocketry, 163
Rocking M Stables, 170
Rockwall, 82; Goliad Place, 82;
    Historical Foundation Museum,
    82; Indoor Sports Expo, 166;
    Lake Ray Hubbard, 182
rodeo, 151
roller skating, 163
Rowlett Nature Trail, 56
running, 163
Rusk, 225

S

sailing, 164, 171, 182
Sammons Center for the Arts, 125

Sandy Lake Amusement Park, 33
Scarborough Faire, 142
science, 59
Science Fair and Destination
    Imagination, 59
Science Place, The; IMAX;
    Planetarium, 34, 55
Science Projects Store, 60
scuba diving, 165
sculpture and murals, 107
Shakespeare Festival of Dallas, 144
shopping, 110
shuttles, 92
Sid Richardson's Collection of
    Western Art, 210
Sierra Club, 56
Six Flags Hurricane Harbor, 35, 132
Six Flags Over Texas, 37
Sixth Floor Museum, 38
skateboarding and rollerblading, 165
skating, 159, 163, 171
skiing, water, 165
slot car racing, 161
Smirnoff Amphitheater, 126, 133
soccer, 149, 165, 172
Soccer Spectrum, 166
South Dallas Cultural Center, 105,
    133
Southern Methodist University, 106,
    126, 150
Southfork, 178
SPCA, 65
special events and ticket/reservation
    hotlines, 238
Special Olympics and Disabled
    Sports Association, 166
Speedzone, 50
sports, 148; arena, 150; collegiate,
    150; individual, family, and team,
    153, 170; major league, 148;
    rodeos, horse racing, and shows,
    151; spectator, 148; summer
    camps, 169, 178
Sports Hall of Fame, Waco, 235
St. Mark's School of Texas:
    Observatory, Camps, 55
Stallions at Lincoln Square, 70

....

T

....

CPSIA information can be obtained
at www.ICGtesting.com
Printed in the USA
LVHW032354100622
721006LV00021B/1252

9 781589 792036